Animals in the Family

Animals in the Family

Tales of Our Household Menagerie

by Edith A. Sisson

The Globe Pequot Press

Chester, Connecticut

Library of Congress Cataloging-in-Publication Data

Sisson, Edith A.
    Animals in the family : tales of our household menagerie / by Edith A. Sisson.— 1st ed.
      p. / cm.
    ISBN 0-87106-443-X
    1. Pets—Anecdotes. 2. Wild animals as pets. 3. Animals—Anecdotes.
  4. Sisson, Edith A. I. Title.
  SF416.S57 1990
  636.008`7—dc20   90-39219
                                                      CIP

Manufactured in the United States of America
First Edition/First Printing

Any glimpse into the life of an animal quickens our own.

—*John Muir*

Contents

Preface *ix*

Acknowledgments *x*

Introductory Notice *xi*

Father Goose *1*

Bringing Up Bandits *28*

The Old Hen *48*

The Egg Came First *73*

Robins Up Front *89*

Flying Free *104*

Jingle Bells *122*

Squirrel in the Tree *144*

The Little Ones *169*

Black and White *187*

Butter's Family *206*

Preface

This book is about animals I have known. It is a personal recollection about my relationships with animals of our household and their relationships with me. But it is also a family memoir. My husband and daughters have lived with these animals. Many of the animals belonged to the children but wove themselves into our family life. Now we extend into the future with our grandchild's enjoyment of our creatures. Appropriate to the book's chief character, the first word I heard my grandchild say was "goose."

The family image enlarges with the many friends, relatives, co-workers, and others who have contributed to the welfare and appreciation of the animals in our custody. My wishes here are to widen the family circle and to share with you the joys, wonders, and problems of the animal characters.

These animals, however, I consider to be representatives of the entire family of animals. Each species and even each individual within a species has its own identity, but they share much with others, especially if we begin to consider our attitudes toward them. My reverence for a tree frog spills over to respect for a pony's needs and to delight in seeing a baby elephant nurse from its mother at a zoo.

Because the human family is part of the animal kingdom, the two families you will meet here make one. May this family book, literally and philosophically, enrich your own feelings about family and the other creatures who share the earth with us.

Acknowledgments

Thanks to Polly, whose photographs of our squirrels prompted early thoughts of this book.

Appreciation to all my students, friends, relations, and others who have listened to bits and pieces from many of these stories. Their interest gave me the impetus to set the stories down. And also, appreciation to all whose names appear in the text.

Thanks to manuscript readers: Biz and Ray Paynter, Chuck Roth, Ellie Horwitz, Dan DeWolf, Mary Ann Bodecker, Binda Parra, and Dr. George P. Faddoul.

Thanks to Jinny, Kathy, Edie, and Polly, whose care of the animals made the fabric for many of the tales, whose love and concern for them increased my own, and who taught me much—and also for reading the manuscript. And to Tom, who contributed as above, extra appreciation for his continued and constant support.

With gratitude for Limerick, a place for soul and spirit, and for my invaluable helper, Mac.

And special appreciation to "my father goose," Butter, and to all the other animals. They give much to us all.

Introductory Notice

For many people, pets offer a link with the natural world obtainable in no other way. People are curious about animals and derive pleasure and fulfillment when they can share their lives and love with other animals. We know that pets and children go together, but so, too, do pets and the elderly, as well as pets and the rest of us.

For centuries people have domesticated many animals, either for farm use or for pets. Some of the animals in this book are domestic; others are wild. Wild animals, however, do not make good pets and do not live well with people. Although these animals temporarily shared their lives with our family, our goal was always to return them to the wild, where they belong.

To protect wildlife, state and federal wildlife regulations generally prohibit keeping wild animals. State regulations vary, but they have become more stringent in recent years because more and more people have been injured by wild animals in their care, or that of friends and neighbors; also, litigation can result. On the other side of the coin, many animals are taken from the wild by well-intentioned individuals, when, for varied reasons, these animals would be better off remaining in their natural environment. Many of my stories illustrate these reasons.

Federal laws also emphasize protection of endangered species, migratory birds, and birds of prey. Federal regulations prohibit people from importing goods made from any part of an endangered species.

Permission for my custody of native animals was granted through permits that I obtained either as an individual or in association with the Massachusetts Audubon Society, the conservation association for which I work. The society has also given me access to expert opinion when I have needed it and referred a number of animals to my care. Before you undertake even temporary custody of any wild animal, check the appropriate wildlife regulations of your state and of the federal government and be certain to secure all necessary permits. Also remember that veterinary hospitals, wildlife rehabilitation centers, and licensed wildlife rehabilitators have the knowledge for dealing with animals with problems.

Fortunately public lands offer everyone the chance to come closer to wildlife. I will never forget seeing alligators at the Okefenokee Wildlife Refuge. The United States has more than 200 national wildlife refuges for all of us to visit. We can also visit national parks, state-owned lands, local conservation areas, and other public lands. Even city parks offer homes for wildlife such as squirrels and pigeons.

Squirrels, pigeons, alligators, and the butterfly in your own back yard, as well as your cat or goldfish, my father goose, and all other creatures—each one has its special attributes. To share the marvel of these attributes is my purpose.

Chapter One

Father Goose

Butter, the goose, desperately wanted to become a father. No mate, no courtship, no nest, no eggs, yet clearly fatherhood stirred within him.

The early spring day had teased us, in spite of the calendar, to have lunch on the side porch. Butter, his white feathers dazzling in the spring sun, paraded back and forth on the wintered lawn, keeping an eye on us: me, husband Tom, daughter Kathy, and son-in-law Rick. Faint cheeping noises drifted through the open kitchen door from the carton inside with chicks for next year's laying flock.

"I wonder what Butter would think of a chick," said Rick, finishing his lunch. He got up, went inside, and reappeared with a downy yellow baby in his hand. Frankly, I thought Butter would make one mouthful—or beakful—of the chick. Not that Butter craved a chick dinner, but one twisting chomp and that sturdy orange bill could finish off the chick: We all knew the dangers of that beak. Geese, especially the males, or ganders, are known for aggressiveness, and Butter had no more restraint than others of his kind.

I said nothing, however, and Rick relinquished the chick to me. Warily I showed it to Butter. He appeared not to see it. I moved the chick closer, ready for a hasty withdrawal. "Cheep," said the chick. We waited in silence. Did Butter cock his head? "Cheep, cheep." Was Butter listening? Did he seem to tilt his head to look? Skeptics all, we could think only about aggression. Butter, after all, believed he owned the side yard, and even a chick could be an interloper. But Butter only cocked his head a bit farther. Tentatively, I put the chick down. "Cheep," again. Butter slowly extended his long neck, and I was ready to grab. We held our breaths. The chick pecked at a blade of dead grass, and Butter brought his head down to chick eye level. That large, feisty gander appeared fascinated by a bit of yellow fluff.

Butter poses.

Innocently, the chick repeated his cry. Butter arched his head over it, oblivious of our astonishment.

Something was going on between Butter and the chick. But what? Having mothered Butter ourselves a year ago, we well knew the "queep, queep, QUEEP" call of a gosling. Queep and cheep—did Butter hear this rhyme? For a moment I considered this anthropomorphic deduction, because it's easy to explain strange phenomena by projecting our human ways. Probably Butter was instinctively responding to the chick's pitch or tone.

By now the chick had taken a few timorous steps, and coincidentally Butter had moved with it. Butter put his head down again to check on the bundle and then he arched his head and neck protectively over his baby. The fearsome gander evidently was assuming responsibility for the absurdly small being beside him. Every time the chick moved, Butter did also, and only once did an ungainly orange webbed foot rouse a cry of distress that was but halfway out before the foot moved off. After a while, not only was Butter caring for his baby, but the baby was also beginning to consider Butter as a possible parent—the chick had begun to follow those large feet.

The chick had no proper parent of its own, only the brooder lamp in the kitchen that kept twelve future laying hens as warm as a snuggle under a real hen mother's feathers. By this time the luncheon group on the porch was becoming aware that Butter *wanted* to be a father. Whether or not he was puzzled in a goosey way when the chick failed to accompany him for a swim in the fish pool, we felt that for the sake of next year's eggs, the chick should be returned to its compatriots in the kitchen, where the foster-parent lamp had neither potentially dangerous webbed feet nor inclination to encourage a swim.

Only a short year ago Butter had come to us in the form of an egg. Nothing like an ordinary hen's egg, Butter's egg was huge to my eyes, as were the three others that my friend Judy entrusted to me. The parent geese, of mixed domestic breeds, had deserted the four eggs in their nest, which was near Judy's home on a suburban pond. She knew that some of the eggs were old, and we wondered if any could hatch.

Into the incubator the four monsters went, making our hens' eggs already inside look small. Incubator directions warn that waterfowl eggs should not be incubated with chicken eggs because the former require higher humidity than others do. But, scheming to outwit the directions, I dribbled a little warm water about twice daily over each of the goose eggs. Parent geese dampen their eggs naturally when they return from swimming to sit on their nests.

In a week I candled the goose eggs by shining a light through them. Two showed nothing happening inside, but the other two revealed faint shadows—embryo goslings had started development. Returning those two eggs to the incubator, I tried to check my optimism, reminding myself not to count my geese before they hatched.

Goose eggs usually take twenty-eight days to develop. Each candling disclosed larger shadows within, and our hopes soared upon hearing a faint peck, peck, peck on the twenty-sixth day. Next day the pecking noises were joined by gentle sounds akin to the cheeping that can be heard from a chick inside soon before it hatches. From experience we knew that a mother hen responds to her cheeping eggs with reassuring, softly guttural cluck, clucks. Konrad Lorenz, known for his ethological studies of Greylag geese, writes that the parent goose will begin to establish a bond with its soon-to-hatch goslings by answering them as they call from within the shells. The tip seemed worth following, but what should one say to unhatched goslings? A greeting seemed in order: "Hello," I answered to the dulcet cells from within. "Hello in there. Hello!"

Butter appeared first, not much to look at. Wet and barely able to lift his head, he lay splayed out on the mesh floor of the incubator. His beak looked as if it were made of yellow plastic, but at least his webbed feet were cute. "Welcome. Hello, hello," I said, almost feeling that his hatching was somehow my accomplishment, not his. Soon the second gosling broke out; having yearned for a gosling, I felt that my cup ran over with two.

A hatchling begins to look soft and cuddly as its down dries. Gosling number one transformed into a ball of fluff, yellow as butter can be, and Tom named him Butter. As for gosling number two, whose yellow down was sprinkled with darker markings, "Pepper," said Tom.

Butter and Pepper found walking tricky at first because of their unmanageably big feet. Just a step or two and one broad foot would catch on the other, toppling over the gosling. They came with the innate knowledge that grass is for geese to eat, but their first tugs at even the slenderest blades were unsuccessful, and over tipped the

One hour old, Pepper rests on the grass.

gosling again. But early inabilities with the grass didn't count, for newly hatched goslings have a two-day food supply from completing absorption of the nutritious yolk sac while still in the egg. On their third day they began to succeed with the grass blades and to enjoy supplemental grain, a commercial starter mash for game birds.

Also, by this time Butter and Pepper were imprinted on me. Lorenz explains that the first moving object a gosling sees after hatching becomes its parent, although the imprinting began with parental responses to calls from within the egg. Imprinting helps survival—goslings immediately know their parents and will follow them; in return, the parents watch out for their young. I have no way of knowing if my cheery "hellos" to egg-bound Butter and Pepper helped with imprinting, but, though I don't look like a goose, I was what they saw when they hatched, thus becoming their mother.

Being an imprintee is a responsibility. If I walked too fast, Butter and Pepper would run to keep up, queep, queep, QUEEPING in distress. As if to add speed they would flap their tiny wings, which still were useless and even looked as if they could fall off; the connection between wing and body seemed absurdly thin. Being a goose mother also requires that you take your babies with you almost everywhere you go. Complete imprinting would preclude the possibility of a substitute, but I was fortunate. Perhaps Butter and Pepper were partially imprinted on human beings in general, for in a pinch they would tolerate a family member as a gosling sitter.

Sitters, as most parents learn, often aren't available. Thus, by necessity, Butter and Pepper became inveterate car travelers. During their first few days while they still needed extra warmth, as from the brooder lamp, they traveled in a Styrofoam cooler in the car. To make a cooler into a warmer, simply add a bottle of hot water, wrapped well in a towel, and be careful to leave the cooler top slightly ajar so that the inhabitants can breathe. Hot-water refills are easily available at rest rooms along the way, and also at roadside stores, but not so easily. The question, "Could you give me some hot water, please, to fill this bottle?" is an eyebrow raiser. And, although proud of my status as mother in my goslings' eyes, I felt that to try to explain this peculiar motherhood, and why I had to have those goslings with me in the car, would be too much for those raised eyebrows. Generally I muttered something about goslings and warmth and hoped that my well-meant thank you would satisfy the donor.

Too much heat, however, is dangerous. We parked once on a hot summer day in a hospital parking lot, with no shred of shade available. We were going to visit our tragically ill friend Myles, and I could understand Tom's feeling that appearing with two goslings was inappropriate. I couldn't leave the babies in the locked car, though, and so in I walked, trying to look as if carrying a large cooler with goslings down hospital halls was nothing unusual. The cooler stayed outside the door of Myles's room, but when the word gosling inevitably entered the conversation, I could not refuse to bring one in. For a few minutes, Myles, only thirty-five and weak from terminal illness, held tiny Butter on his large hand as he lay in his hospital bed. What Myles said, if anything, I do not remember, but I picture a warm light in his eyes, perhaps because our gosling brought him contact with something of the soul of the natural world, far from the hospital's aseptic confinement.

Soon Butter and Pepper outgrew their need for the warmer and traveled instead in an open carton. On any long trip we had to stop at intervals to administer water, because we had learned that leaving water in the carton invited trouble. The goslings either dribbled messily while drinking, manners that we later realized were accepted goose etiquette, or they dunked their heads, inadvertently overturning the container. Either happening reduced the bottom of the carton to the strength of a few soggy newspapers.

After frequent water stops on the seven-hour drive to daughter Polly's college town to celebrate her twenty-first birthday, I neared the motel at dusk. I had requested a first-floor room, thinking I could drive directly to the door of my room and whisk the gosling carton inside before anyone noticed. But that plan was foiled. Instead of the typical long, two-storied building the motel was a converted home on a crowded street, its only entrance up steps from the sidewalk into an office vestibule. There the clerk cheerfully said that my first-floor room was "just down the hallway there, take a left at the corner, go through the door, and then go right and. . . ." Something warned me that if I asked about the motel's policy on goslings, I might face a travel-weary search for another place to sleep. The only alternative seemed to be to fold down the top of the suspicious carton, hold it on a hip, proceed up the stairs, and hasten through the office and then down the labyrinth of halls. Thank goodness, we made it. Better still, I found the room pleasant and the bed comfortable, and Butter and Pepper could have a refreshing bathtub swim after the long trip.

Our final exit two days later, however, proved perilous. Halfway down the hall network whom should we meet but the manager. Knowing that I would have to tilt the carton to sidle by, and fearing disapproving noises from its contents, I thought I should mask such giveaway sounds with conversation. What better subject than the weather at such moments? "Nice day, isn't it?" I said firmly. "Mmm—warmer than last night," I added, with some apprehension because I thought I heard something from within the box. I had neglected to realize that goslings in a dark carton, happy to hear mother's voice, would exuberantly respond. By necessity the weather discourse became more earnest; the manager agreed that we probably would have a thunderstorm. I, with my carton, passed safely by. Moments later, hastily tucking the noisemaker carton into the back of the car, I thought that, even had our subterfuge become known, the manager could not have minded much. Butter and Pepper had left not even a tiny feather behind. The room would be in fine order for the next guest, with or without little geese.

On her birthday Polly took us to visit the university's formal gardens, and we were proud of our goslings' behavior. Like good children they followed along in the grassy pathways between the flowerbeds. Not once did Butter or Pepper test a rare calendula or a marigold border, or crush a delicate herb. Later we walked with some of Polly's friends, who were unacquainted with geese, but Butter and Pepper quickly taught them basic goslingese, and soon we were all saying "queep, queep, QUEEP" to the goslings as they dutifully followed us. The imprinted goslings wouldn't have let us out of their sight anyway, but maybe so many queeps made them feel more secure. In return the goslings, still looking comical when they flapped their undersized wings trying to catch up, subtly advertised the marvel of imprinting as they followed the group with complete trust, giving everyone much more education than a few words of goose babytalk.

The goslings and I visited the university's famed bird sanctuary by ourselves. At its entrance the No Dogs Allowed sign caused a hesitation, but, no, I thought, geese are not dogs, and in we went for our stroll. Soon we encountered our first bird-watchers, and momentarily I wished I had brought along my binoculars, but the birds I was watching that afternoon were easy to see. In fact, Butter and Pepper were nearly one foot tall then. The bird-watchers were standing in the middle of the trail, peering through binoculars, intently scanning the upper branches of a tree. I approached with my followers and tried to look nonchalant. Utterly absorbed by those remote branches, the watchers did not look down, and we passed by, unnoticed. As a prejudiced mother, I thought the watchers had missed a special sight. The next group of bird-watchers, although at first busy with their binoculars, kindly noticed us. "Those goslings belong here . . .," one said, something between a statement and a question. "You found them?" A little daunted that goose motherhood didn't radiate all over me, I tried to explain, but as we walked off, I felt they had their doubts.

Shortly we came upon geese that did belong there, a flock of Canada geese gracefully swimming nearby in a pond beside the trail. A chance for Butter and Pepper to meet relatives for the first time: how would the goslings react? And the wild flock, what would they do when they saw domestic cousins in their pond—I did not doubt that Butter and Pepper would try a swim. But our children often surprise us. Butter and Pepper didn't see the Canadas, or acted as if they didn't, despite my entreaties. And as for going in the pond, no, they wouldn't so much as stick a webbed foot in while their mother remained on the shore. The Canada geese simply swam slowly away and out of sight.

Within days of returning home from the trip, misfortune came. It was a sultry, hot evening, and gosling bedtime. "Queep, queep—time to come in," I said, and as I held the kitchen door open for Butter and Pepper to enter, I noticed that Pepper was holding his wings slightly out from his body, much as chickens do when they are hot. But were his wings drooping as well? Although worry flashed through my mind, I lifted each gosling into the box under the kitchen window as usual. Sleep well, little ones, I thought, and went up to bed myself.

A worried voice awakened me in the morning. "Something is wrong with Pepper," Tom was saying. "He can't stand up." When I reached the kitchen I realized how wrong things were. Poor little Pepper was lying on his side in the box, looking disjointed and feeling limp when I picked him up. What had happened? Disease—but what kind? Poison? Could Pepper have eaten something toxic? No, we couldn't think of anything harmful he could have found, but neither could we think of any other explanation.

It's difficult to be with an extremely sick animal and do nothing about it. Something, anything, might be better than nothing. I tried forcing a little water into Pepper's beak with a medicine dropper. Water couldn't be harmful, and, if he had ingested something toxic, water might dilute the poison. Within half an hour, though, Pepper died. Just a gosling, but we grieved. One takes a risk when allowing oneself to love a creature. And how did Butter feel? If she (we thought Butter was female then) missed Pepper, it didn't show. Of course we watched Butter for the mystery killer's telltale drooping wings, but fortunately we saw none. Understandably, Butter became more dependent on me, her "mother," and on other human "parents," and therefrom hangs a tale.

Toward the end of July Butter had grown to be a young goose, her yellow down replaced almost entirely by sleek, white feathers. On a Sunday morning some early riser in the house had kindly let Butter out of her kitchen box and into the side yard. Butter's mother slept on and, upon wakening, had the audacity to read the Sunday morning paper in bed. Lazy, cold-hearted mother! When I went downstairs, the side yard was empty—no young goose with feathers white as snow. "Butter, Butter—queep, queep, queep. Where are you?" No goose appeared. Tom, Kathy, and Rick searched the back yard and field beyond, and I took my bicycle to hunt up and down side streets. No luck, and we felt helpless. How could such a large creature simply vanish? On an off chance I called the police at the nonemergency number so as not to interrupt important police matters with my silly-seeming inquiry. "I have a odd question," I said, "but by any chance has anyone reported seeing a white goose?" "Just a minute," was the reply. I considered what else we could do, but then the voice returned, "Lady, your goose is here," and continued, "Someone in a car found it walking down the middle of Sudbury Road and brought it down here to the station." Incredible! "I'm on my way," I replied, and within a few minutes arrived to find Butter placidly eating grass on the police-station lawn, guarded by two policemen. My relief was immense, but Butter, intent on the grass, didn't even offer so much as a "queep."

I wanted to thank the person who had brought Butter in but was disappointed to learn that she had not left her name. "Write a letter to the local paper," suggested an officer. Regretful that I couldn't do more, I sent this letter, which appeared in the next edition.

GOSLING IS RETURNED HOME

I wish to thank the kind person who rescued my young goose from the perils of traffic on Sudbury Road last Sunday morning. Apparently the gosling took off on a little stroll, seeking companionship because her foster parent was not yet up. It was a great relief and joy to find "Butter" happily grazing on the police station's lawn under the protective custody of several officers. Many thanks to the gosling's rescuer (I hope she behaved in your car), as well as to the police for their good care of perhaps an unusual charge.

Edith A. Sisson (and Butter)

After all, not every person would have both care and courage to pick up an impressive-looking bird walking down the middle of a street. Furthermore, the person might have realized the likelihood of goose droppings in her car. I never found out whether or not Butter had "behaved" during her ride. Her rescuer did phone some weeks later; I was away, but Tom spoke with her, thanking her again.

Perhaps the police-station incident made me more appreciative of Butter. She was beautiful. Although large, she carried herself with noble stature. The erstwhile useless wings had grown to functional proportions. The ends of the long flight feathers crossed over each other on her back just in front of her tail. Incidentally, I've read that the flight feathers of adult geese were the chief raw material for quill pens from the fourth century until steel pens were invented in the nineteenth. Butter bore her flight feathers proudly, as if she understood their historic significance.

Her eyes were a deep azure blue, contrasting strikingly with her radiant whiteness, as well as with her matching orange beak and feet. Her dulcet queeps were beginning to change into strident honks. When threatened, she hissed, an unmistakable harsh, fearsome noise. I remember her first hiss when she was small; safely in the car, she spotted a dog through the window, and opening her beak, uttered a little hiss. Though it was a mere whisper compared with a grown-up hiss, it showed her instinctive reaction to a potential enemy.

She ate copiously, grazing on the lawn and occasionally nibbling supplemental grain. Because much goes in to the front end of a goose, a lot comes out the back as well. Geese are well known for their numerous droppings. During growing seasons the droppings are usually green from the grass ingested and are not objectionably smelly.

Butter taught us much about geese as the summer continued. For one thing, geese don't like heat. The summer's sun always sent Butter to the shady side of anything—building, tree, or even me. After all, geese are the progenitors of goose down, the insulating material stuffed in comforters for centuries and, more recently, in jackets and sleeping bags. Butter had a luxuriant coat of this insulation under her outer contour feathers.

One day in the country I drove with Butter on the seat beside me to the local plumbing supply store. Butter was obnoxious; she kept trying to wedge herself behind my back as I kept on trying to drive. Luckily the trip was brief, but only after Butter hopped from the car, beak open and panting, did her insensitive mother understand: an uncomfortably hot goose had been trying to find relieving shade behind Mom.

Butter joins family lunch on the picnic table.

After completing the business transactions at the plumbing store, a thought occurred: "By any chance do you have some kind of large container that a goose could bathe in." Most country people can understand such a question. No, he didn't have one that he could sell, but . . . and he called to his wife down at the house to bring up that old tub used for something I've forgotten. The tub arrived promptly, a hose was fetched, and the tub was rapidly filling before I realized what was going on. Apprehension gripped me because, knowing Butter as I did (she and Pepper had refused to swim at the bird sanctuary), I could envisage her cocking one blue eye at the proffered cooling bath and calmly walking away. Well, children are unpredictable, and even before the tub was full Butter clambered in and began to duck her head in the water, shake her wings, and splash cold liquid over herself again, and again, and again. Her message was clear, "Oh, a million goosey thanks. I felt as if I couldn't stand the heat a minute longer." Wife, store owner, and I watched, transfixed by the sight of

such a happy, bathing goose, and I felt relief that the hauling and filling of the tub had not been in vain.

On the return trip, while a cooled-off goose sat contentedly beside
me, I conjured up a solution to a goose's problem with heat at a
cabin in the woods that had neither bathtub, nor running water, nor
any other plumbing amenities. I procured a large carton from the gro-
cery store in the old mill building, and back at our cabin I lined the
box with plastic, while Butter eyed the proceedings as if she could
understand the makings of a goose tub. Butter and I had been staying
alone together for a few days, and she never let me out of her sight,
not even when I walked down the outhouse path. As I carried the
makeshift bathtub to the well and laboriously filled it bucketful by
bucketful, Butter was there, ready and waiting. She did not need
encouragement from me. When the water reached some goose-
acceptable amount, in she climbed. She bathed, she splashed, and in
so doing thanked me for attending to her needs. Afterward every trip
to the well was highlighted by a cooling bath for Butter. Her bathing
combined exquisitely graceful action with efficient use of strength. It
was an intense experience. Undulating body motions, especially
through her long, supple neck, brought her head under the surface,
and then up rose head and neck, allowing water to flow over her
body. As in a dance, she repeated the motions over and over. Toward
the end she extended powerful wings to force cascades of water
splashing over her, as the water of a fast-flowing stream rills over
boulders. Butter's bath rituals were obviously efficient—no need for
soap or scrubbing brush. With the last water droplets glistening as
they rolled down her snow-white back, she clambered over the edge
of the cardboard tub to the mossy ground and began a preening job,
carefully setting her feathers in order with her beak.

Butter's first swim in the open water of a lake dramatically
revealed to us her aquatic prowess. A goose on land is hindered by
those large webbed feet, and newly hatched goslings frequently tum-
ble over the clumsy things. Despite her footwear, though, Butter
could accompany us on a woods walk, on the trail or through the
bush, keeping up with reasonable ease. When she waded into Long
Pond behind daughter Jinny, our friend Rich, and me, she suddenly,
almost mysteriously, began to glide through the water with tranquil
grace. We discovered the simple fact that Butter was designed, built,
and adapted for water. Yes, geese are water birds, no matter how

adroitly they manage on land. Of course many geese are superb flyers too, but that is another matter.

Soon, as she swam after me at the pond, the water was deep enough for me to plunge in. Surfacing, I found my gosling at my left side, only a few inches away. Perhaps Butter was anxious in this new environment, for not only did she swim near, at times encumbering my arm trying for the next stroke, but also several times she endeavored to hop aboard my back. She resembled a toy, moved by some quiet mechanism. From close by, you could look through the water at her legs paddling and her feet opening for the pushing stroke, then closing as they came forward, decreasing water resistance. Butter sparkled white against the blue sky and clear water, and she arched her neck elegantly, as if she knew how beautiful she looked. I swam beside, my heart full with the majestic sight.

Then, without warning, Butter dipped her head into the water and disappeared. I saw a vague, white form below, and within a few moments she reappeared at the surface at my other side. She repeated the performance, swimming under me again. I was astonished because I hadn't known that geese could dive underwater. Diving ducks swim underwater to catch fish or other prey, but geese are primarily herbivores. What was Butter doing? And why? Perhaps she wanted to play, something I could enjoy too. At her next dive I went under with her and we swam through the underwater world together. Without goggles, my view was blurry, but even so I could clearly see the brilliant shimmering of her white feathers that were catching reflections from the sun's light above. We dove and played together again and again; at least I felt it was play and enjoyed some moments of unusual good fun.

What Butter's intention was I do not know. A need for underwater exercise? A way of streamlining the bath rituals? Or a feel of playfulness? After all, many young animals play to develop skills needed later in life. Kittens and lion clubs both practice stalking and pouncing on prey as they play. Young roosters engage in spritely little mock battles, anticipating the adult fights to establish dominance or position with the flock's peck order. But Butter's underwater "play" still baffles me.

Even more astonishing was an August episode in the gentle surf by a sandy beach at a national park. My friend Binda and I were wading out through the waves for a swim, and Butter was swimming unusually close by. Maybe she was worried by the waves, and, if so,

Butter steps into Long Pond with Jinny. **(Photo courtsey Rich deCampo)**

her worry had due cause. Suddenly a wave larger than the others pulled her away from us and dragged her back toward shore, where it tumbled her in the foam. Recovering quickly, Butter swam with frightened determination straight back to us. Three times more Binda and I watched waves wrench Butter away. Next, however, we were amazed to see Butter turn deliberately and swim with a wave toward shore. Then, in a few moments, she briskly reversed direction and swam confidently back to us. Of a human being we would say she had it all figured out, something I had never seen an animal do in this way before. What caused Butter to "think" of turning and going toward shore with the wave? How did she "know" the right moment to turn again and successfully swim against the current of the wave back to her "parent," who was anchored by human legs to one spot? Furthermore, Butter did not turn to go with every wave, but only the bigger ones. For the smaller ones she simply stayed put and floated over. I still feel wonder when I recall how that little goose learned so quickly that day in the waves at the beach.

Salt water increases buoyancy; thus Butter floated higher in salt than in fresh water. Would she still be able to swim underwater, I wondered? No problem. When she and I swam together in the ocean she dove under me (for her own reasons), and down I would go with her (for my own reasons—enjoying play). Generally Butter ended our underwater frolics by surfacing and beating her wings with a crescendo of force until her body rose almost perpendicularly out of the water. Then, seemingly satisfied, she would settle down for a period of quiet swimming.

I had learned that I was no match for Butter in speed, for I could never leave her so much as an inch behind, but her towing power was a surprise. To have a ride you simply swim up behind her and hold the front sides of her chest. Then Tugboat Butter will demonstrate the strength of her marvelously engineered webbed feet by towing you along behind. You would enjoy the ride.

Although Butter was a natural swimmer, we speculated about her flying ability. Wild geese are known for their airborne power, especially during migrations. Butter, however, was a domestic goose, and I had never seen a domestic goose manage to get even both feet off the ground at the same time. People have bred domestic geese over the centuries for the purpose of having them end up on the dinner table rather than in the air. The simple result is that domestic geese

I could never keep up with Butter. **(Photo courtsey Rich deCampo)**

are woefully heavy for their wing area. As a gosling, Butter's ridiculously small wings looked as if they had been stuck on as afterthoughts. But by midsummer her wings were sturdy and had their required flight feathers. Could these wings take Butter up into the air? Unrealistically, perhaps, we hoped we might have a goose that could delight us as much with graceful flights above us as she could with her waterborne talents, and Butter's first flight encouraged us. We were by a rocky shore at low tide, and Kathy, Rick, and I went down to the water's edge. Butter, however, paused at the top of the rocks, possibly considering how to manipulate webbed feet over slanted rocks covered with slippery seaweed. Suddenly, Butter flapped her wings and took off. Hooray, I felt, hooray for our flying goose. She landed easily nearby and I don't know if she felt proud, but we did.

She has flown many times again, but never so dramatically or so high and far. Sometimes in the morning, a run and a short flight hasten progress toward her breakfast in the side yard, and occasionally she flaps her way over something that appears perilous to step on.

A special flight was one with a group of children in the fall. Butter accompanied me often to the school in the city where I was teaching. From kindergartners to eighth graders, the students admired and loved her. They liked to go out to the school's large playing field with

Butter, who walked along with the group holding her head high. When we ran, Butter, of course, ran with us. One day with a large class that combined kindergartners, first graders, and second graders, Butter changed her run into a long, low flight. We kept up our pace and she kept up her flight, and when we reached the end of the field we were out of breath and happy. The running children, laughing as they went, with Butter flying in their midst, is a sight I won't forget, and I think the children may remember running with the flying white goose.

The children got first-hand experience with imprinting, but Butter had much more to teach. Students thought they saw teeth in Butter's beak and were intrigued to learn that instead she had serrations enabling her to use her beak as a sieve. She could grab a mouthful of water plants in water, bring her head up, and let the water drain out through the serrations while the plants stayed inside for her to swallow. Many other waterfowl have beaks similar to Butter's, for the same purpose. The serrations also helped Butter to be an efficient grass clipper. Students were surprised to find that the webbing in her large feet felt warm; unlike her beak, which was of a hornlike material, her feet have blood circulating through them.

The children enjoyed watching droplets of water roll down Butter's back like miniature glistening marbles, a goose illustration of the old saying, "as easy as water rolling off a duck's back." Waterfowl have an oil gland at the base of their tails, and with their beaks and heads they rub oil from the gland onto their feathers, waterproofing them like an all-covering raincoat. Other birds have oil glands, too, but they use theirs less. Waterfowl need waterproof feathers, for the feathers would become wet in water and the birds would lose their buoyancy and sink.

The soft down feathers under the outer feathers of a goose increase its buoyancy and also keep the bird warm by the air trapped among them. One thing the children especially enjoyed about Butter was reaching their small hands and fingers into her chest feathers and feeling the thick covering of the soft, warm down.

Not everything about Butter's school visits went perfectly. It was an independent school that parents often visited to consider sending their children there. Following me down the hall one day, Butter carelessly left a dropping practically under the noses of a group of prospective parents seated at the side. I don't know what effect Butter's action had on the next year's enrollment, but I do know that the inopportunely timed dropping was easily removed with a paper towel. At times Butter honked, loudly, at school. Her former gentle queep, queep, queeps had evolved into strident calls that frightened some of the younger children, but comforting easily assuaged their fears. Once as a teacher passed close to Butter, she lunged her head as if to bite. I was surprised, but, because I did not understand the warning, I didn't think much about it. I preferred to accept what the large, white goose was giving the students. When they are adults and see geese flying overhead, will they warm with an inner stirring caused by having known a large white goose many years ago?

During our commutes to school Butter traveled in a box in the back of the car. Her long neck and head stuck out of the box, and she appeared to be looking around at the sights we passed. And I enjoyed the sights in my rear-view mirror, especially when we were stopped in traffic. Inevitably a face in the car behind would burst into surprise and then smiles. If another person was in the car, the news would be communicated: "Can you believe it—there's a goose in that car in front. Look." I suspect that sometimes duck was specified rather than goose, but that's a confusion we've learned to live with. Some people have even thought Butter was a swan. Ducks have short necks; geese, middle-sized; and swans, the longest. As a prejudiced mother I sometimes think that Butter arches her neck as elegantly as do swans.

When winter drew near, we noticed that Butter was becoming aggressive and starting to act like a watch goose. Her vigorous honkings announced any person or car entering the property, and she assumed the duty of protecting the place against strangers. People she didn't know found themselves at the mercy of an attacking goose whose bites were painful. Within a second she could close her beak in a hard bite that ended with a twist. Ouch! I began to understand my premonition when Butter had looked as if she might bite the teacher at school.

Often we had to go out to escort visitors past our watch goose. Diana, who bought eggs from us, suffered one of Butter's particularly distressing bites and relinquished use of the driveway, entering instead by our seldom-used front door, well out of the way of any goose. A salesman once walked down the driveway while we watched through a living-room window, but his steps became slower and slower, until he stopped. Though we couldn't see Butter, we knew what was happening. As you might guess, the salesman proceeded no farther, but retreated to safety, and we were spared having to explain that we didn't want any more magazines or that our old vacuum cleaner still did its job. Thank you, Butter.

Our watch goose even distinguished our cars from others—we hadn't known she was so mechanically minded. Strange cars that came down the driveway she attacked, but fortunately a determined beak is no match for a metal fender or a rubber tire.

But conditions worsened. As I returned from teaching one afternoon, Kathy greeted me, saying, "Mother, YOUR goose bit me today." Shortly after, Kathy, Rick, Tom, and I were sipping hot cocoa in the kitchen after shoveling snow, discussing a familiar subject—Butter. Tom interjected a novel question, "Do you think Butter is really a girl?" Months earlier I had taken a close look, and, according to pictures on sexing geese, I had decided Butter was female. Mature geese, however, are easier to sex. You hold the goose on its back on your lap, in a position the goose may feel is undignified, and slightly evert the cloaca, which is the opening all birds have for genitalia and expelling wastes. If you see a corkscrewlike object, it is a penis, and your bird is a male. During the cocoa party that day I hefted Butter onto my knee, turned her upside down, and beheld the corkscrew. Our girl was a boy—our goose, a gander. Then we understood the biting and other awful actions because ganders are well known for their aggressive behavior.

Soon, even I, his "mother," lost my immunity. Feeling threatened, or even not feeling threatened, he would bite the hand (arm, leg, or any other convenient anatomical part) of the mother who fed him. One reason for ganders' aggressiveness is defense of territory. For Butter, that territory was our side yard and a portion of the back. But one day he decided to expand his territory.

It happened on a Tuesday, as I remember, because Mrs. Murray, our eighty-four-year-old neighbor, had died that Monday. Butter had not set so much as a tip of a webbed foot in Mrs. Murray's yard before, but on the day after her death, over he went and annexed a large portion of her yard to his territory. In fact, he found a sunny little corner of her house particularly attractive in the middle of that late winter day. As I said before, that was Tuesday. On Wednesday when I came home from work, Tom and Kathy related that people coming and going at Mrs. Murray's house were holding brooms. By this time relatives had arrived from out of state and one even from Switzerland. Brooms are useful weapons against an attacking gander, and so we had no doubt about what Butter was doing.

On Thursday morning I attempted to put some fencing between our yard and Butter's new territory. Then I kept watch to see that our gander did not go over and again add to the problems of the deceased's relatives. But nothing's like a determined gander, and suddenly Butter was missing. Over I went, immediately, and scooped Butter up from his sunny corner of Mrs. Murray's house. Then I knocked on the back door and was admitted with a few wary looks at the large white bird in my arms.

"Will he be all right now that you are holding him?" inquired the daughter-in-law. "Oh, certainly," I responded. But Butter, who was perhaps indignant that I had summarily removed him from his favorite new corner, made a liar out of me. The daughter-in-law was large and buxom under her shiny pink blouse. She walked by us, just a little too close, and before I was aware of what was happening Butter had extended his graceful neck and had bitten, right on the part of her anatomy that stuck out the farthest. Confused by the inappropriate placement of the bite, I blurted, "Oh, I . . . I'm sorry," and I don't remember the mumbled responses. I did, however, express my feeling that they had enough problems during those days without having to cope with the neighbors' aggressive goose.

But these were plucky people. One told me how she returned the last evening with a friend, and there was Butter, blocking their route into the house. Not having a broom with her she sat down, removed her shoes, threw them at him, and she and her friend passed safely by. I reassured the relatives that I would try to prevent any further need for throwing shoes or carrying brooms and kept Butter practically under lock and key for the next few days. At the gathering of family and friends after Mrs. Murray's funeral, the story of Butter's taking over the property added a welcome light touch and gave the great-grandchildren something special to remember.

Why, we asked ourselves, did Butter annex Mrs. Murray's land, and why did he do it when he did? Mrs. Murray died on Monday, and by Tuesday he had taken over part of her yard. Did he sense that the owner had gone? Did he "feel" something was changed? Mrs. Murray had enjoyed watching Butter over in our yard; one of her children suggested, "Perhaps Mother is not in heaven where she is supposed to be, but is here and calling to him." Or was it simply because all the relatives' comings and goings in the formerly quiet yard stirred his aggressive tendencies. To our knowledge, moreover, Butter has never again gone over to Mrs. Murray's yard.

Soon spring was on its way and, with it, the yearly inundation of chicks at our house. One of these was the chick that Rick had brought out to meet Butter. We noticed after the chick episode that Butter even eyed the bantam chicken families that scratched about in the yard. Mother hens are watchful of their brood, and protective too, but if Butter decided on chicknapping, the outcome would be doubtful. Therefore, I began to search for a webfooted baby for him.

Soon I found a potential solution in the form of two domestic mallard duck eggs. Mother mallard belonged to Josephine, my friend in the country, who said the mallard's nest abounded in eggs and that they were partially incubated. I knew they should be kept warm during the trip until they could be put into our incubator at home, but saw no problem. People and birds have about the same body temperatures, and so I carefully placed the mallard's eggs between my shirt and my stomach and wrapped a down parka around the outside. This expedient is effective as long as you don't forget your responsibility and leave the car without holding on to your inner cargo. No mishap occurred, though, and the two eggs were popped safely into the incubator as soon as we arrived home.

The incubator already held many chicken eggs, but, as with Butter's egg a year earlier, a little water sprinkled daily on the mallard eggs helped the duckling incubation. Several times I candled the eggs and saw signs of developing embryos. After the last candling my estimate, based on the size and shape I saw in the eggs, was that they would hatch in about a week. I've drawn reasonable conclusions by candling eggs for years—but one hatched the next morning, and the second, a day after. Yes, I was surprised.

As soon as the first duckling had dried off in the incubator, I took the soft brown and yellow baby outside to meet its foster father. Feeling that I was about to witness an unusual happening, the imprinting of a duckling on a gander, and the fatherhooding of the gander, I wrote notes. Here they are:

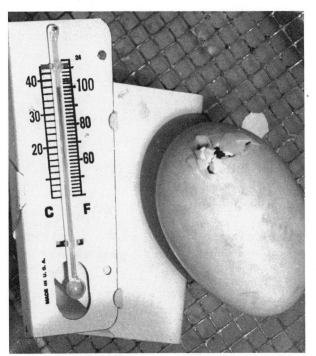

In the incubator, a mallard egg shows signs of hatching.

Duckling feels at home on Tom's hand.

11:40 A.M.	Put duckling down in front of Butter. B immediately drove me away. B paid some head-down attention to d.
11:44 A.M.	B drove me farther away.
11:45 A.M.	B bathes in fish pool.
11:47 A.M.	B looking at d out of side of head, i.e., cocking head.
11:48 A.M.	D crying. B goes to fish pool. B returns. Head down to d.
11:50 A.M.	D going toward B. B eating grass off and on.
11:53 A.M.	B to pool. D cries. B returns. B makes comforting, soft honks.
11:57 A.M.	B swims in pool. D crying, heading vaguely in the direction of pool. B swimming back and forth—low, soft, honks. D hurries to edge. B swims back and forth in front of d. D crying at edge. D tangled in some bricks. B keeps inviting.
12:00 noon	Guinea fowl comes very near. B looks menacing.
12:09 P.M.	B leaves water. Attacks me (trying to take photograph). B walks off. D following.
Until	
12:50 P.M.	B walking around and d following everywhere. D seems absolutely imprinted. (I'm trying to take pictures of them but keep getting big, aggressive goose head in viewfinder.)

At 12:50, reality intruded into my witness of wonders. A newly hatched bird seems a miracle in itself, but I had been privileged to see the mallard hatchling "choose" (my own anthropomorphism) its parent, as well as to witness the big white gander's response in accepting the duckling. A two-way wonder, it seemed, and I had to leave then to teach my class.

Herein lay a number of complications of the kind that occur when anyone is responsible for the care of others, be they creatures or people. Could I, should I, leave my father goose with his baby alone while I taught class? What if . . . and I could think of too many "what-ifs," from roaming dogs to an accidentally misplaced large webbed foot. Telephone calls, arrangements, an old baby's playpen for Butter, and a small aquarium for duckling, as well as my teenage friend, Kim, to baby (goose/duckling) sit at the place where I taught, and—it worked. At the end of the class Kim reported that Butter in the pen was satisfied because he could see his baby through the aquarium glass, also in the pen, and that the duckling had neither become lost nor stepped on, but was safe in the aquarium and contented to see Dad nearby through the glass.

That night the duckling slept with Butter in his cage at the top of the pony shed. The next morning duckling number two hatched, and we had another time of wonders as Butter enlarged his family by including the newest baby. We also had more teaching on my part, and thus again we needed the playpen, the aquarium, and Kim. Again all worked out well, and that second night the two ducklings slept with Butter at the top of the pony shed.

It had been an extremely hot day. As soon as we returned from teaching, the family had hastened to the fish pool for a long, cooling swim; Butter's babies looked like windup toy ducks while they swam right beside him. We were going out to dinner that evening to cele-

Proud father goose swims with his babies.

brate our wedding anniversary, and so Tom and I put the new family to bed early. Was the swim too long? Bedtime too early? Or were there other influences? We do not know what caused the ensuing misfortune.

The next morning when I went to let Butter and his babies out, the babies were dead.

They were on the floor on the covering layer of wood shavings by the door of the cage in the shed. Two limp little bodies. Two brown and yellow rag-doll ducklings. It took me a few minutes to believe what I saw.

Why? The hot weather? Dehydration? Misplaced large webbed feet? No explanation seems particularly plausible—as for Pepper's death, another mystery. Far preferable are the mysteries of such things as imprinting of the baby mallards on Butter, but we have to accept death as a partner of life's mysteries.

We lamented losing the ducklings, the generous gift from the nest of the country mallard. And Butter? He guarded the driveway, swam in the fish pool, and went about his business as usual that day.

Further Thoughts

Aesop's fable about a goose that laid golden eggs was written in the sixth century B.C., but our relationships with geese go back to prehistoric times when our primitive ancestors hunted wild geese for food. The Mesopotamians are credited with having domesticated geese, and the early Egyptians considered geese sacred to one of their gods. In 388 B.C., according to Plutarch, the sacred geese of the Temple of Juno saved the citadel of Rome by honking at the enemy's stealthy approach in the night, thus alerting the Roman soldiers. Similarly Butter, highly regarded but not quite sacred in our eyes, warns of arrivals in our driveway. Stories and folklore, such as the Mother Goose poems of the nursery, attest to the long and close relationship between human beings and geese.

Domestic geese, such as the Embden, Toulouse, Egyptian, and Pilgrim descended from the wild Greylag goose, while the African and China breeds may have evolved from the wild Chinese Swan goose. Butter, we feel, is part China goose because of his arched neck and the small knob on his beak. Of all domestic animals, geese have the reputation for being the easiest to keep, because they forage for most of their own food. Anyone wanting to keep geese can find books with helpful information on the subject.

Konrad Lorenz's ethology studies of Greylag geese won him a Nobel prize, and his writings about these studies are fascinating, even for people who may not feel themselves to be ardent goose admirers. I recommend his book that helped me to understand imprinting, The Year of the Greylag Goose *(Harcourt Brace Janovich, 1978). Lorenz's approach to animals, his insight, care, and reverence have universal appeal—I urge you to read his earlier* King Solomon's Ring, *which deals with many animals, geese included.*

Lorenz's Greylags that imprinted on human beings when young did adapt to life in the wild as adults. My limited experiences indicate that imprinting by one species on another (such as the mallard ducklings, had they survived, on Butter) is not harmful. Some wildlife specialists, however, discourage imprinting a young waterfowl on another species because they feel that it will grow up with an improper identity and will not be able to court and mate with its own species.

I've mentioned that goose flight feathers were traditionally used for quill pens. You might like to experiment with one. Almost any feather that has a reasonably large shaft or quill will do, although our forebears would scoff at such a suggestion, for they used top-quality feathers to make pens that would both write clearly and endure. To make a crude pen, cut off one-half inch from the end of the shaft at a sharp angle (about thirty degrees). Cut a slot down the middle of the leading edge of the slant about an eighth of an inch. (For a more professional pen, make two scallops in the slanted cut, and omit the front slit.) Then find some ink (drawing ink will do nicely), dip the pen into it, and write. You may need to modify the pen so that the ink doesn't come out in blobs, or perhaps start afresh with a new feather, but you may also find yourself trying calligraphy with your own quill pen.

Chapter Two

Bringing Up Bandits

"Mum, could I have a baby raccoon? I would take care of it during the summer, and we could let it go when it's old enough in the fall." Nine-year-old Edie's question many years ago was unusual only in that she wanted a raccoon. After all, most kids at some time or other want an animal of their own. The effects of Edie's question, however, are still with me.

Why? The answer comes with the story.

Not one, but two orphaned raccoons joined our family that summer. Our twin daughters, Jinny and Kathy, were twelve then, and Edie's younger sister, Polly, was nearly six. Edie was to take primary responsibility for the babies, although the rest of us would help. I had the proper permit for the undertaking and a local wildlife rehabilitation center had two sister raccoon babies that they would entrust to our care, because our goal was to release them at summer's end. We chose the names Bonnie and Gay, and everything seemed in order.

Except that we did not know then that even young raccoons do not make good pets, nor did we know much about the pros and cons of raising wildlings. Also, we could not foresee the inevitable involvement of the entire family with these orphans, nor could I guess their direct influence on me. Furthermore, we found that "release" was not the right name for the final act.

Baby raccoons are undeniably adorable—winsome little beings with black-button noses, matching bright eyes set in the traditional raccoon bandit's mask, and short, stubby tails that scarcely hint at their future ringed splendor. We have succumbed to four of these irresistible babies over the years, and Bonnie and Gay were our first.

They captivated Edie and me the moment we met them. And when Gay made soft, chittering noises as Edie held her, and Gay's smaller sister, Bonnie, snuggled in my hands, they won us over completely. They had been born six weeks earlier with but little fur and with eyes closed in a den that was high up in the hollow of a tree. Recently their mother had been found dead, and, because father raccoons do not help to raise their young, the babies were orphaned. Now we were to assume their mother's responsibilities.

It's not easy to take over for a raccoon mother. To begin with, what could we give the babies as a substitute for their own mother's milk? Raccoon milk isn't a supermarket item. We tried a milk formula for puppies, laced with vitamins and served in bottles made for human babies. Fortunately, Bonnie and Gay accepted this milk and guzzled it from bottles at every feeding, no matter whether Edie, Jinny, or some other family member held the bottle. Their vocalizations were as delightful as they were varied—chitters, trills, purrs, and subtle variations on each, as well as growls. Mother raccoon would have understood the nuances; we had to guess as best we could. Their wobbly steps slowly evolved into surefootedness, and soon they became so adept with their manipulative little paws that they held their bottles themselves, lying on their backs. They were thriving, and shortly we introduced solid food in the form of high-protein baby cereal mixed in formula. They gobbled this mixture, but just like human babies starting to eat on their own, a lot of food ended up on rather than in them, and we quickly found that baby cereal, when dried, resists removal from a furry snout. Surely mother raccoon would have started them on something less messy.

Their substitute den in our kitchen was a wooden box inside a spacious cage that has housed many of the animals in our family. The babies were naturally toilet trained. All we did was provide a baking pan, half filled with sandy earth, as a potty in the corner of the cage, but a cat-litter box would have done as well. After a tiring playtime in the kitchen, Bonnie and Gay always returned freely through the open cage door to their den box, where they snuggled together for a nap.

They played much like puppies—biting, snarling, and rolling over each other in mock battles that taught them the self-defense techniques they would need as adults. They also played with balls or anything else that came within reach—pencils, fallen house plants, electric cords, bottle caps, anything. A full wastebasket, once tipped over, offered a treasure trove of intriguing smells for raccoon noses and varying textures for their tactile paws. Our efforts to raccoon-proof the kitchen were in vain, for, unlike toddlers, our curious little imps could climb, especially aggressive Gay.

Polly holds Bonny and Gay.

Our little raccoons peer from a cider press.

Gay quickly turned family breakfasts into a shambles. All it took was a brief climb up someone's trouser leg and a slight jump from lap to table to be in a place filled with things that little raccoons like most: salt to spill and feel, soft-boiled eggs in their shells to roll, or honey-sweetened tea to taste. Generally by the time Gay had tipped over the cereal box, strewing its contents over the table, an exasperated family member would put the interloper firmly back down onto the floor. In the meantime Bonnie, who might have been eating and playing with one of the eggs Gay had kindly rolled over the edge of the table, would have slowly climbed another trouser leg with eggy paws to arrive at this fine raccoon playground just when Gay was deported. Next morning they would repeat the performance of the breakfast shambles because none of us had the hardheartedness to resist our mischievous charmers. By this time we had learned that little raccoons do not make good house pets, but sometimes we chose to ignore our knowledge.

Gay soon educated us further about wildlings as pets. She gained access to forbidden territory, a lower kitchen cabinet, which for her was dark and safe and filled with items awaiting exploration. A clatter of pots and pans proclaimed her enjoyment, but with kitchen orderliness in mind, innocently I reached in to remove her. A sudden, fierce noise that was something between a snarl and a growl greeted me, and I realized that even such a "tame" young raccoon might not hesitate to bite when threatened.

Two weeks later, Gay gave an unfortunate demonstration of her ability to use her small but sharp teeth. While our backs were turned, Gay's constant curiosity led her to climb into a large carton that held a dozen or so baby quail that we were rearing. By the time we noticed what was happening, Gay had decapitated three.

Gentle Bonnie, on the other hand, lacked her sister's aggressiveness. Bonnie had injured herself in a fall from her den tree soon after her mother had disappeared, which may have contributed to her timidity. She was hesitant to try new experiences, and, although her injury had long since mended, she would not climb far up anything. Gay, however, had already demonstrated raccoon climbing ability—a surprise to us because we hadn't known how well adapted raccoons are for being in trees. She used her tail as a balancer in the way squirrels do, and her sharp claws were perfect for clinging to bark or even for hanging upside down to walk with ease along the underside of a branch. Gay distinctly preferred to come down from the tree at a time of her choosing, not ours, no matter how frustrated we became by delays she caused. Encourage as we might, however, Bonnie would not follow her sister to any frightening height of more than a few feet. But we knew that climb trees she must, if ever she was going to survive in the woods as an adult.

Soon Edie devised a solution. Armed with chicken bones with enough meat left on them to create an irresistible aroma for a creature with a keen sense of smell, she climbed our side-yard cottonwood tree to a comfortable branch for sitting, about seven feet up. The tree had beginner's-level rough bark for inexperienced raccoon climbers, and Bonnie, lured by seeing her foster mother up on the branch or by the tantalizing chicken smell or perhaps by both, began to climb slowly, hesitantly, and carefully. At the seven-foot level she nestled into Edie's lap and crunched on one of the bones of her well-earned reward. When finished she played with one of Edie's braids until curiosity, along with her new climbing confidence, led her to cautiously explore more of the cottonwood. Then we had another problem—how to entice Bonnie to come down from her new jungle gym. Edie decided we should wait to see what Bonnie would do, and about an hour later a tired raccoon clambered down the big tree trunk.

A vital part of the raccoons' education was to give them experience in finding their own food. Raccoons are omnivorous; they eat berries, acorns, and corn, as well as frogs, grasshoppers, and even young rabbits. They are, however, classified as carnivores along with such animals as wolves, skunks, and bears, as well as dogs and cats. Gay had already shown her instinctive talent as a carnivore when she decapitated the three small quail. Because wild raccoons obtain much of their food in swamps and shallow streams, or along pond shores, we took Bonnie and Gay to a local brook thickly populated with young horned pout. Without hesitation the raccoons started to explore in the water with their handy front paws, paddling in a dancelike motion. Then, as if savoring tender horned pout had been a daily routine, those paws brought up small, shimmering black fishes that disappeared speedily into hungry mouths. The raccoons needed no teaching from us. Obviously fishing was a skill they innately possessed, along with the equipment for doing it. We marveled at the efficiency of what we perceived as instinct. We were fascinated too by their seemingly nonchalant fishing style, for they did not look at what they were doing. Instead they appeared to gaze upward, as if contemplating the upper branches of trees like bird-watchers. It was fishing by feel, and we began to understand the delicate sensitivity of those front paws.

"Raccoons wash their food," instructs an old saying. In fact, *lotor,* the second half of their scientific name *(Procyon lotor),* means "washer." Once I had even heard that raccoons must wet their food because they do not have salivary glands. But Bonnie and Gay disproved these myths. They swallowed sticky peanut-butter sandwiches, dry dog biscuits, or popcorn as easily as wet horned pout. And yet, putting paws into the water dish, pouncing on the jet from a garden hose, and sneaking a splash in a toilet bowl, were favorite pastimes. Even my morning shower was perceived as an invitation to climb into the tub and join the watery fun. Clearly they had a passion for water. Why? Is it because so much of their natural foods come from watery places that raccoons' front paws have developed extra sensitivity to touch in water? "Ahh, the lukewarm tea in your cup FEELS so good," we could almost hear Bonnie say just before spilling the tea over the table, to be followed by "Oh, great, now I can get all four feet into it."

Those tactile feet are reflected in several American Indian names for raccoons. The Algonquian *arakun* means, I've heard, "he who scratches with his hands," and the name became corrupted to our "raccoon." I've read that the Sioux Indians' name is *wica* and that it means "little man." Raccoons are almost smart enough to deserve such a title. Also, they can use their forepaws almost as handily as we use our hands, and their back feet resemble human feet in shape. Raccoons, like bears, skunks, and us, have plantigrade feet, which means that in walking the sole and the heel both touch the ground. After Bonnie had played with the spilled tea on the table, her hind feet made wet prints that looked like those of a human baby. Should you see such babylike prints in mud by the edge of a puddle, you will know that the "little man" has been there.

Bonnie and Gay grew rapidly during the summer as did their capacity for making mischief and trouble. We moved them from the kitchen to a large outdoor cage in the side yard, but when they were not confined and needed control, we found that a harness for a cat or small dog was useful, although slipping the harness onto the supple, furry body, and doing it up before the youngster slipped out, was a challenge. With a rope for a leash we could go outside together, reassured by the knowledge that our charges wouldn't disappear up a tree for an hour or so, go into traffic on our busy street, or pay a surprise visit to the neighbors.

Although our neighbors have always been kindly tolerant of our assorted creatures, Bonnie and Gay were armed with sharp teeth and claws, for which we, as their guardians, were responsible. We were concerned about our raccoons' potential for biting or clawing, especially if threatened. And I hadn't forgotten how easily Gay had decapitated the quail when she was much younger. When my children had friends over to play I was particularly watchful to keep an inexperienced raccoon admirer from provoking an aggressive response. A photo in our family album shows Gay clambering over ten-year-old Charlie's shoulder, while Bonnie, perched atop his brother Steamer, appears to be contemplating the view. Charlie smiled and Steamer looked a trifle apprehensive, but neither Bonnie nor aggressive Gay ever bit them or anyone else.

Bonny and Gay meet Charlie and Steamer.

At least we had little fear that our raccoons could transmit a disease, for they had been robust since infancy. It is dangerous, however, to handle an unknown mammal from the wild, no matter how "friendly" that animal may appear. Such behavior generally is unusual and can indicate sickness, possibly one that is transmittable to people. Rabies, for instance, is carried not just by cats and dogs but also by wild mammals, particularly skunks, foxes, bats, and yes, raccoons. Wild-animal parasites can also cause problems. I never saw even one flea on any of the four raccoons that we raised, but I will have a tale to tell about hungry fleas from a most innocent-looking infant squirrel.

As the summer days passed, Bonnie and Gay continually educated us in the ways of raccoons. Despite the artificiality in our human parenting, we felt as if we had been admitted into a secret world like flies on the wall of the wild, to witness and ponder the wonders of raccoonhood.

For instance, we discovered that sometimes two raccoons can seemingly multiply. I remember a tennis game that started with two raccoons enjoying a climb around the fence surrounding the court. We saw no new arrivals, but then a raccoon appeared testing the tennis net for a swing, and next several more raccoons were carrying off tennis balls under the misapprehension that the balls were intended for their play. Furthermore, our friend Jimmy found that every time he served, a raccoon was at his feet to trip him up. That totals six raccoons at least. Bonnie and Gay were indeed ubiquitous.

Their innate alertness, agility, and endless curiosity contributed to this talent, as well as a penchant for fast travel in short bursts. I've read that they can run as fast as fifteen miles an hour, although typically they move at an ambling pace.

An ambling raccoon viewed from the side reveals a distinctive rounded-back shape. The back rises, starting above the middle of the rib cage, reaching a height of several inches (a guess; I never measured it) over the haunch, then descending to the beginning of the thick, ringed tail. Once you can recognize this shape, you will find it easy to differentiate a raccoon from the neighbor's cat, or any similar-sized mammal, when your car headlights at night illuminate an animal on the road.

Occasionally raccoons sit up. After catching a tasty grasshopper in the meadow, Gay would pause to sit up on her hind legs to peer over the long grass and check her whereabouts. She'd look like a small bear in this pose, which isn't surprising because bears sit this way too, and raccoons are sometimes called bears' small cousins. The tropical coati are more closely related to raccoons, but I know nothing about coatis' sitting habits. I do know that near the tropics raccoons are smaller and more sparsely furred. I met one once panhandling in a Florida campground; no insult is intended, but it seemed puny to my eyes, accustomed to its larger and more lustrous relatives to the north.

And lustrous indeed were both Bonnie and Gay by summer's end. Our intimacy with them enabled us to see differences between them that otherwise we would never have noticed. Darker Bonnie had an appealing delicateness compared with her bigger sister, but Gay's tail was exceptional. It was luxuriantly thick, and against the lighter brown the seven dark bands stood out in splendid contrast. If you think we were prejudiced parents—well, perhaps we were.

Like normal parents, however, we worried about our kids' future. How would they make out in their real world? Had our lessons in tree climbing, fishing, and insect hunting been sufficient preparation? How long would it take them to lose their affinity for human beings? Would they become wary enough before hunting season? None of these questions were answerable, though we did know how hard all of us had tried to maintain Bonnie and Gay's essential raccoonness despite our human influence.

Yet our adolescents were becoming increasingly independent of us. We had cut down on their daily ration of canned dog food and appropriate leftovers as they began to forage for themselves. At that time we were vacationing beside the sea and at a low tide we took them down to the seaweed-laden shore. Bonnie delighted in feeling the wet seaweed with her front paws, and within seconds Gay had captured and eaten a tiny shrimp relative and another small seaweed dweller. Bonnie followed suit, and we recognized that under the seaweed lay a raccoon cafeteria, bountifully supplied. After that they were responsible for finding all their own food, except for an occasional peanut-butter sandwich snatched at a picnic.

We had decided to return them to the wild on the day before our departure, which was just before the beginning of school. But where should we leave them? Our first choice was a swampy area where they would find frogs and other freshwater delicacies; our second was the shoreline with its seaweed cafeteria; and our third was a place remote from human beings so that the raccoons could forget the human side of their identity. We consulted a topographical map, and, after some of the usual family debate, in which six individuals have six opinions, we reached a consensus. Far from houses was a stretch of back road. It passed over a small brook that led through a swamp and onward to the shore. We could ask for nothing more, except perhaps for the inevitable parting not to have to happen.

We feared that the raccoons might search for us during their first few days on their own, and yet we felt reasonably assured that our work in educating them to be on their own would help them to adapt to their new life-style.

But what about us? During the summer Bonnie and Gay had been like family members. Despite their mischievousness, despite our intellectual satisfaction in returning them to the wild, we would miss them, greatly. And I underestimated the effect on me.

But there was no turning back. Adult raccoons become "vicious," we'd been told. I knew that the label meant simply that raccoons, which are wild creatures, become that which they must be to survive in their environment. Whatever the semantics, though, the danger from bites and clawings was real. And they would have to be caged, permanently; we could not do that to them. No, we had no alternative.

We drove them to the stretch of back road seen on the map, all eight of us together. And when we left them, Gay immediately began to explore in the brook, followed by Bonnie. Before the raccoons could know what was happening, the six of us dashed back to the car and drove quickly away with empty places in our hearts that could be filled only with memories. I can see Bonnie and Gay still.

And I give them credit for rejuvenating my sense of wonder about the natural world. Other family members were strong agents, but these two creatures were the tangible turning point. They were the catalyst that led the full-time mother and former history major toward conservation pursuits and natural-history studies, and to become a teacher of nature and science. They also caused me to sell the raccoon coat that my mother had given me years earlier from a trunk in her attic.

Perhaps I would be more pragmatic now about the coat, but I like to feel the sense of wonder remains.

Four years passed before we relished again the sparkle of black-button eyes set in a black bandit mask and the gentle touch of sentient front paws on a cheek. Blithe, we named her. She was darker than Gay but lighter than Bonnie, and her black mask was nearly separated over her nose. The undertaking was the same as before: Edie would be the primary caretaker for the orphan over the summer, and we would return her to the wild in the fall. Tom and I had found that with our own babies it was easier to care for a singleton than twins, and so we felt that this time with only one raccoon it would be easy—but were we wrong.

Perhaps it was quicker to dispense only one bottle, and maybe it was easier to account for just one mischief maker in the kitchen wastebasket or up the cottonwood tree. But two raccoons can amuse and play with each other, while one raccoon will seek out the nearest human being for sociability and play. We began to realize that we hadn't fully appreciated how serious was Bonnie and Gay's play; they had been truly practicing the aggressive and defensive tactics that they would need as adults. When baby Blithe started to give play nibbles to our hands, we thought it cute. Gradually, however, her tussles with fingers became bolder and stronger. As her enthusiasm for this play grew, ours waned because—ouch—her teeth and claws could hurt.

Picture yourself lying abed still half asleep on a warm and hazy summer morning. A young raccoon appears, deftly climbs up onto the bed, and slips down under the covers. Suddenly your left foot has been seized as an imaginary enemy and is victimized by needlelike teeth and sharp claws. Move your foot away and the intruder perceives this as a playful defensive gambit, clinging to the nearest toe to prevent its escape. By this time your luxurious sleepy state has dissipated, and when you reach under the sheet to remove the perpetrator of the bites and scratches, such a move will be interpreted as a further inducement to play. What you might do next I will leave to your imagination, but remember, please, that the little raccoon only means to be playful.

Although occasionally we indulged our playful Blithe with such goodies as ice cream or elderberry fritters, we taught her how to eat as an adult, when such raccoon junk food would no longer be available. Gay had killed three quail early and easily; to ensure that Blithe would know how to kill, we gave her the opportunity to practice on a surplus, young bantam rooster, which she could then eat. Our giving Blithe the rooster may sound grisly to you—I was squeamish about it myself, even though I know killing is both normal and essential in the natural world. I'm accustomed to watching robins catch earthworms on my lawn in spring, and I've seen many a cat with a mouse, but never have I seen larger predators in action, like a fox catching a rabbit. Although we may witness such aspects of nature's violence on television, we can feel comfortably remote and secure in our living rooms. The television experience is not like a first-hand encounter. I didn't watch Blithe and the rooster, but I know that afterward she was better prepared for life on her own, and that she had enjoyed a chicken dinner.

On her own Blithe learned that toads differ from chickens. Polly and I were picking raspberries in the garden with Blithe; our raspberries went into our baskets, Blithe's into her mouth. A huge toad hopped out from under the bean plants, and we saw it as another healthful raccoon meal. Blithe evidently had the same idea. She watched the toad a moment, pounced on it, and bit—but just once. Immediately she curled back her lips and looked as if she were trying to rid her mouth of a puckery taste. We could almost hear her saying, "Yuk!" And then I remembered reading that toads emit a poison with a foul taste that efficiently protects them against predators. Our toad apparently thought nothing of the incident, for it hopped into the shade of a squash leaf to continue its work of consuming our garden's insects.

Blithe followed us everywhere she possibly could, whereas Bonnie and Gay had often preferred each other's company. After all we were Blithe's only family, and from her viewpoint survival depended on staying with the family group. From the family group's viewpoint, however, this dependence had disadvantages. Try to take a long walk, probably too long for a young raccoon. Therefore, leave your raccoon at the other side of the house with a bribe of several cookies. Then, sneak away for your outing. In about fifteen minutes though, don't be surprised if an undaunted raccoon comes hurrying at your heels. We never had the heart to take Blithe home when she outsmarted us in this way. How did she find us—by smell, by hearing, or how? She shared no clues with us, and we never knew.

Fortunately, her following urge gave her a valuable swimming experience. On a low-tide walk Edie and I waded through a deep tide pool, and we wondered if she would, or could, swim across to join us. She had been nimbly searching with her front paws for tasty small creatures under a piece of seaweed, when she looked up and saw us at the other side of the pool. She hesitated for a mere moment, then walked into the water and paddled easily across, holding nose, eyes, and most of the black bandit mask above the water. As soon as she clambered out onto the seaweed, she gave a hearty shake that showered us with salty drops. But how could we mind when she had just revealed what a good swimmer she was?

Gale winds from the tail of a hurricane indirectly caused Blithe's next swim. Just after midnight the winds blew a large sailboat, dragging its anchor, to smash into a dock. In the howling darkness rain-suited rescuers in boats and on shore were working to free the boat before the tide fell too low. Pelting rain obscured flashlight beams and gusts of wind muffled shouts, a tumult you would think a young raccoon would shun. But be with her family Blithe would, and at the critical moment of success, suddenly I recognized her dark form as she deftly maneuvered her way down a broken ramp. The instant the boat began to move from the dock, Blithe nonchalantly hopped to its deck, possibly curious to explore. A raccoon aboard was not what the frightened cruisers on the boat needed then. "Toss her overboard," my husband called with an assuredness I didn't share. I needn't have feared. Blithe swam directly to shore through the frothing waves and shook off the salty water as casually as she had done after her first swim in the tide pool.

Shortly after the shipwreck it was time for the inevitable parting. Unanimously we decided upon the beach where the little brook— beside which we had left Bonnie and Gay—emptied into a brackish pond at the rear. I had promised Blithe a peanut-butter and honey sandwich for the occasion, and we added delectable-for-raccoons lobster remains from last night's dinner. It was harder to escape from one raccoon than from Bonnie and Gay, who had each other's company, and so while Blithe explored her goodies, we ran back to the car and drove off—fast. The next summer, remnants of the lobster shells were still there with fresh raccoon tracks nearby, and "Blithe's Beach" we have called it to this day.

Our last family raccoon was Jesse, our first male. Also, he was our first raccoon that caused us to worry about his potential for taking care of himself as an independent adult. He had the condition that educators call a developmental lag; more concretely, he acted babyish, and we despaired of his ever growing up.

Even during his first twenty-four hours with us his behavior was surprisingly infantile, and I mean that literally. His surrogate mother, Jinny, who had just finished her college freshman year, was away on a long backpacking trip, and so you can guess who was left holding the baby—me. Jesse guzzled down a number of bottle feedings during the day, and, as a measure of extra care, I gave him a ten o'clock bottle before saying a final goodnight. At 2:00 a.m., however, I awoke—somewhere a baby was crying. A baby? Oh no—Jesse—I thought. He was hungry and demanding a bottle, which I groggily gave him. Night after night infant Jesse cried, and, as all human parents know, that middle-of-the-night crying is difficult to ignore. Ironically, by the time Jinny returned to take over mothering duties, Jesse had just begun to sleep through the night.

Jesse continued babyish all summer, and we worried about abandoning him in September. He showed little interest in foraging for his own food, and, if a pillow was about when he was tired he would surely find it for his napping spot, the softer the pillow the better. He had "101 cute and adorable sleeping poses." One of the 101 that I especially remember was on a porch-chair cushion, a most comfortable one, of course. Jesse was sprawled out on his back with front and hind legs akimbo. His head was turned slightly so that one paw touched the mischievous-looking black mask, his closed eyes and utter relaxation imparting a contradictory, innocent look.

In August, Jesse had progressed so well that he was able to follow

Jesse investigates a watering can. **(Photo courtesy Polly Fleckenstein)**

us up a small mountain, but he collapsed into a nap as soon as he reached the top and was so tired that he slept in Jinny's knapsack all the way home. Annoying child, he even once in a while forgot to use his potty, and someone had to clean up his chosen corner on the porch.

He did, however, appear to appreciate music. Invariably he climbed atop the upright piano when Jinny played. He lay in front of a seven-masted schooner model, contentedly stretched out, listening and maybe enjoying the feel of the vibrations as well. When I think back, I can hear the piece we considered his favorite. Perhaps he felt as if it was his mother's special lullaby for him.

Near the end of the summer Jesse showed encouraging signs of maturing. Although by day he could be found sleeping on a luxurious pile of pillows on the porch, at night he was up and about. He was, in fact, the only one of our raccoons to become nocturnal before release, and raccoons are nocturnal animals. One evening by the ocean shore I heard a soft pattering on the pebbles and through the semidarkness I spotted the familiar rounded-back shape. Jesse drew near, then went right on by me, as if following an established evening foraging route. Another time, Jinny went to investigate strange rattling noises emanating from under the house. Down in the semidarkness she found Jesse rolling an empty raspberry-jam jar about, as he maneuvered his paws inside to obtain every last savory, sweet morsel. Possessive of his sticky treasure, he turned on his foster mother and bit. The bite didn't break the skin, but Jinny had no doubts—she knew then that her Jesse was grown up.

By the time for parting he had weaned himself of all human needs, except for the pile of pillows. We were not generous enough to leave him a pillow or two, but instead we left popcorn under a wild apple tree near Blithe's Beach.

Bonnie, Gay, Blithe, and Jesse often come alive for me in stories I tell when teaching. Generally, I hear a tale or two in return about nighttime raids on garbage pails. Raccoons find that a life alongside human beings is filled with free soup kitchens. Most closed containers with anything that might smell edible are no match for those dexterous paws. My friend Mary Ann has a story about her cat door—the neighborhood raccoons would come through it into her kitchen to eat the cat's food. To solve the problem she removed the food to an upstairs room, but she underestimated raccoon abilities. Next evening

Mary Ann went into the kitchen after dinner and found mother raccoon calmly pattering down the stairs, followed by her four babies.
The family then trouped through the kitchen and exited through the
cat (and coon) door. Raccoons live well in the wilderness, but they
are extremely well adapted for living near people. Decidedly, they are
not an endangered species.

Over the years we, too, have had difficult times with these clever
wild creatures. We've been exasperated by nightly raids on our just-
ripening sweet corn, and we have lost many chickens, including
recently Henrietta and her seven bantam babies, when a raccoon has
manipulated its way into the henhouse. Many of these marauders outwit us, escaping capture in the live trap we set, while stealing the
peanut butter and honey sandwich bait. The ones that we outwit and
trap are relocated to new homes away from chickens and vegetable
gardens. I have another friend who makes raccoon stew, but—thank
you anyway—I could not.

Yet, there is one more story. Brief. And gory. After a first night of
slaughter when we lost fourteen young and specially-bred chickens,
and after a second night when eight more were killed, Tom and I
went out at dusk to save our remaining young birds by moving them
to a safe place inside until morning. We were horrified to find that we
were already too late—inside the cage with the chickens was a mother raccoon and her three youngsters. We had a grievous decision to
make because we could find no way to extract the intruders and avert
the danger of losing our entire new flock. Fervently wishing it could
be otherwise, we felt we had only one option. I will spare you the
details, except to explain that in the end, with a local policeman's
help, four raccoons had been shot and killed. Previously we had
returned four raccoons to the wild, yet now we had taken four.

The paradox is hard to understand, just as our high technology
society faces environmental issues that are difficult to comprehend. If
we are going to live within environmental constraints, we have to
compromise at the very least. Issues such as pollution or destruction
of habitat, or even of a raccoon family versus the new chicken flock,
do not have easy solutions.

With raccoons, however, generally people can coexist and even
with pleasure. Should you have difficulties with your local raccoons,
install a raccoon-proof top on your garbage container (or, as we did
too late, a raccoon-proof door to the outside chicken cage). Use a live

trap (but check wildlife regulations first, because in some places moving wild mammals is illegal). Try an electric fence around ripening corn. If you have no close neighbors, experiment with a portable radio where you don't want raccoons, tuning it to an all-night talk station. Perhaps you can find your own ways of adjusting your needs to those of raccoons. Then you will be free to appreciate the wily and wonderful ways of your special neighbors, those relatives of Bonnie, Gay, Blithe, and Jesse.

 *Further Thoughts*

Edie's question that opens this chapter, "Mum, could I have a baby raccoon?" brings up the issue of the ethics in raising wildlings. I discuss some of the problems in this chapter, and in others. These are complex problems, and my sharing of our family's joys and experiences with our raccoons is not intended to offer encouragement for temporary adoption of wildlings. We may have had luck. Also, we had some of the necessary knowledge and ready access to more, and we were willing to try hard. But maybe we weren't even successful. We do not know what really did happen to Bonnie, Gay, Blithe, and Jesse after we left them on their own.

Here are questions that must be answered by anyone considering the responsibility of caring for a young wild mammal.

1. Does the animal need help? The young of many species may appear orphaned or abandoned, though in reality the parent is giving good care but is temporarily out of sight.

2. Should the animal be given help? It may be injured, diseased, genetically defective, or parasitized, and therefore deliberately abandoned by its parents or unable to compete with its siblings. Many veterinarians have little or no training in handling wild-animal problems. Unless successful treatment can be obtained for the animal, it is generally kinder not to prolong its life. Also, the risk is there that the animal may transmit disease to its human care-giver.

3. What kind of care will the animal need? Human care should approximate as nearly as possible the care that the animal's parent would provide. It is difficult to know the details of the normal parental care and how best to translate them into possible human care. Furthermore, it is next to impossible to give as much time and devotion to the task as the true parent would.

4. Will the animal be able to adapt to life in the wild when grown? What difficulties may occur? Unless we can monitor the animal, we cannot know if or how it has adapted. Dangers may await if it is too trusting of human beings or dogs and cats, and it may not have learned to be wary of its natural predators. If it was raised on human-provided foods it may not be able to find adequate food for itself. It may not be able to compete successfully with other members of its own species; nature overproduces, and even in normal times many young animals in the wild do not survive to adulthood.

5. If the animal does not seem able or healthy enough to adapt to life in the wild when grown, can it be kept as a pet? Almost always, no. The animal cannot appreciate what people have done for it, because normally it must become independent of its parents to live on its own. Thus it can be dangerous to people and should be confined, which is unnatural and stressful for the animal and gives little pleasure to its human captor.

6. Is it legal to care for wild animals? State laws and regulations vary depending on the state and the species, but almost always a license or permit is required, and these permissions are not given readily. Some species are protected also by federal law. Consult the Introductory Notice for further details.

Anyone who contemplates rearing a wildling must thoroughly consider the attendant problems. The difficulties, however, are not necessarily insurmountable, and some sources of help can be found. Many wildlife rehabilitation centers accept care of orphaned or injured wildlife and may give advice to individuals about wildling care or suggest one of the many informative books on wildlife rehabilitation.

Books on raccoons are abundant, but the classic is Rascal *(Dutton, 1963) by Sterling North, which is about his boyhood raccoon. For assistance in watching raccoons in the wild, consult field guides to mam-*

mals or to animal tracks and signs and also Charles E. Roth's Wildlife Observer's Guidebook *(Prentice-Hall, 1982). This is the only book I know entirely devoted to how to watch animals in the wild.*

If you find raccoon footprints you might like to keep a track record. A simple way is to trace the track with a waterproof pen on a piece of clear plastic. Or make a plaster of Paris cast of the track. Cut a strip of cardboard so that you can encircle the track with it. Mix the plaster according to the directions on the box and pour it onto the track within the cardboard circle. Wait for the plaster to dry before removing your cast.

A long time has passed since the raccoons were in our family. Although much of the material in this chapter is from memory, with some jogging by family members, many of the details are from Edie's writings about the raccoons that she cared for: Bonnie and Gay when she was nine, and then Blithe at thirteen. I would like to share with you her version of leaving Blithe.

She has grown up so much that it makes me afraid because she is ready to go back. She is my borrowed child for the summer and when I finish writing this we will return her to her wilderness mother. I think she will miss people for a few days, but adapt easily.

We picked a beach that was stony and dropped her off behind a salt-water pool that moved with the tide. Into this runs a small, fast stream. She loved running water. We left her with a pile of food and ran through the woods. I didn't cry, and my father thought I was incredible, but my mother cried. I realized that Blithe would be happy now and that it was right for her. But later, now, I do cry when I think of her and the good times we had.

Chapter Three

The Old Hen

The three bantam chickens were an unusual housewarming present, but then my cousin Ellen is an unusual person. She has an uncanny way of sensing people's needs and acting upon them. Her action this time was to present a young bantam to each of our three children (Polly was not yet born) when we moved from the city to an old house in the suburbs. And now, a quarter-century later, we have never been without a chicken. Descendants of the three housewarming gifts still scratch about in the yard and a laying flock of hens provides the stock for our small egg business.

Kathy promptly named her trim brown bantam hen Cluck Cluck, a name that made up for any lack in originality by its suitability as a five-year-old's choice. Jinny's hen was plump with white and gray feathers and a feathered tuft on her head, like a hat. Tom intervened and wryly called her Anne Boleyn, but she survived well despite the historical implications. I collaborated with two-year-old Edie to name her little rooster Chanticleer after Chaucer's famous cock that outwitted the fox.

How were we to care for our feathered presents? "Chicken mash from the grain store, plenty of water, and a simple shelter—really, very easy," experienced chicken-keeper cousin Ellen informed us with a breezy casualness that masked the understatement. The first two requirements were easy: chickens will naturally eat and drink anything palatable and potable wherever they find it. Chanticleer and his two hens supplemented their diet of grain-store mash with tender bits of grass and other plants and worms or whatever it was they found when they scratched holes in the lawn or under shrubbery; puddles were a change from fresh, clean tap water. It was the "simple shelter" that was a first problem.

We assumed that Chanticleer, Anne Boleyn, and Cluck Cluck

would instantly welcome any protection from the environment that we provided. How could I foresee that the lean-to I so easily created by propping two old doors at an angle against the side of the garage would not only fail to capture their fancy, but also fail to lure them in out of the rain? Then I recalled the old expression about chickens coming home to roost at night. That explains it, I thought. Our birds need a roost to come home to, and so I propped up a stick inside the makeshift lean-to. We were to be rebuffed, though—the three birds spent the night contentedly perched in the lilac bushes at the other side of the garage. The next night was no better. At dusk Chanticleer flew up to a lilac branch, Cluck Cluck chose one alongside, and Anne Boleyn took a liking to a branch just a little farther up. Night after night we could see three forms at the same place in those alluring lilacs. What the allure was I don't know, although I suspect it was chance. Needing a place to roost on their first night with us, when darkness came on they looked up and there were the lilacs overhead, and up they flew. Being creatures of habit, they took to that spot in the lilacs as their home roost. Why they eschewed my lean-to soon became apparent, and I laughed at my naive attempt, realizing that such a small, low area with a stick in it had little chicken appeal.

But where were we to house our birds? After all, cousin Ellen had said chicken-keeping was simple. The solution turned out to be not only relatively simple, but also effective enough to be still in use today. I don't know if any other houses in our suburban area still had outhouses then, but ours did. It was an old three-holer at the back of the shed between house and garage. Close down the seat covers, adapt the window to serve as an entrance, spread shavings on floor and seating area, put in food and water, don't forget that all-important roost, and there it was, a fine home for bantam chickens—except that ours still preferred the lilacs. When we closed the chickens into their renovated outhouse, however, they gave all appearances of enjoying it. They had food and water aplenty, shavings to scratch about in, and, of course, that roost to sit upon. Occasionally, even with the entrance open, they would roost inside at night, by choice.

During this time of tussle between lilacs and new henhouse, a potential solution appeared in the form of a small black bantam hen, which, for reasons I've forgotten, was being ejected from home in a nearby stable. Our reasoning was that if she came and spent her first nights with us in the henhouse, she wouldn't be subject to the lilacs' lure and would instead entice the other banties to roost in the hen-house with her, for we knew that chickens liked to stay together.

But Blackie's arrival only compounded our troubles. She was immediately and brutally attacked by our three bantams, none of which had ever before displayed an unfriendly gesture. Fearing injuries, to say nothing of outright murder, I immediately isolated Blackie from our bullies. I put her in a small cage, which I left in the henhouse. I hoped that through the cage bars they could all become acquainted without animosity. By degrees this strategy worked and ultimately Blackie was accepted into the group.

Again in hindsight I snicker at my naivete. Cluck Cluck and Anne Boleyn should be excused from charges of brutality, for upon Blackie's arrival they were only trying to establish pecking order, a ritual in any group of hens. One hen is dominant above all the others: she has first rights to food, water, and anything else she wishes. The second-place hen is dominant above all others except the first, and so on, right down to the hen at the bottom of the peck order, with no rights at all. The system is not exactly democratic, but it works and keeps social orderliness within the group. My interference by isolating Blackie in the cage only prolonged the seemingly hostile procedure. And as for Chanticleer's role with the new hen, he was only making overtures to let her know how ready and willing he would be to mate.

At least the lilacs were finally abandoned and each night four bantam chickens roosted in the henhouse. In fact once winter set in they stayed inside; chickens disdain snow and avoid walking in it if they can. The bantams didn't move from their henhouse until the ground was snow-free early in April.

Several weeks later Cluck Cluck produced our first egg. This egg we felt had the ideal shape—gently oval yet finely pointed. The color was a clean white. Cluck Cluck was Kathy's hen, and so Kathy had the privilege of consuming that first egg. She reported it to be tasty, what there was of it. Our egg of perfection was, I have to admit, tiny.

You see, bantam chickens are small—not young, just small—in the same way as a pony is a small horse. And being small, a bantam hen lays an egg appropriate to her size. Her first eggs are smaller than her later ones, but the later ones never get as big as even the smallest eggs that you buy at the supermarket. With tongue in cheek we call ours low-cholesterol eggs, but the yolks have nothing extraordinary—they are simply smaller, thus giving you less fat. And they can be extremely useful when your recipe needs only half an egg.

Cluck Cluck had found that the corner shelf, the toilet-paper holder in earlier days, made a fine nesting box, and left an egg there for us about every other day. She was an orderly, punctual sort of hen and was especially friendly to people, perhaps because Kathy often took her along for company on shopping trips while Mother attended to decisions of little interest to a five-year-old. In mid-May Cluck Cluck laid her seventeenth wonderful egg, but it was her last. Next day, while peaceably scratching about in our yard, she was killed by dogs.

This was the first of our many experiences with the busiest predators in the suburbs, neighborhood dogs, and these dogs, which we could neither catch nor identify, also killed Blackie, the refugee from the stable. Chanticleer and Anne Boleyn seemed upset and sulky for several days. Two weeks later, Anne Boleyn was missing, but this time Chanticleer did not appear upset at all, and several days later Jinny discovered Anne Boleyn eating mash in the henhouse. We began to see her periodically after that and we strongly suspected that practical, sensible Anne Boleyn had hidden a clutch of eggs and was brooding them. Neither she nor Chanticleer let on about the nest's whereabouts although we guessed it might be under the henhouse where we couldn't see it. Then, on June 20, Anne Boleyn appeared in the yard, followed by four fluffy brown-striped balls with little legs. We rejoiced at the sight.

We kept the new family in the chicken house for safety against dogs. Anne Boleyn, an old-fashioned apple-pie and motherhood type, took great care of her chicks, but even so, one died of unknown cause. Not until the remaining chicks were about six weeks old were they able to fly up to the window entrance to the chicken house, and we did not discourage them from coming out because if they could manage that flight they at least had some power to elude the dogs. It was a fine sight to see them following their mother about that day, but come dusk they showed no signs of heading back to the henhouse. We could hardly believe it when we later found Anne Boleyn and chicks happily ensconced in the old favorite roosting spot in the lilacs by the side of the garage. We moved them inside and that was the last time the lilacs were used until many years later when Chanticleer was old and, as if pressures from younger generations in the henhouse were too strong, he occasionally sought refuge there.

When the chicks needed no more mothering, Anne Boleyn started laying again. By this time, realizing how delicious the home-raised
bantam eggs were, we decided to enlarge our poultry flock with the
hens we've always called egg-layers to differentiate them from the
banties. We purchased eight Buff Sex-Link pullets, young hens about
twenty weeks old, ready to lay. They seemed like brutes compared
with our dainty bantams, but Chanticleer saw them otherwise and
immediately deserted his family in favor of the eight glamorous new
arrivals.

Problems soon arose, however. The new pullets required more
room than we had anticipated, and the bantam house was too small
to accommodate all. We figured an area in front of the old outhouse
could be converted for the laying hens. Tom added a door for an
entrance, but to me fell the job of building roosts and nesting boxes.
The larger birds needed more substantial roosts than the bantams.
Though nails often did not go in straight and the hammer would hit
fingers instead of recalcitrant targets, roosts began to take shape. They
were wobbly at first, but my few props worked so well that the roosts
are still in use today, although my nesting boxes have had to be mod-
ified several times. You may wonder as we did: why nesting boxes? A
hen will naturally seek out a safe, dark place for her eggs, just as
Anne Boleyn had hidden hers, we figured, under the henhouse.

The eight pullets soon repaid me for my carpentry by laying six
eggs in my nesting boxes almost every day—plenty for our family,
which by this time included baby Polly. And Chanticleer? He resumed
life with Anne Boleyn and the chicks in the bantam house as if he
had never granted his attentions elsewhere.

We enjoyed the layers, but they were bred to be egg machines,
and they never developed singular personalities. We have had many
breeds of layers since, such as Rhode Island Red, Plymouth Rock, and
Black Sex Link, all of which, like the Buff Sex Link, have been indis-
tinctive, but friendly and docile. The breed most noted for egg-laying,
however—the White Leghorn—is something else. Enter the henhouse
in a hurry, and swoosh, the Leghorns fly up in a distressing panic,
and outside the more enterprising ones fly over a chicken-yard fence
of normal height. They find the grass literally greener on the other
side of the fence, for in the chicken yard busy beaks prevent any
plant from taking hold. One solution we tried was to make the fence
higher. Some of the Leghorn super-flyers still found their way to free-

dom. The ultimate solution is to clip their wings. Simply cut off the ends of the primary flight feathers on one wing, which does not hurt the bird but limits its flying ability. If clipping one wing does not sufficiently ground the bird, clip its other wing. The most difficult part of this procedure for me is catching the hen, for I'm the most butterfingered in my family, and more often than not the bird slips out of my grasp to seek sanctuary at the other side of the henhouse. Wing clipping is not permanent; when the bird molts (chickens do shed their feathers for new ones once a year) the flight feathers grow in again—long, strong, and useful for outwitting chicken-yard fences.

Unlike most of the egg-laying hens, the banties are creatures with wits and personality. Chanticleer was always the gentleman, gallant as roosters can be. Throw a rooster a tasty morsel from your luncheon sandwich and he will not eat it himself, but will pick it up in his beak and drop it, while calling to his hens to come and enjoy the delicacy. Chanticleer constantly watched out for his family, except in his older years when younger roosters superseded him. He was handsome— mainly reddish brown, but with golds and blacks that in some lights showed a green sheen, especially on his curving tail feathers. At the backs of his legs he had spurs, useful for protecting a family from other roosters, and he crowed frequently to assert his masculinity. His crow was always recognizable, for it ended with an extra note that

Edie pats Chanticleer.

sounded as if he were breathing in rather than out, and sometimes now when we hear that same extra note in a descendant's crow, we feel nostalgic, for Chanticleer was an integral part of the bantam family and our own for about thirteen years. At the end he simply vanished one day. Mangled remains or scattered feathers would have increased our sense of loss. Although we knew better, we dulled our sorrow with the idea that he had flown straight up to chicken heaven.

As for our Anne Boleyn, you could not imagine a hen being more of a typical old-fashioned housewife. If she'd been a person, her life would have hovered close around her home, and she would have been a totally dependable friend, the one who would always have time to listen to your woes or take care of your kid when you had a dentist appointment. Once we hatched some eggs from an aristocratic Polish bantam hen. Perhaps I was tempted because the Polish breed had tufts of feathers, far larger than Anne Boleyn's, atop their heads, like large hats. The chicks were cute, but if a dog came through the yard the other bantams would sensibly take flight with tremendous cackling and other alarm sounds, as the young Polish birds stood around, uttering distressed cheeps, as if to say, "maybe something's wrong, but we don't know what to do." We began to realize that these young aristocrats were so highly bred that little remained inside their fluffy heads of wits, wisdom, or instinct. Fortunately we acted before misfortune struck. We couldn't pen them in with our big egg layers because the latter would have shoved them so far down the peck order that their lives would have been miserable. Instead I traded them: four aristocrats with brains bred out of them for one sensible bantam like Anne Boleyn. I felt it was a good deal.

Over the years many bantams have seemed special, but Clucky stands out. She reminded us of the original Cluck Cluck, in both looks and disposition, and she became my first teaching hen. She accompanied me to classes of all kinds. Students could meet a hen close up, learning from her what makes a bird a bird, patting her, and feeling her hard scaly legs, her soft down feathers, her comb, her beak, or just holding and admiring her. How many classes she visited, how many thousands of desks and laps she sat on, I cannot say. One co-teacher, who always liked to use Clucky with a class, was so prejudiced in Clucky's favor that, when seated with students on a rug, she claims, Clucky would move off the rug to the floor to deposit a dropping, and then return to the rug—much too polite to do such a thing amid the group. We have had many other teaching hens, but none has ever equaled Clucky, nor have we used her name again. Perhaps a grandchild will revive it some day.

There have been other notable banties. We even had a "Champion Jumping Hen." We called her champion, though there had never been a contest, because she could leap nearly four feet straight up for a piece of a peanut-butter sandwich held temptingly over her head. Another hen was so taken with our first guinea pig, Squeakie, that she earned the name Squeakie's Little Friend. Squeakie lived in the kitchen in an old wooden box with CHAMPAGNE stamped on the outside, and whenever indoors, the little hen stayed in the box with Squeakie, who never willingly left the box's confinement although the sides were a mere seven inches high. If you took Squeakie out he hopped back in immediately. Guinea pigs seem to have a conservative outlook, but I am fond of them, a weakness noticed by my family. Both Squeakie and the hen, Squeakie's Little Friend, lived to ripe old ages. Several years after Squeakie's demise I received an unusual birthday present—a guinea pig for me from daughter Edie. Generally it's the parents who give their kids the pets, isn't it?

A son of Chanticleer that turned out to have a villainous side was Henry the Eighth. As a youngster he disappeared, presumed to be permanently missing until some weeks later our elderly neighbor, Miss Abbott, remarked matter of factly that one of our "cockerels" (her word) had taken a liking for her thoroughbred horse, Bufo, and was living in Bufo's box stall. We assumed that this bird was our Henry, but knowing how difficult it is to change roosting habits, we decided to let Miss Abbott and Bufo continue to enjoy our cockerel.

One night after Christmas when the temperature was around zero we heard a clucking outside the kitchen door. There in the darkness was Henry. We brought him inside, of course, and then reunited him with his family in the bantam house. Although they received him tolerantly, when spring came I arrived home one afternoon to find Henry chasing Chanticleer, his father, around our house. After the third go-around, I refereed, separating the two. Although I realized the two roosters were trying to establish who should be at the top of the peck order, I did not know the extremes to which such strife could go. Inside the henhouse Henry unstintingly attacked Chanticleer, and outside, the round-and-round-the-house drama inevitably kept on. Evidently Henry was dominant, but he could not let matters

Polly hugs her rooster, Hank.

rest there. One of them had to go, and it assuredly was not Chanticleer. We found a new home for Henry the Eighth and we'll have a story later about his progeny hatching in a shoebox incubator.

One of our first big chicken roosters was another Henry, named for Henry Wallace, secretary of agriculture back in Franklin Roosevelt's administration. Mr. Wallace also bred chickens, producing an especially fine egg-laying strain of White Leghorns. Our regional poultry specialist, Dr. Faddoul, maintained a small flock of direct descendants from Mr. Wallace's birds, and kindly gave me a surplus rooster, immediately named Henry Wallace. He was big and glistening white, with an impressive contrasting red comb. At that time Polly, in charge of chicken care, came into the house one morning saying "Mummy, Henry attacked me when I went in to check the food and water." I hope I refrained from saying, "nonsense—he'd never do such a thing," although I probably felt it. I do remember, with some shame in retrospect, saying something casual, like, "Oh, good heavens, if you think he's going to cause you a problem, just take a broom along when you go in. Don't worry, that'll make everything all right." Several days went by, with no comments from Polly about brooms or attacking roosters. Then, one midmorning when all the children were at school, I went into the henhouse needing a few eggs for a meat loaf I was making. As I left the henhouse I had a vague impression of something large and white descending behind me, and I felt little stings on the back of each leg. In the kitchen I put down the two eggs and pulled up the corduroy trouser leg and the long underwear underneath, and was surprised to see blood trickling down the back of my leg; the other leg was in the same condition. Henry Wallace had not only attacked almost quicker than the eye, but also his spurs had pierced trousers, long underwear, and me. The wounds were minor; the results of the incident were not. I hope my apology to Polly was adequate—I know that Henry Wallace quickly hit someone's stewpot.

We were keeping a rooster in with the layers because I had embarked on a breeding program that was totally casual but reasonably successful. However peculiar it may sound, I have been trying to breed for bigger and better green eggs—yes, I did say green. Some breeds, including our Leghorns, lay white eggs. Others, like our Buff and Black Sex Links, lay brown eggs, and, despite regional prejudices, these eggs are all the same inside. One breed of chicken does in fact lay a green egg—the Araucana breed, which comes from the Araucana Indians in Chile. Known for its colored eggs but little else (it is closer to wild chicken ancestors and its eggs are small), and, much like the bantams, an Araucana hen will lay a number of eggs and then take time off from production. Years ago I was given three Araucana eggs, each a delicate shade of light green. These eggs hatched in my incubator and about six months later we began to enjoy our first green eggs. As in Dr. Seuss's green eggs and ham story, they were good, although their taste did not differ from that of our fresh brown or white eggs. I was curious to see if I could breed the Araucanas with our egg-laying strains to produce hens that would lay larger green eggs more frequently, making the green egg layers more akin to the modern egg-laying machines. Luckily, the green-egg gene has generally been dominant, and we now have descendants of the three original Araucanas, that lay large green eggs with reasonable frequency.

A special Araucana-descended hen was First, who earned her name because she was always first out of the henhouse in the morning when we opened the door. She was an exceptional layer; her eggs were not as large as others of Araucana descent but she laid and laid all year long with modern egg-laying frequency. But it was First's personality that won her a place in our hearts where we keep room for special chicken feelings. She was not only first out, but she also became independent of other chickens, learned how to scale any enclosure she was in, and won complete freedom of the yard as well as a free pass to whichever henhouse she chose to roost in. Never has such an honor been conferred on any other hen, before or since. The sight of First scratching about in the yard gave one the feeling that all was well, at least in our home environment, and with the world the way it is, the all-is-well feeling is welcome. Inevitably, though, First (beloved especially of Elizabeth, our animal sitter) began to show signs of aging. Subtle signs, to be sure: an egg mislaid in an open place, a slower-than-usual approach to grain being scattered with the "Here chick, chick, chick" call. At the end, First was one that in our family lore flew directly up to chicken heaven. She disappeared and we never found so much as a feather.

We do often find eggs in surprising places. We have a perpetual Easter-egg hunt (except in winter, when the bantams stay inside and lay few eggs). In this game the bantie hens hide their eggs and the

Sissons try to find them. We look in bicycle baskets, under woodpiles, or in the hayloft, and if we find the eggs, we've won, and we can keep them to eat. If we don't find them and the hen accumulates enough eggs in her nest so that she starts to brood them, she has out-witted us. She can then incubate her eggs until they hatch, as Anne Boleyn did with her (and our) first chicken family. Often if we find where the bantam is brooding we will move her as protection against predators. But moving is more easily said than done. Many's the time I've moved mother and eggs to a fine nesting box that can be put in a safe place, only to have mother leap out at the first chance, cackling wildly as if to protest, "Help, help, this is not where I'm supposed to be!" I try to put her back without breaking eggs and then put heavy raincoats or anything else at hand over the box to darken the inside and keep the hen in. Sometimes even this isolation doesn't work, but if I persist long enough, generally the hen will acquiesce and contin-ue incubating her eggs in the strange place before too much chilling damages the embryos. One of our bantams earned the name Mrs. Nails because she chose to hide her eggs in a box of roofing nails in the workshop. When we found her brooding the eggs on the nails, we moved her and the nail box inside but then began to worry. How could she possibly turn her eggs over on those rough nails? Eggs need turning while incubating so that the embryo won't stick to the side of the eggshell; we moved Mrs. Nails to a box with easy-for-turn-ing shavings. In her own chicken way she may have been grateful, for she hatched a fine family.

Droves of chicks pass through our kitchen every spring. But in some years when Chanticleer was three or four we had no chicks. We weren't raising big chickens and were puzzled that the bantam hens brooded eggs that did not hatch. Pure chance gave us the surprise answer when Chanticleer came down with a respiratory infection. Because of his special importance to us I took him to Dr. Faddoul, who dismissed the infection as nothing serious, but he took one look at Chanticleer's long spurs, which we thought handsome symbols of our rooster's masculinity, and asked if Chanticleer was able to mate. Thinking of all the unhatched eggs I suddenly realized what had not been going on and answered, "No." "Those spurs are interfering with his mating," Dr. Faddoul told me, "You should cut them back, but you'll need to be careful because they will bleed if cut too far." Back home I first used scissors on the spurs but could not make a dent.

After trying several other implements I ended up with the tin snips, which did the job nicely. And next spring we again began to have baby Chanticleers in the kitchen.

When a hen has laid enough eggs she will incubate them by brooding, and a broody hen is impressive. Her body looks enlarged into a mounded pancake shape to cover all her eggs. Her eyes have a glassy look and she growls if you come too near. Put your hand under her and you can expect to be pecked. She'll sit tight in this way for three weeks, leaving the nest once a day to eat, drink, and defecate. A broody hen on a clutch of eggs is reassuring, like pussy willows promising spring.

But not Snowflake. Her pristine white beauty belied her viciousness as a brooder, and here is her story. Snowflake is setting on a clutch of eggs in the dining room and five-year-old Edie along with her kindergarten friend Brigham want to candle Snowflake's eggs to see if embryos are developing. "Something special for the kids," I think, and I adapt an oatmeal box for candling as Cousin Ellen had demonstrated. (Note "Further Thoughts" in chapter 4 has more detailed information about candling.) Snowflake tries to protect her eggs but amid her snarls and pecks I carefully remove her eggs, one by one. Candling them is fun, especially because all nine reveal developing embryos. Brigham soon learns how to tell—we use an unincubated bantam egg for comparison. The light shines through that one without a shadow; all the others are three-quarters dark.

The children watch while I return the nine developing eggs to their mother. "Isn't it wonderful how mother hen carefully uses her beak to push her eggs back underneath," I point out, when that beak instead lunges at my hand returning the last egg and pecks, hard. We all hear the crunch and I do not have to look to know that Snowflake has pecked a hole in her egg, which must mean death for the embryo inside. "It's my fault, kids, Snowflake was trying to protect her eggs and meant to peck me, not her egg. Let's open it up and see how the chick has grown inside." Calmly covering my own consternation, I start peeling off bits of shell and get a bowl to hold the contents of the egg. Brigham says he doesn't want to see the chick and fortunately I don't press the issue, because out comes the chick with a gunky yolk sack and other gunk, and then . . . the chick wiggles. And not only wiggles, but kicks its feet, opens its eyes, and is unquestionably still alive. "Oh, no," I think, as I realize how helpless we are. The embryo, though alive, is doomed, and I feel guilty that I allowed the vicious beak to break the eggshell.

Edie is interested and wants to see the embryo, and then she suggests keeping it warm to help it live. I can't find much to say and am horrified.

From then on everything goes wrong, as things just do sometimes. One of the pots of maple sap boiling on the stove burns. The acrid smell is still in the kitchen when I remember that I forgot to put into the dryer the skirt that Edie is to wear to afternoon kindergarten, and the fire we light in the Franklin stove doesn't burn. I worry about the egg episode and if Brigham will ever dare eat an egg again, and so I hard-boil eggs for lunch; they turn out runny, but the bad-luck streak breaks as both children happily consume their eggs. And I go to check on vicious Snowflake; she is still sitting on her eggs like a large pancake in time-honored chicken style. She doesn't know she has one less.

Snowflake's violent saga didn't stop there. When her eggs began to hatch, she pecked at the chicks, tossed them bodily out of the nest, and ended by slaughtering two. Was she simply mean and nasty or was she not yet ready for motherhood, regarding her own chicks as intruders—rats perhaps—after her eggs. Whatever it was, on advice from Dr. Faddoul I tried putting her down in our dimly lit cellar with one chick, and quietly, from time to time, slipped her remaining chicks underneath. It worked.

Please remember that Snowflake was the exception. Our bantie hens usually made model mothers. They'll raise their own chicks and will adopt others, never questioning what comes out of a shell, be it pheasant, quail, or guinea fowl. Sometimes they'll even take on mothering babies without having been through the brooding stage. Almost no other species equals the continual caring exercised by a typical mother hen. They talk in distinctive cluckings to their chicks frequently, calling them to food or water and to come in underneath for warmth. Our Champion Jumping Hen obviously was the worrying sort and kept after her chicks constantly with a barking kind of cluck. "Over here, dears, come quickly. You must eat enough. Watch out, watch out, don't stray too far. Come back now. Surely you're thirsty now. Let's. . . ." Well, perhaps you've known that kind of mother. However good her intentions, we could stand her constant nagging in the kitchen only so long, so that she and her chicks were always moved out to the bantam house long before other families.

Because all our hens and chicks have the privilege of spending their first weeks in a box in the kitchen, it is easy for me to take a chicken family along on a teaching day, for all I have to do is put box and contents in the car. Lugging the box and coping with heavy school doors can be a nuisance, but I'm repaid for any trouble as soon as I enter a class and hear the gasps of delight when the children catch their first glimpse of what's in the box. Not long ago Henrietta and her seven babies visited a record number of classes—thirteen in two schools in one day—and the children could watch Henrietta call her chicks to feed, see how they went under mother for warmth, and sometimes see a chick poking its head out between wing or tail feathers to look around. One class was delighted when some of the chicks hopped onto Henrietta's back. Something about a mother hen and chicks is comforting, reassuring, and fun. Perhaps they rekindle in us a primal memory of our own need for such care when we too were babies.

A bantam mother always protects her chicks. When Butter the goose spotted a chicken family in the yard, which he felt he owned, he would slightly lower his long white neck and sidle in a seemingly unintentional way toward the family while cocking a blue eye at the chicks. Mother bantam would not let him come near, and Butter never had even a remote chance to kidnap a bantam chick. And yet, on Blithe the raccoon's first day with us, she tottered after a chicken family in the yard, possibly with the misapprehension that anything that moved could be her own missing mother. But the bantam mother was not at all worried about the harmless raccoon baby and let her continue her wobbly chase.

Older raccoons, as I've recounted, have taken their toll of our chickens, as have dogs, but we have also had other predators. Occasionally skunks come into the henhouse at night. They love eggs and might enjoy a chick, but our skunks have been pleased simply with raiding the chicken feeder. Rats probably come in more often, though we seldom see them. Grain left about anywhere is an invitation to rats, and mice as well, as any farmer knows. Polly discovered an unusual invader one evening while collecting eggs. She dashed into the house, shouting, "Mummy, Daddy—there's an opossum in the henhouse!" As we ran out Tom grabbed a broom and I called to him, "Don't forget, opossums have lots of sharp teeth!" But my warning was needless for we found the opossum cowering under the nesting

Incubator-hatched bantam chicks stay under the lamp for warmth.

Henrietta and her chicks perch on a school classroom sink.

boxes. Occasionally it opened its mouth, which was surrounded by ugly, curly whiskers, to utter a noise combining a growl, hiss, and yawn. We put an open cage down near it, and Tom began to push the opossum into the cage with the broom. I wouldn't say the opossum actively resisted; it simply acted as if nothing much were happening, and once in a while made its growl-hiss-yawn noise. We removed it from the henhouse and released it in a chicken-free area. I've since learned that it wouldn't have mattered where we let it go, for opossums wander and do not stay in any one area. We could probably have freed it right outside the henhouse and it would have meandered away.

This opossum I found singularly ugly from its pinkish-tan nose and small eyes to its pudgy, purplish feet to its hairless and scaly tail. When I read that the brain of an opossum is one-seventeenth as big as that of a raccoon, my prejudice grew. But I was unduly harsh. I've worked with several opossums since and have discovered that they have their own special attributes and can be friendly, even lovable. Their tails are marvels of strength because they are prehensile. Then too, opossums have the great distinction of being the only marsupials in North America. In that way they are treasures.

Our most unusual henhouse predator was a goshawk, another story for a later chapter. Besides predation, however, diseases, parasites, and accidents take a toll. Dropping a baby chick can kill it (I'm glad I don't remember which of our youngsters was the dropper), and last year a chick got its head stuck where two pieces of my amateur carpentry did not quite meet, and strangled. Avian leukosis and the highly unattractive scaly leg mite have been household diseases. I guess I wouldn't have made a good doctor because when I've leafed through chicken-care books to diagnose an ailing bird and then have taken it to higher authorities, invariably my diagnosis has been far off the mark.

Bumblefoot, however, is an infection anyone can recognize—a swelling on the bottom of the bird's foot that causes lameness. The cure is simple. All you have to do is lance the foot to remove the infected material, and I can still picture myself seated on the kitchen floor with a hen suffering from bumblefoot in my lap and I have a knife in my hand. But the picture goes no further, for I cannot make the initial cut into the foot. A vet can, I thought, and decided to pay for my queasiness by asking the veterinarian at a small animal clinic to do the job. Now mind you, this was one of our laying hens and nearing the end of her egg-laying career with us at that. The vet put her on his shiny stainless-steel table and confirmed my diagnosis, as I expected. What happened next I did not expect. He carried the hen away, and I was hearing unbelievable words from his secretary—that I should return in three days to pick her up. I had been set to pay for the treatment, but not for hospital room and board for a laying hen. Though I have a heart for my creatures, our layers are part of family economics. I must have muttered something that sounded cold, cruel, or calculating to the secretary, for all I can remember is her astonished voice, "But you want the best care for your hen, don't you?" I slunk out, returned at the prescribed time, paid a bill that at least was smaller than I had imagined, and returned home with a hale and hearty hen that perversely would not lay us a golden egg for gratitude.

Although golden eggs seem to reside only in folklore, our eggs are of many other colors—shades of brown, speckled tans, and greens, mingled with those of pure white. We sell them in several stores and even with our fifty layers nowadays we have to spoil and cajole the hens to keep up with the demand. Never (well, almost) do the hens want for food or water, and yet chicken chores often bring a curious reversal that nourishes me as well as the hens, albeit with different sustenance. Morning chores especially make a peaceable rhythm, what with hauling water buckets and pouring grain into feeders. I find joy in watching the hens exuberantly run through their door to their yard, like kids running for the schoolyard at recess. An inner strength comes from deep breaths of morning's fresh air. Later today I'll clean out the chicken houses. That I've never been a clean housekeeper I admit, and anyone in my family will readily agree, but there's something about shoveling out the chicken house and putting down fresh shavings that goes further than enjoyment from the pine smell of the shavings; it's an anomaly within me that I can't explain. But, as any farmer knows, these are not utopian chores: chicken droppings do stink and frozen water dishes are a bore and will freeze in one's hands if, in haste to leave for work on time, one forgets gloves. Furthermore, right now it's Tom who does the bulk of the chicken work, and his thoughts about it may be more pragmatic.

Yet another side of chicken-keeping is never rhapsodic. What do you do with your old laying hens, all those extra roosters you've raised (like the one we gave to raccoon Blithe), or any other bird that you don't wish to keep? They all have good meat that is tasty and has valuable protein. But it's one thing to pick out your plump plastic-wrapped chicken at the supermarket and another to confront the same creature running around with all its feathers on. When we buy meat at the store, most of us don't think about someone having to kill an animal for us.

A hen lays well for a year, then lays fewer and fewer eggs in each consecutive year. Sooner or later she becomes an economic liability. Large commercial poultry operations renew their laying flocks every year, but we've done a little of everything. The first time we renewed our flock we killed and dressed off the eight old layers ourselves. Tom wielded the ax, the kids probably still remember the chickens running around with their heads cut off (literally), and I recall the hours it took for me to remove feathers and innards. It was years before we did that again. Finding someone to do this work for you, however, isn't easy. For a time Mr. Christie in the next town would dress off our old hens but only after I spent twenty minutes on the telephone before coming to the purpose of the call, whereupon he would say he was far too busy to do anything for me. Like a game of Ping-Pong slowed to twenty-minute intervals, the ball would ultimately come to rest on his side of the net and yes, maybe he could fit in my birds. Once when I didn't have the nerve to take on Mr. Christie I tried a live poultry place in Chinatown and made an appointment to bring in twelve "pieces," as the man on the phone put it. Polly and Edie, both rather young, accompanied me and the twelve pieces in grain bags on the drive to the city. Upon arrival we found, of course, no place to park. I can still see my two little girls trudging into the Chinese poultry store with the grain bags over their backs. Finally having dispensed with the car I retrieved my carriers and we enjoyed egg rolls and fried rice before taking the twelve freezer-ready pieces home again. Off and on I tried to find a way to reach someone who might be hungry and also able to cope with living, feathered meat. I was unsuccessful. Ultimately we came full circle and again began to tackle the job ourselves.

Over the years I've become a reasonably efficient plucker and eviscerator—hens, roosters, guinea fowl, ducks, geese, turkeys—I've had a hand in them all. Still, I have hang-ups about this business. I would have to be extremely hungry to eat an animal that I've known well. And I don't want to do the killing myself: So far I've avoided it, although I realize I am being illogical. I came close once. Neither Tom nor Edie, who could handle the entire operation, were to be here on the Saturday when my backyard chicken-flock course was meeting, and I had no one to kill the bird that we would dress off at the end for interested students. All week long I kept rehearsing the killing procedure with Tom. Let's see, first you do this, then you do that, and so it went. But just as he was going out the driveway late Friday, he leaned out the car window with words that for me were inspired: "Why don't you see if someone in your class wouldn't like to learn how to kill the bird?" The next day when the time came I fetched the ax and asked the question. A student willingly assented and I gave him the instructions that Tom had so carefully taught me. Like Tom Sawyer, I got my work done for me.

Thus, in one way or another, chickens have been coming and going here ever since Cousin Ellen's gifts. You find a flavor of the chickens' influence on our household in an anecdote told me recently by Torsten, a young man who used to visit our house as a child with his brother Niels. "We each went out to the chicken coop and were allowed to pick a chicken friend to bring to tea. We then brought them into the kitchen. I had a wonderful image of Niels and myself having tea with your daughters while the chickens perched themselves on the backs of our chairs. It seemed like a very sophisticated tea party."

The chapter title, "The Old Hen," is a name that my children invented for me ages ago. Jinny is especially liable to address a letter to "O. H. Sisson." I'm not old enough yet to mind being called old (even if I were, I don't think I would trade an ounce of the knowledge the years bring for a younger stage). And so locally I'm sometimes known as The Old Hen, which for a whole bunch of reasons I consider a term of endearment.

Further Thoughts

You may have some chicken questions not covered in this chapter. How many eggs does a hen lay? A modern egg-machine chicken will lay an average of two-thirds of an egg a day, or two eggs every three days. Can you tell if a hen is in good laying condition? Yes—our first pullets came from a flock owned by a blind man, who said he had tried to select for me those that were ready to lay. I didn't think to ask him how he could tell, but since then I've learned the signs that indicate if a hen is in good laying condition, such as a bright and glossy red comb, yellow pigment in the legs, and a wide opening between the pubic bones so that eggs can come out. The blind man chose well; our pullets soon began to lay. Yet often when I try to cull from my flock hens that aren't laying, having all my senses I have never been able to tell the layers from the nonlayers as well as he.

Has chicken care changed since modern egg machines were developed? Yes—commercial poultry enterprises are mechanized and many use the caged layer system, which isolates hens in small cages that restrict their activity, so that more of their energy goes into producing eggs. We are old-fashioned in allowing our birds to go outdoors, but we do use lights in our henhouses, a modern practice that fools the hens into thinking they have perpetual summer. Wild birds naturally lay their eggs and rear their young when the weather is warm and food plentiful, rather than in winter when it is cold and food scarce. Chickens normally slow down egg production in fall when shorter days bring cooler weather. It is not the temperature that runs chickens' biological clocks, but length of day. A light that extends their "day" to sixteen hours stimulates their pituitary glands to produce hormones that result in egg laying for hens and semen production for roosters.

What about chickens grown for meat? Modern breeding tech-

niques have developed meat-machine chickens, and we raised some once. They were even lower on the chicken scale of wits than the egg machines. Their main activities were eating and growing—rapidly. After a scant three months, we had a dozen tubs that could scarcely walk because their legs could barely support their gross weight. But they did taste good.

Is it economical to keep a back-yard flock? Yes, but barely. With our first pullets I kept a tally of how much the eggs were costing us. Excluding labor, the cost of the pullets, plus capital items such as the henhouse, and counting only the food that went into the front end of the hens to get the eggs out of the other and shavings underfoot, made our eggs cost 40 cents a dozen, which may sound like a bargain except that in those days eggs were selling for 50 cents a dozen. We weren't saving much with our project, but we were enjoying it—our fresh eggs were delicious, and we had the rewarding feeling of self-sufficiency.

How can you tell a fresh egg from an old one? An opened fresh egg has a rounded yolk surrounded by firm layers of white that mound up if you look at the egg's profile. An older egg has a flatter yolk, and the white layers too are flatter. If an opened egg spreads out wide on your plate, you know that the egg left the henhouse a long time ago. Try this experiment. Use three eggs as fresh as you can get them. Open one onto a flat plate and notice the firmness of both yolk and layers of white. Leave the other two eggs at room temperature. Open the second in two weeks and the third in another two weeks. What differences do you see? Try taste testing each egg after thoroughly cooking; I'd vote in favor of the freshest.

Can you eat fertile eggs? Yes, and some people believe them to be superior in nutrients to infertile eggs, but taste and looks are the same. Supermarket eggs are nearly always infertile because commercial poultry farmers do not keep roosters with their laying hens.

Did you wonder why Chanticleer's long spurs interfered with his mating? Many people are confused about how birds mate, but the most startling question I've been asked about this came at a formal dinner before an opera. I had been making mundane conversation about my chickens when the man at my right, looking suave in his tuxedo, *solemnly lowered his voice and asked, "How does the rooster fertilize the egg? Does he . . . er, um . . . peck at it, or something?"*

First, a hen will ovulate and lay an egg whether she has mated or not, just as mammals ovulate and pass on their eggs without having mated. Roosters often put on a short courtship dance around the intended hen, circling her with outside wing held down, perhaps both to show himself off and to prevent her from moving away. Then he mates by hopping upon the hen's back from the rear and holding her down with his beak at the nape of her neck. He brings his cloaca down to join with hers and deposits his semem, but this move generally happens too quickly to be seen. Without fail, however, the hen rises afterward, ruffles, and shakes her feathers as if to say that's enough of that, then resumes her own business. Chanticleer's long spurs got in the way when he tried to assume the mating position.

One rooster for every ten to fifteen hens generally ensures fertile eggs. After rooster and hen mate, the sperm travel up the hen's oviduct, remaining viable for about two weeks at the beginning of the oviduct near the ovary, which makes the egg yolks. Fertilization takes place when a mature yolk leaves the ovary. Fertilized or not, though, the yolk then starts down the oviduct, where the procedure is much like a factory assembly line: first, layers of white are added; next, two membranes; then, the calcium layers of the eggshell; and last, the pigment—white, shades of brown, or green if the hen has the green Araucana gene. Twenty-three hours after the yolk started its journey, the wonderful egg, symbol of fertility for thousands of years, is laid.

How does one learn about keeping a back-yard flock? Try to find a chicken keeper for first-hand advice. Local 4H clubs usually include poultry groups, which are helpful for youngsters. Otherwise look for practical library books or use publications from the U.S. Department of Agriculture. Before starting to keep a flock, remember to check local ordinances. A book that is a delight for both poultry and nonpoultry keepers is The Chicken Book, *by Page Smith, a historian, and Charles Daniel, a biologist. They give an extraordinary blend of chicken information, from history and mythology to raising and cooking them.*

How did Clucky help people understand about birds? She gave them a first-hand opportunity to observe a bird's hard beak, nostrils,

*eyes at the side of her head (for all-around spotting of predators),
wings and flight feathers, contour and tail feathers, down feathers
(which keep her warm, like long underwear), scaly legs (a clue to her
reptilian ancestry), feet adapted for scratching, and four, yes four, toes
(people often guess three, four, or five). Opening Clucky's beak proved
the adage "as scarce as hen's teeth" because birds do not have teeth,
which are heavy. (Birds need to be light for flying. They also have hollow bones and an aerodynamic shape.) Lacking teeth, birds swallow
their food whole. It goes down the esophagus to the crop, a large moist-
ening sac. If we fed Clucky grain, we could feel pieces of grain in the
crop at the base of her neck. The moistened food next goes to the giz-
zard, a tough grinding organ, which "chews" the food using small
pebbles the bird has swallowed.*

*What about Clucky's ears? Could birds fly efficiently if they had
large, protruding ears like a rabbit or a donkey, or even ears with sim-
pler superstructure like ours? Such ears would increase wind resistance;
birds' ears are simple little holes at the sides of their heads, generally
under an ear tuft of feathers. Hold back the ear-tuft feathers to reveal
the hole underneath. The tiny hole of Clucky's ear fascinated everyone.*

*I have read that chickens are the most numerous of any kind of
bird in the world and that they are found on every continent except
Antarctica. Many sources say that the chicken* (Gallus domesticus)
*was first domesticated in Northern India and Southeast Asia from Jun-
gle Fowl. Charles Darwin believed that the Red jungle fowl was the pro-
genitor of the modern chicken, but now some people believe chickens
have a multiple origin and that other types of jungle fowl are also
chicken ancestors. As members of the Galliforme order, chickens are
related to grouse, quail, pheasants, turkeys, ptarmigans, prairie chickens, and even peacocks.*

*Chickens have been associated with people since prehistoric times;
their influence is reflected by the numerous chicken-related words in
our language. Consider these expressions: chicken-hearted, henpecked,
spring chicken, and the many words that include "cock," such as
cocky, coxcomb, cocktail (whiskey drink that originally was decorated
with a rooster's tail feather), cocked hat (a hat with a side turned up
like a rooster's tail), and cockpit (originally a reference to the pit in*

which cockfights were held). Chicken sayings are numerous, including don't count your chickens before they're hatched; mad as a wet hen; get your hackles up; or, ruling the roost.

Chickens are also common in fables, poems, and songs, as well as traditional children's stories such as Henny Penny, the Little Red Hen, and Chicken Little. With our current environmental worries about the ozone layer and greenhouse effect, perhaps Chicken Little's worry about the sky is more pertinent now than when her story was first told.

Chapter Four

The Egg Came First

Which came first? I've read about a Chinese fable that tells of a cosmic egg—how in the beginning neither heaven nor earth existed, but only chaos shaped as an egg, and how from this egg a heavy, dark yolk fell to become the earth and the light, white part became the sky. The fable favors the egg as first. I, too, find many beginnings in eggs. After all, that is how Butter the goose came to us, and at our house we celebrate the rites of spring yearly with hatchings from many eggs.

We prefer to use the real thing, a broody hen. She is the most reliable but also we use incubators because we never have enough broody hens to do all the work. To function as properly as a mother hen an incubator must maintain a temperature of 100 to 103 degrees Fahrenheit and 50 to 55 percent humidity; someone also has to turn the eggs at least two, and preferably four, times daily. The incubator that we use now, Polly made for me from a Styrofoam cooler box, and it is the best one we've had—it did a fine job of incubating Butter as well as the mallard ducklings, and yearly it hatches numerous chicks.

Remember how our raccoon, Gay, decapitated three young quail? These were the foreign coturnix quail (also known as Japanese or Pharaoh's quail), prodigious egg layers and our first venture into raising birds other than chickens. Coturnix quail, imported as domesticated birds, are unlike any of our native quail. Our first two, Queenie and Quenton, were brown with light streaks and came in a box by air mail from California. Although Queenie was only six weeks old she had laid an egg in the box in transit. Soon, after recovering from the stressful trip, she laid an egg a day, constantly, and we were bombarded with tiny delectable eggs, which I can best describe as tasting like a fresh chicken egg with a hint of butter flavor. These mini-eggs were good boiled, fried, or in any other usual style, but it took six quail eggs for one normal scrambled-egg serving.

We wanted to develop a coturnix quail flock, and Queenie was unlikely to brood for a long time, so we put a dozen of her eggs under the bantam hen, Squeakie's Little Friend, who was broody. Sixteen days later in the afternoon every egg hatched and we had twelve brown-streaked babies that made bantam hatchlings seem huge. These chicks looked like softly fuzzy brown bumblebees with miniature legs. Squeakie's Little Friend took no notice of the eggs' hatching five days earlier than her own, or that her babies looked more like bumblebees than chicks. She immediately started talking to them about what and when to eat and all the other usual things that mother hens impart to their chicks. The babies understood her and communication went well between the species. Under the hen's good care the little quail grew rapidly. In six weeks the males had the bolder coloring that distinguished Quenton, and the females began to lay eggs—nearly one a day each—and we began to make culinary hits with stuffed quail eggs and quail eggs in aspic.

To give all our coturnix quail a suitable place to live outside, we constructed a large penned-in area that became known as the aviary. I remember that making it was a family endeavor, thus subject to uneven workmanship. Its chicken-wire construction, especially for the roof, has collapsed several times over the years, requiring extensive repairs. But a special feature I call the air lock is still intact and functioning well. This system consists of an entrance with two doors, one of them always closed so that birds cannot fly out. Years later the mother raccoon and her three young entered the aviary through these two doors for several nightly binges of chicken slaughter. I visualize the mother prying open each door at the bottom and holding it so that her youngsters could enter. That is an improbable picture but I'm unable to imagine another.

The quail felt at home in the aviary and we enjoyed watching them there. The males made a strange noise that we called quirkeling. It sounded like "quirkel," just as the rooster's call is supposed to sound like "cock-a-doodle-doo." When we moved quail in or out of the aviary one or two escaped, and, once gone, we could never retrieve them—that brown-streaked camouflage worked too well. Such escapes bothered us beyond loss of the quail themselves, because, even though only a few went and we believed they could not survive the winter weather, accidentally introducing a new species often upsets the established ecosystem. Sometimes the newcomers

Eggs! From left to right lie an ostrich egg, a basket of our mixed-colored chicken eggs, a bantam egg, two coturnix quail eggs, and a goose egg.

take over, as did the imported gypsy moths that escaped from a laboratory a great many years ago. Because the moths had no natural predators here, cyclical blights of gypsy-moth caterpillars still defoliate our trees.

We began to have trouble with our quail especially when we brought them indoors for the winter. The males fought and if males and females were confined too closely, everyone fought. Closeness exaggerated peck-order rituals, which went disastrously out of control—Quenton, for example, died after being brutally pecked by females. Because we did not have a roomy enough cage in which these quail might coexist peaceably, we resorted to a caged layer system. We felt the arrangement was unnatural for the birds but better than letting them kill each other. Even though we prevented killing, after a few years natural attrition gradually phased out our flock.

We liked quail, though, and the next year on Jinny's eleventh birthday we gave her thirty-four bobwhite quail eggs. For these native North American birds we obtained the eggs from a local farmer, who grew everything from prized bulls and a productive vegetable garden to bobwhites. Twenty-two days later, two dozen babies hatched, some in the incubator, some under Clucky. They weighed only about seven grams, compared to the average fifty grams of a big chicken chick, and like the coturnix quail babies, they resembled bumblebees. We transferred the incubator-hatched quails along with the incubator-hatched chicks into a box with a brooder lamp.

Clucky with her own chicks and the bobwhite bumblebees seemed at first such a fine family group that Edie and I took them to visit seven classrooms at her school. One morning soon thereafter a cold and lifeless baby lay on the shavings in Clucky's box. Without hope I immediately warmed the tiny body in the top of a double boiler (careful not to cook it), and to my astonishment it responded with signs of life. Several hours later I returned a lively baby to its family. Other accidents—some fatal—followed. It appeared that the bobwhite babies, unlike the coturnix quail babies, could not understand mother-hen language, and that Clucky could not understand her strange offspring. Would this failure in communication have happened with other bantam mothers rearing bobwhite quail? I don't know because we never tried the combination again, and to save Clucky's remaining bobwhites we put them under the brooder lamp with the incubator-hatched quail babies and chicks. At first even the sight of one of the fluffy chick-giants was enough to send Clucky's baby bobwhites into a frenzy of fear. East was east and west was west until the following morning integration started, and soon they slept in a chick-bobwhite heap, all snuggled together.

When Jinny put the bobwhites into the aviary, they had outgrown the bumblebee stage and had become adolescent-looking, as young chickens do—they looked gawky, with disproportionately long wings. Soon, however, we had the trim but chunky adults, ruddy colored with short dark tails. The males had conspicuous white throats and eye stripes, delighting us when they were old enough to give the call from which this species gets its name, sounding like "bob why-ite" and sometimes, "poor bob why-ite." We live at the northern edge of the bobwhite's range and hoped to raise a covey of at least thirty that we could release, especially because our birds were descended from cold-hardy stock. Bobwhites live together in coveys during the winter but separate in summer. At night the individuals in the covey form a circle with tails in, heads out, as covered wagons made circular camps for protection against Indian attacks. The birds share warmth with those on either side, and if a predator attacks, the entire flock flies up with such a startling commotion that the predator is confounded and often fails to grab a meal.

Our small bobwhite covey began to make their protective circles at evening in the aviary as the weather turned colder. They survived winter nights well in this style until below-zero weather was predicted. Late that afternoon the children and I brought the roosters to the cellar for the night so that their combs wouldn't freeze (a magnanimous habit of ours because early morning crowings from a cellar easily awaken an entire household). When Tom came home he announced that a strong wind was advancing the chill factor and asked what we should do about the bobwhites. Once the question was raised none of us felt we wanted to pass the evening guiltily wondering if our little quail were surviving, and so out we went to bring them in. With confidence about our good deed, Tom and I entered the aviary, but our bobwhites did not see us as the rescuers we felt ourselves to be. Instead, their reaction was, "Marauders approaching. Fly up, everyone!" The quail circle exploded and when the action was over the birds were scattered to the four corners of the aviary. Next, our dilemma was would or could they regroup themselves into their warming circle now that they were dispersed in the darkness or should we try to find them and bring them inside as we had planned? Would we be able to locate all of them? We chose the latter solution, and by the time we had found every bobwhite we didn't need a weather forecaster to tell us about the wind-chill factor. We settled them for the evening in our biggest cage—the one that housed Bonnie and Gay the raccoons in the kitchen. It was ample for all the quail but not for the diameter of their circle. What did they do? Resourceful little beings, they spent that night and several others in the cold spell snuggled into a rectangle that conformed nicely to the shape of the cage.

We never achieved a large enough covey to release, and their numbers declined. Jinny wrote me recently about her last two bobwhites, which in winter she kept in her room.

I called them Robert and Roberta. They were skittery and flew around wildly if disturbed by loud noises or sudden movements. It was a challenge to go quietly and say hello without their trying to escape the confines of their cage. Robert was quite a gentleman, always protecting his lady. He would wake both me and Roberta with subdued coos and a few bobwhite calls. They would sleep side by side, trying to emulate their missing covey.

Roberta died during the summer, and the next winter I had only Robert. He was silent without Roberta and rarely did I hear him say bobwhite to me. He needed minimal care—just clean water, a bit of food, and a clean cage. I always thought he died of a broken heart after losing Roberta, but those are the romantic thoughts of a child.

In two springs I've been given a ring-necked pheasant's egg that, for reasons I forget, could not be restored to their nests. Both times I've tucked the egg under a broody bantie and both times a fine young pheasant has hatched that looked much like some of the brown-streaked bantam chicks that hatched with it. Each time the mother bantam accepted it as her own despite the hyperactivity that is typical of pheasant. Even having come out with other bantam chicks, the young pheasants never learned the chicks' shrill "cheep" distress call, nor did they understand their hen mothers' talk, and, worse still, the hens never learned one word of pheasant, not even the pheasant call for help. We were reminded of the difficult communications between Clucky and her bobwhite babies but found that as long as the baby pheasant remained with the bantie chicks the language barrier was not significant. But if the baby pheasant got out of the box in which the family was living and began to cry for help when it became cold, the mother, not understanding the distress call, would neither answer nor go to find her missing baby.

The pheasant's hyperactivity was unpleasant to live with because even one's calmest approach could startle them into flying up against the cage bars and we gladly released each in the field at the back of the house when old enough to be on its own. The first one, though, Kathy found a day later in the field, dead. Why? I don't know, but our efforts in raising it had been fruitless. We hoped the second one, released a few years later, fared better and found others of its breed. Ring-necked pheasants are naturalized in our area. They are not native birds, however; they were imported to North America from Eastern Asia during the nineteenth century and are now quite common especially where farmland is abundant.

We've also raised golden pheasants, another Asian native, but these have not been naturalized here. The pair of goldens, like my guinea pig, was a birthday present, this time not from family but from my friend Biz, who knows my idiosyncrasies. Male golden pheasants live up to their name: among their iridescent and brilliantly colored feathers gold predominates, especially on the long curving tail feathers. Visits to the aviary, where our handsome Jack and his mate Charlotte lived, became mandatory for newcomers to our house. Unlike Jack, Charlotte's feathers were a mottled brown, as are those of female ring-necked pheasants and many other female ground-nesting birds. This camouflage protects the female and thus her progeny both during the time she sits on her nest and while she raises her young.

In the fall Charlotte developed a lame left leg, and we brought her in from the aviary to a cage in the dining room to restrict her activity so that her leg could heal. Thus she did not have an opportunity to become acclimated to the cold weather. Even though her leg mended, we had a dining-room visitor until spring, one we all enjoyed. My memory is that she was like having a rare flower with subtle shades constantly in bloom. Arrive downstairs first thing in the morning and there was a beautiful being of soft browns, graceful demeanor, and gentleness, unobtrusive yet responsive to attention. She returned to the aviary in spring but always she remained tame and friendly.

When she laid a clutch of eggs in May and they hatched, gentle Charlotte was a fine mother; we enjoyed our golden pheasant family. But handsome Jack soon succumbed to unknown causes, and later in the summer a dog caused the first collapse of the aviary roof, and, jumping through it, killed the remaining golden pheasant family members, including our lovely Charlotte.

The guinea fowl that we raise are also immigrants, originating in Africa. As with Charlotte and Jack, we started with an adult pair, refugees from a farm whose barn was destroyed by fire. Known as common or pearl guinea fowl, they have dark gray feathers with white polka dots and are stunning birds from the neck down. Their heads, unfortunately, look like a cross between a vulture's and a turkey's—bare with bluish-white skin, pink wattles, a gray knob on top, and a few scraggly feathers sticking up at the back. Guineas have been called feathered watchdogs because of their propensity for setting off a huge racket when disturbed by intruder, predator, or unknown causes. They like to roost in trees and, because they make their watchdog racket when they wake up in the morning, we do everything possible to prevent tree roosting, both for our neighbors' sleep on summer mornings and our own. Most of our guinea fowl we keep with a flock of big chickens; clipping the guineas' wings keeps them down and out of the trees. But we keep one unclipped pair with the bantams (these two are supposed to think they are bantams and roost inside), and these guinea fowl delight us as they go about the yard in a style different from that of chickens: they strut, they run so fast that their legs become a blur, and when they come to the little fence around the terrace designed to keep the geese out, their wings stay in position—one little spring and they are up and over, like playing hopscotch with your hands pinned at your sides.

I've never given guinea fowl credit for much intelligence. They spook at the least excuse and are so flighty that they make Leghorn chickens seem docile; they are almost impossible to catch or to steer back into the henhouse before dusk (they'll walk right by the door as if it weren't there); and the females do not make good mothers. Yet who am I to judge their intelligence? These birds have undergone little domestication, and what I see as nuttiness could be interpreted as good survival techniques for life in the wild. And once a father guinea fowl communicated with me in a way that no other bird has ever done. He was one of the pair living with the bantams, his mate brooding eggs somewhere under the back-yard brambles. Maybe I am the unintelligent one, for when he spent several hours on the porch table by the kitchen door making short strange calling sounds I thought nothing of it. He did the same thing next day and finally I caught on: he was communicating something, and my hunch was that the news was bad. Sure enough, after searching through the brambles I found the empty nest with eleven cold guinea-fowl eggs and no mother. Completely gone. Was the male telling of his loss? Whatever it was after a few days he was back to his normal self, but I have never looked at guinea fowl in quite the same way since. Intelligence after all may depend on the brain of the one making the judgment.

And yet, I have not changed my opinion about the guineas' motherhood ability, at least not compared with that of bantam mothers. Guinea-fowl mothers are easily frightened off their nests, subjecting the eggs to dangerous cooling. Our first guinea-fowl mother to successfully hatch her own eggs nested in our neighbor's pachysandra ground cover. We worried about where she might take the keets (as baby guinea fowl are called) once she left the nest, and the obvious solution seemed to be for us to go over in the dark and simply lift mother and babies from the nest, and bring them home to the safety of the aviary (we had repaired the roof since we lost the golden pheasants). With hindsight, however, our plan was foolish because we hadn't considered the creatures we were dealing with. I remember creeping slowly in darkness up to the nest in the pachysandra and then an explosion, much like that of the bobwhites on the cold night, and probably for the same reason. My well-intentioned, creeping self probably became a predator in the mother's eyes and clearly she ordered her children to disperse, quickly. This story ends less pleasantly than the one about the bobwhites, for in looking through the pachysandra for the scattered keets, we inadvertently trampled and killed several, and also we probably missed finding some.

We let the guinea-fowl mother raise the remaining keets and it can't be said that she didn't try, but her innate skittishness made her appear absent-minded about her young, so that several times she lost a few. Almost ever since, I have used bantam hens or the incubator and a brooder lamp for raising guinea fowl. The bantams are best; they can raise the keets as well as their own chicks.

Even though we hatch several batches of guinea fowl every year, we have many extra eggs. The guineas lay well and their eggs are tasty once you get into them. The eggs, which are between the bantams' and big chickens' in size, have surprisingly tough shells; only a few years ago I found out why. Contrary to usual practice, I was letting a female guinea fowl brood her eggs. She was in a safe enclosure and, because she had few eggs of her own, I added a few chicken eggs to the clutch. When she returned to her nest, she jumped onto it, and under the weight of her landing feet—squash—the new additions at once became scrambled eggs. The thick shells of her own eggs protected them from the rough treatment.

What makes a bird go broody? I suspect it is a natural hormone change, as if she'd laid enough eggs for a family and now it was time for her to incubate them. Most of our egg-laying chickens have had the tendency for broodiness bred out of them. Chickens that go broody cease egg production, and poultry farms do not want to pay the price for maternity leave.

The warmth of the broody hen (or of an incubator) causes the embryos to grow inside the egg. Cell division, though, the beginning of embryonic growth, begins in the hen's warm body during the hours after fertilization while the egg travels down the oviduct. After the egg is laid, the embryo can wait for about two weeks in suspended animation, allowing the hen to start incubating all her eggs at the same time. If she had to incubate each egg as it was laid, the first egg incubated would hatch many days ahead of the others, and the hen could not both care for the new chick and incubate the remaining eggs at the same time. The hen is a servant to her eggs; Samuel Butler said, "A hen is only an egg's way of making another egg."

One could say that using an incubator frees the hen from brooding, as if part of a modern hen-liberation movement, but incubators are not modern. We read that both the ancient Egyptians and early Chinese civilizations built incubators that could hatch thousands of eggs. I wonder at the skill of the ancients, for I find incubators tricky to operate. But I knew a teenager who made an incubator with a shoebox and a light bulb. We had given her Henry the Eighth (Chanticleer's nemesis) to accompany her three hens, and she telephoned me about a month later to tell me that she had rigged up a shoebox with an electric lightbulb and had put several eggs in it to incubate. She wanted to know what preparations she should make for the chicks. I did everything to prepare her for disappointment, reminding her that not counting the chicks before they hatch is practical though timeworn advice. I told her how many times I'd had trouble with incubators, that you must keep the temperature from going above 103 degrees and cooking the embryos, and also keep it high enough for proper development of the embryos. I added that the humidity should be at about 50 to 55 percent, and by that time I knew I had been discouraging, but those eggs probably wouldn't hatch. At least I said to call back if any chicks began to hatch, although I knew I wouldn't hear from her. How wrong I was—three weeks later she called to say that her chicks had hatched and what should she feed them? Despite her shoebox success, I still find incubators less reliable than our bantie hens.

Every spring, though, our incubator generally works for several months because we usually don't have enough broody banties. Into the incubator go Araucana, guinea fowl, duck, goose, and any other kinds of eggs that need hatching. One year someone slipped a starling egg into the incubator. The pale-blue eggshell was so thin that just by holding the egg up against the light we could see what was going on inside: first a spread of blood vessels; later a dark, moving shadow; after a week a large shadow; and then on the twelfth day I opened the incubator and was greeting by Starling Darling in person. Starling Darling was naked and looked more like a four-footed creature than a two-legged bird, for it supported itself on its tiny wings and legs. It looked surprisingly ugly to me, but, remember, I was only its foster mother.

This was first experience with an *altricial* baby, one like a robin, blue jay, sparrow, pigeon, or hawk, which upon hatching is featherless and helpless, and stays in the nest to be cared for by its parents. Altricial birds generally have nests that are off the ground, and so the young are reasonably safe from predators while the parents obtain food. Birds such as chickens, quail, pheasants, guinea fowl, ducks, and geese have *precocial* young that have downy feathers, can leave their nest, follow their parents, and feed themselves. These are generally ground-nesting birds, and it's an advantage for the babies to be able to leave the nest immediately, because otherwise they would be unguarded and subject to predation while the parents sought food. Precocial babies, as the name suggests, are further developed than altricial ones.

Naked, helpless Starling Darling needed to be fed about every fifteen minutes during daylight hours by hands that were already full with four children of my own. I did my best, but the little one survived only a few days; never have I managed to bring up an altricial baby from hatching to adulthood. In recent years we have had barn swallows raising families in our garage and under the porch eaves. The parents catch insects on the wing, which they bring to the nest constantly, but the gaping mouths seem never to be satisfied. No, even without having to catch the insects, I could not give that kind of care, and I understand my failure with Starling Darling.

Our incubator also hatched our first webfooted baby from a duck egg given to me by my friend Biz. I was up early on the morning it hatched and found the novelty of the little webbed feet exciting enough that I took the duckling around to all five sleeping members of the household for admiration. As I recall, no one grumped about being awakened early—the family has been remarkably tolerant about Mum's priorities. Within several days the duckling was able to swim in a kitchen bowl, earning the name Cork because it floated just like one. Cork's stay with us, however, was short. When he was living in the aviary, a predator got him, probably through the leaky roof.

Another egg episode in the family was occasioned by a Mrs. Buchan, who taught at a day-care center and telephoned (many calls about animals are referred to us) to ask if we had a broody hen that she could borrow, with eggs, for her day-care center. It happened that Eleven, one of our Araucana-related hens, was broody, and I appreciated a kindred spirit who would want a setting hen to visit kids. I suggested that she come over and we would see what we could do. When she came I had ready a nesting box with Eleven inside, sitting on a number of eggs. I told Mrs. Buchan to keep the box covered until she had it at its destination and then uncover it carefully. I also had chicken food ready for her to take and said that when the chicks hatched she could come to me for chick starter mash. I added that should the eggs not hatch we would replace them with new ones. Kathy, who had been in the kitchen while these arrangements were being made, said "Mum, you sound like you're selling a product with a guarantee—mmm, Rent-a-hen." And so, Rent-a-hen it was, and it worked well. Eleven brooded contentedly among the children, and when all the chicks hatched the children were delighted, gave each chick a name, and enjoyed watching the daily mother hen and chick show. Eventually Eleven and her family were returned to me, but in summer the whole day-care center came to visit Eleven and admire the growth of the chicks.

After Rent-a-hen came Rent-a-dove. A Barbary or ring-necked turtle dove had appeared one day in our garage. Probably an escaped pet, the dove is a nonnative species. My attempt to capture it failed, but I succeeded two days later when it landed on our porch—I quickly popped a wastebasket over it. It looked much like our native mourning doves, but was lighter in color: a soft fawn shade with a black half-ring around the back of its neck. Barbary lived in a roomy cage in our house and also in my school classroom. During the first summer it laid two eggs, and so we knew it was a she. Next spring she was out of her cage in my classroom one afternoon, flew to the desk where I was correcting papers, and began to pick up elastics. I watched, fascinated. Why elastics? She kept taking them with her beak and putting them beneath her in a pile. Suddenly I grasped the idea: she was trying to make a nest. I began to hunt for a mate, calling the owner of a nearby pet store and, admitting I had an odd question, asked if I could rent a male Barbary dove. The owner transferred my call to the head of the tropical-fish department, who apparently kept doves. Oh yes, he responded, he had a fine male that I could borrow. Would I like to come next day? I did and picked up Eric, a handsome white dove. Eric and Barbary hit it off immediately. Courtship ensued, the bits of hay I had put into the cage were taken to the nesting bowl I had provided, and then came the first egg, followed a day later by the second. Both Eric and Barbary shared the incubation, and when the eggs hatched they shared the parenting. I had forgotten when I became involved with Rent-a-dove that I, or rather Barbary, needed more than a male for mating. With pigeons and doves both parents incubate and care for the young; what's more, they feed the young "pigeon's milk," which is semidigested food regurgitated from the parent's crop into the beak of the young. The babies therefore have huge beaks, and to my eyes anyway do not look prepossessing.

The two little doves grew like weeds and shortly became known as Fore and Aft. Although we never quite knew which was which, they always sat in the nesting bowl, one facing in one direction and the other, the opposite. When the young were grown, I reluctantly called the pet shop to say that Eric had done a fine fathering job and I would return him that day. We had become fond of him. His whiteness, which neither Fore or Aft had inherited, was striking. What a pleasant surprise it was when the keeper of the tropical fish said "Well, why don't you keep Eric?" I assented at once, and Rent-a-dove became Keep-a-dove. Some years later we still have one of the doves. It's hard to tell which—not Eric anyway, because he died of an illness—but probably either Fore or Aft. It had been living alone for a time when an injured mourning dove was brought to me. At the moment they are sharing a large enclosure, and Fore (or Aft) seems delighted with company, paying courtship bows and coos to the mourning dove, but the mourning dove does not reciprocate. Anyway, its injuries are improving so that soon we can release it. Mourning doves I find to be beautiful birds, and we once raised an orphaned one, whose story we will come to.

Further Thoughts

Take an egg in your hand and you are holding a symbol of life; if it is fertile, you have a potential piece of the future. Eggs as a symbol have been associated with birth, renewal, and good fortune in many cultures over the centuries. Today, Jews use the egg in the Passover feast and Christians decorate eggs at Eastertime, though the custom has its roots in pagan tradition. A few Hindus do not eat eggs because they believe any form of animal life is sacred and eggs can be a source of animal life.

The smallest egg is the hummingbird's, about the size of a pea. About 120 hummingbird eggs would equal an average chicken egg, whereas it would take 3,000 hummingbird eggs to equal the largest egg, the ostrich's. An ostrich egg is about six and a half inches long and weighs a little more than three pounds. Boiling one for breakfast would take forty minutes, and you'd need a lot of hungry breakfast eaters.

The eggs of birds vary in color and shape as well. Some eggs appear to be colored for protection by camouflage, like the brown speckled eggs laid by our coturnix quail, but other egg colors are not so easily explained. The ovoid shape of most eggs has protective value. Roll a hen's egg and you will see that it tends to roll in a circle; if lost from the nest it will not roll far. Birds that lay their eggs on cliffs have eggs that are especially pointed at one end as a protection against rolling off the edge of a precipice. Although we all know how easily eggs can break (a piece of advice: never put an egg in your pocket; I speak from experience), but they also have remarkable strength, from end to end. Hold an egg lengthwise between the palms of your hands and squeeze your hands together, hard. Unless the shell has a crack, a chicken egg can support about nine pounds, end to end, because the egg's curvature distributes the pressure evenly, rather than concentrating it at one point. If, however, you are apprehensive about trying the experiment, put the egg into a plastic bag before squeezing it.

Chickens, as I have mentioned, hatch their eggs synchronously, and most other birds do too. Owls, however, incubate their eggs as soon as they are laid, resulting in owlets of different ages in the nest. In seasons of poor hunting, the first, stronger hatchling will be able to grab most of the food brought by the parents, and it will be the one to survive rather than its younger and therefore weaker siblings. Thus little food is wasted on the ones that won't make it anyway.

In running an incubator many manuals suggest starting the eggs together so that at hatching time, proper conditions, particularly a slight rise in humidity, can be maintained. Sometimes, however, I take my chances and add eggs at different times. Butter's and Pepper's goose eggs, for instance, were added to an incubator that already held chicken eggs. Small incubators that hold four eggs are inexpensive but may be erratic in temperature control. Incubators designed for thirty eggs are generally reliable, as is the one Polly made. Commercial ones hold thousands of eggs and are the most effective. Of course you can always use a shoebox and a light bulb, but I don't recommend it.

Making an egg candler at home is easy. Take a round twenty-four-ounce cardboard oatmeal or cornmeal container (or adapt these directions to suit a quart-sized cardboard milk container). Remove the loose end and in the other end cut an egg-shaped hole slightly smaller than the eggs to be candled. In a dark place aim the candler's end with the cut hole at a 75-watt bulb and hold an egg over the outside of the hole so the light can shine through it. Unincubated, or underdeveloping eggs show only the dim round shadow of the yolk, but dark shadows indicate growing embryos. Candling can also reveal egg quality. The air space, which is visible at the pointed end, is small in a fresh egg; but because an egg's liquid contents evaporate slowly through its porous shell, the air space of an older egg may be three times larger. Blood clots, which are not embryos as people often think but remnants from small hemorrhages during the egg's formation, also show up. Two dim round shadows indicate double-yolked eggs, which are caused when the hen ovulates twice in a short time, so that two yolks start down the oviduct together and are made into one egg.

An embryo shows up with candling first as the blood vessels that the embryo sends out around the yolk. Soon a dark spot shows at the center of the red vessels, and the spot becomes larger as the embryo grows. Snowflake's eggs that Edie, Brigham, and I candled showed dark shapes that filled about three-quarters of the egg—those embryos were ready to hatch in five or six days.

The embryo uses the yolk for nourishment through the network of blood vessels. It also uses nutrients and liquid from the white. Egg protein is of high quality, supplying all the amino acids and many essential minerals necessary for animal growth. Many reptiles, birds, and mammals, ourselves included, eat eggs. The yolk, however, contains cholesterol (sometimes reported to average 250 milligrams), and much current medical opinion specifies that a healthy human diet should be low in cholesterol.

When the embryo's growth is nearly complete, it pecks the eggshell with its egg tooth, which is not a real tooth but a tiny pointed bump at the top end of the beak. The egg tooth is an adaptation for breaking eggshells and drops off the beak several days after hatching because it won't be used again. If you hold a chicken egg up to your ear about a day and a half before hatching time, you will hear faint pecking noises. Shortly before hatch you will hear louder sounds and even cheeps. The embryo can breathe air from the egg's air space and will absorb the last of the yolk sac into its body (leaving a visible mark after hatching, like a belly button). It revolves slowly within the egg, making a crack all around the shell and then thrusts its body to break its way out. Even though hatching is a normal occurrence in the life of every bird, from chickens to hummingbirds and ostriches, I am awed each time I see a baby bird come forth—it seems like a miracle.

Chapter Five

Robins Up Front

The two girls who burst into the classroom were breathless. "Mrs. Sisson, Mrs. Sisson," one said, "we found these eggs, and they've fallen out of the nest, and we don't know what to do." Without pause the other chimed in, "They were right on the ground beside the school. I nearly stepped on one, and we picked them up so no one else would step on them, and then we thought we should bring them to you because you would know what to do with them." The girls showed me two light-blue robin's eggs. My fifth graders, with hand lenses ready to observe small pond creatures, were silenced by the outburst, and so I had a moment to gather my thoughts. "Could you see the nest?" I asked. "Well, we think it must be in the tree at the corner of the school building," one responded. Knowing that the restlessness of my twenty-seven fifth graders would soon overflow, I had to be quick with advice although I knew it might be hard for the girls to follow. "See if you can spot the nest," I said. "If it is low down try to put the eggs back in it. If you can't do that, find a little container for the eggs and put them in the container on a surface as near to the nest as you can. That's the best you can do. Good luck!" With a "thanks" and an "Okay" the girls left and my class was soon engrossed in watching tiny aquatic creatures with their magnifying glasses.

That was my first class of the day. In the middle of the third, the two girls interrupted again, more breathless than the first time, "Mrs. Sisson, Mrs. Sisson—the eggs are hatching!" Moments ago in the class Terri had spilled pond water on her desk and her partner's lap, Jose was complaining that his partner wouldn't give him a turn with the hand lens, the paper-towel supply had just given out, and I had to hear "the eggs are hatching." I knew that those eggs were not hatching; I've had too many experiences with kids mistaking a fleck of dirt or other spot on a hen's egg in a nest for a sign that the egg was hatching. Flustered as I was, I stepped out into the empty hall with the girls to minimize further confusion in the classroom, ready to calm the girls down and reinstruct them about what to do with the eggs. Fortunately, before I opened my mouth I looked at the eggs and was astounded to see that, yes, they were hatching. Unmistakably. One had a tiny hole and the other was further along with the telltale crack that develops into the break around the shell. What next? I thought. By this time I had managed to tell the girls how right they were, that it was good they had brought the eggs back to me, and that I would do my best to take care of them. "Thanks, Mrs. Sisson," and the girls left.

Maybe it sounds confusing to teach a class and at the same time care for two eggs needing warmth during their crucial hatching time, but I had promised the girls to do my best. It was no idle promise because years ago I had learned the advantage of being female when something small needs life-giving warmth—just put it down in the front under the bra and in the cleft between the breasts and you have an instant incubator all set at body temperature. In the school's hall I put the two eggs into position and returned to the classroom to deal with the spilled water, who should use the hand lens, and . . . oh, no, I could feel that my instant incubator had a problem. Something was slipping, and I realized that one egg would easily stay put, but the second didn't quite fit. I put my hand over my chest and gently coerced it back where it belonged. Both eggs stayed in position, I found, if I stood straight and still, but I had to assume a Napoleonic pose, hand over chest, to move about and especially to lean over to share enthusiasm with kids about small animals they discovered in their pond water.

Modesty prevented me from explaining my inner circumstances, and so I finished classes three, four, and five, all on each other's heels, using my Napoleonic gesture and wondering what might be happening with the eggs inside and if the students noticed anything peculiar about Mrs. Sisson that day. When the fifth class ended and the students left the room still excited about the pond creatures they had seen, I had a moment to myself. The eggs—how were they? I reached in to find out and, as if by a miracle, brought up a baby robin, pink, with bulging closed eyes, floppy but very much alive and wriggling helplessly in my hand. I reached down front again and pulled up a baby that was lifeless, just partially hatched and looking as if it might have been squashed.

I returned the living baby to its warm spot and tended to picking up: stacking pans, putting away the hand lenses, and carrying everything, including buckets of pond water, to the car. I drove home with a wonderful tale to tell the family and a baby that would need to be fed every fifteen minutes. In the kitchen we made a less intimate home for it in a small box lined with paper tissues on a heating pad and then faced the regime of feeding the orphan. Every fifteen minutes? We did the best we could from dawn to dusk, though sometimes more than an hour went by between feedings. We used natural items such as earthworms, a product of our dependably fecund compost pile, and also unnatural foods such as hard-boiled egg yolk and lean hamburg. Quickly the baby became known as "Folly," a name that is self-explanatory.

When Folly grew and began to develop feathers, we couldn't resist some cautious optimism about his chance for survival. When he was about ten days old, he accompanied me to a teachers' workshop that involved a field trip to a beach where the water remained shallow for nearly a mile out. We were wading in the water and I had Folly down front keeping warm and a supply of worms in a plastic bag in my pocket. It was chilly and windy and when it came time to give Folly another piece of worm, Sally, one of the organizers, would call out, "Robin feeding time," and immediately everyone would gather around to make a windbreak while Folly ate a piece or two of worm. Folly received such good care involving many people that it seemed especially wrong two days later when he appeared weak at the first morning feeding. By noontime I had to open his beak myself to get the worm in and by evening the little robin was dead.

Why? I have no concrete answer, except that I was not a mother robin and lacked the necessary skills. Of course nature continually overproduces and I could console myself with the thought that even with its own parents Folly might not have survived, but I doubt it. I mentioned earlier about Starling Darling that I've never brought up an altricial bird from hatching to adulthood, but I have managed with some of these babies when they came to me older.

About six years ago a student's father brought me a young English sparrow. I asked if he knew any way to return the sparrow to its nest or even to leave it near the nest—questions I always ask before accepting a baby bird. No, the father responded, the baby had been all day in the parking lot next to his business firm. No nest was in sight, and cats in the neighborhood posed danger for the baby. I took the little bird and told the father I would do the best I could for it.

I had noticed that the sparrow's feathers had begun to come in, meaning it was about a week old—old enough, I felt, to have a good chance for survival with foster care. Had the bird been a week or two older I would not have taken it. Often people spot young birds that are feathered and able to fly a little and believe them to be orphaned and in need of help. Not so. These young birds are merely adolescents, old enough to leave the nest but not yet mature enough to care for themselves. They are still being fed and looked after by their parents. Should you see such an adolescent, watch quietly from a discreet distance. Chances are that soon you will see a parent bird arrive with food for the youngster, which will flutter its wings and open its beak, anticipating the meal.

The sparrow orphan was insatiable. At the slightest tap on the edge of the box that was its substitute nest it gaped its beak, which was enormous when open, dwarfing the small body underneath. Gaping is the natural reaction of young nestlings when the parent bird alights on the edge of the nest with food. The yellow outlining of the little bird's beak makes it a target for food that would be hard for any parent, bird or human substitute, to ignore. The sparrow thrived and grew rapidly on a diet of worms, bits of lean meat, and egg mixture with chicken mash, all fed with a pair of tweezers.

Some of our experiences together are worth telling. One was on a ferry trip. I needed hot water to put in the jar in its box to keep the baby warm but none of the rest rooms on the small ferry had hot water, and so I knocked timidly on the door that said "Crew only—Private." I was invited in and, although the practical purpose behind what I wanted may have remained obscure, the idea got across—I needed hot water for this baby bird. Hot water was provided and I was allowed to stay (a female in an all-male bastion) and cared for the little bird, feeding it earthworms and warming it in the box with the bottle filled with hot water. The several crew members, who lived on the island where the ferry was headed, cared as much about the welfare of the orphaned bird as if it had been a rare species, not a common English sparrow. How had it become orphaned, they inquired. How long would I keep it? Would it be able to fend for itself when I released it? And did I need more hot water, or could they do anything else for the bird? When I hesitantly knocked on the private door I did not expect to find such reverence for life inside.

Later on, the sparrow accompanied me in its box and with all its feeding gear to a job interview for a position as science teacher. I'm not certain if bringing the orphan (and having to feed it during the interview) was a help—perhaps it told something about myself—or a hindrance—why can't this person arrange to have her bird cared for by someone else when she has a job interview? After the interview I took advantage of having had to go into town to the school and went to several big city stores. I managed one feeding time unnoticed in the section where all the television sets are on full blast, but the next feeding coincided with my wait in the checkout line. Some adults do not notice such things as someone feeding a baby bird in a checkout line, but children are generally more observant or less inhibited about speaking up. Anyway, with help from a few kids' curiosity, the little sparrow's meal turned out to be a lesson for the people in the line on bird specializations, the care of wildlings, and the relation between birds and their environment. No small order, that.

As the sparrow matured it grew brown-streaked feathers on its back, and its breast was grayish brown without streaks. Young English sparrows resemble the adult females and lack the males' stronger colors. When our orphan outgrew its box, we moved it into a cage that was easily portable. It was not large enough, however, to give the bird room for the flying practice I had planned. The little bird, however, took things into its own hands. It was in its cage on the table on our side porch and the day was July 4. I opened the cage to add some food and, almost quicker than I could see, out flew the young sparrow. It went in a straight line and with strong flight about thirty yards to a neighbor's convenient tree, where it stayed for a few moments, and then, as if had been flying every day, it took off and disappeared. I was startled and slightly worried about the bird's ability to adapt to being on its own so abruptly. Tom thought the whole happening was only fit and right for Independence Day.

English sparrows are common, the opposite of an endangered species. Starlings, the chunky black birds that sometimes have a spotty appearance, are even commoner; some ornithologists believe they are the most abundant wild bird in the western hemisphere. Aside from Starling Darling, whose survival was brief, we have brought up three other orphans of this abundant species. The first was brought to us by our neighbor, Jeremy, who is canny about animals and wondered if the young starling might have been the victim of a toxic substance, perhaps an insecticide. The baby was uncoordinated, perhaps partially paralyzed, and looked contorted. Because it was not old enough to have left the nest on its own, we wondered if the parents, recognizing the handicap, had forced the youngster out. We did not know if caring for the baby and giving it a chance for survival would also give time for the effects of the poison, if that was the cause of the coordination problems, to wear off, but we could not refuse to try. Were we witnessing the kind of event that Rachel Carson described in her book *Silent Spring?* It is one thing to read about the results to wildlife from toxic elements that we put into the environment, and it is quite another thing to see the results first hand.

The baby looked pathetic, and when it tried to move, it ended up sprawled on its side with wings akimbo or helplessly upside down, and it soon earned the name of Topsy Turvy, or Turvy for short. He could not hold his head up to open his beak and gape as do normal bird babies, so he needed to be helped with feeding; I had to open his oversized beak and put the food in. But to our surprise, Turvy grew, and as he grew he became more coordinated. At first we weren't sure if this was wishful thinking on our part, but when Turvy began to eat on his own, we knew he was improving. After awhile he began to walk, and along about this time he began an irritating habit that I have since found is common to other starling youngsters as well. When he was hungry he would squawk. Not just one squawk, or two, or even a half-dozen, but a nonstop series of loud, raucous, and demanding squawks that distinctly denied ignoring. Obviously this squawking must have survival benefits for young starlings, though it is hard to conceive that any bird parent would need the impetus of such a constant racket to give proper care to its young.

Turvy continued to grow and improve. He began to be able to perch and would sit on my typewriter and watch me write. One day he hopped from the typewriter to my teacup and tried to take a bath in it. Fortunately, I had finished my tea and had refilled the cup with cold water, and when Turvy returned to the typewriter, he shook water on me, the machine, the paper, and anything else within a two-foot radius. And soon Turvy started to fly. His landings were often uncoordinated, and over he would go in a fashion befitting his name. And sometimes he would fly into a wall or a piece of furniture. But,

Turvy learned to perch.

as with the rest of his development, his flying too showed signs of improvement.

I wish I could say that Turvy became sufficiently coordinated that we felt he had a good chance to survive in the wild. When he was old enough so that he did not need constant care, we went off overnight, and, instead of taking him with us, left him at home in a large built-in cage at the top of our pony shed. We were dismayed to find upon returning home that he had disappeared. Somewhere in the cage was a hole roomy enough for a small starling's escape. We felt pessimistic that with his handicap he could suddenly learn to take care of himself. Perhaps he managed to find enough food; perhaps his coordination improved faster than we expected; perhaps.

The other two starling orphans that we raised did not reach our hearts as Turvy had. Two of my students found them by the school's playing field on the floor of an enormous shed that housed at least thirty starling families (no exaggeration: I counted them one time with a class). Usually the children brought me baby starlings that had fallen and were dead; I think the kids felt that because of my interest in all creatures I would want to know even about the dead ones, and, besides, I think it's hard for a child to see a dead animal and not do something about it. But this time the two young starlings were so alive that I thought I could even detect the faint beginnings of that raucous squawk. Two orphans take more time to care for than one, and later the squawkings from two young starlings were doubly annoying, but the orphans finally were old enough to be released, and probably some of their many-times great-grandchildren are among the thirty or so families still living in that shed.

English sparrows and starlings are rivaled in commonness, particularly in urban areas, by pigeons. The colonists brought the ancestors of these pigeons as a source of food, along with other domestic animals. Because city buildings offer suitable nesting spots for these birds, also known as rock doves, and because a pair of pigeons can raise as many as five families in a season, it is understandable that we have vast numbers of pigeons in urban, and also suburban, habitats. A neighbor once called and reported that her son had found an unusual bird that, although rather large, was too young to take care of itself. Would I be willing to care for it? I came as near to not being "willing" to care for a creature as I ever will when I saw the contents of the shoebox she brought. I could hardly believe my eyes, for the "unusual bird" was a pigeon. Although starlings may be more numerous, pigeons have always seemed to me the most banal of birds. Even so, I don't believe that my care for life should be discriminatory—after all, everything in the natural world is connected—and the pigeon received good treatment. Parent pigeons, like the Barbary doves, the homing pigeons that Edie reared for a short while, and all other birds in the dove family, feed their young "pigeon's milk," a substance a human foster parent cannot imitate. I consulted my books on animal care, which suggested mixing a raw egg with baby cereal, or moistened dry dog food, or other grains. I administered the mixture with a medicine dropper, which was a messy procedure, but the pigeon thrived and several weeks later we let it fly away in the field behind our house, sure that soon it would find other pigeons and become one more member of a flock.

The experience with the pigeon's milk proved to be valuable in the following spring. I had just finished dinner and was loading into my car violet jelly, nettle soup, various plants and books, and everything else needed to teach my evening wild-foods course, when the telephone rang. I was running behind schedule, nothing unusual for me, and wondered if I should ignore the telephone, but I didn't. It was a local librarian who asked if I might help. A young mourning dove had fallen from its nest near the top of the tall spruce tree beside the entrance to the childrens' room, and. . . . I responded with a hasty yes, ran to the attic for a small box into which I put some paper towels, added the box to the materials in the car, and left for my course, but via the library. The librarian was relieved to see me, and we put the little bird into my box so quickly that I scarcely had time to notice its ungainly appearance. Curious though I was, I taught my class and refrained from opening the box until I returned home several hours later.

Peeking in, I saw a squishy-looking little bird nestled in the paper towels. Its skin was pink but blotched with gray where feathers were beginning to come in, and its beak was bulbous and huge in proportion to the rest of its body. Our newest family member was ugly. Even though it was beyond the little dove's normal feeding hours, I thought a meal would be in order, because it might not have had food for a long time. Thanks to the experience with the pigeon, I was quickly able to make a pigeon-milk mixture and administer it to that bulbous beak. The dove was smaller, however, and it was harder to get the sloppy meal down the beak. Much of the homemade pigeon milk dribbled over the baby and onto my hands and lap as well. While cleaning up both of us, I was musing about the dove's birthplace by the library and thought of a name for the orphan: Biblio.

The name stuck, as did the food that leaked onto poor Biblio at every feeding. He was ugly enough to begin with, and that dried imitation pigeon's milk encrusted on his new feathers did nothing to help his appearance. Wherever I went during the day, Biblio came too for feedings, and, despite his looks, many classes of children enjoyed meeting him and learning about how young pigeons and doves eat, as well as many of their other adaptations. Doves and pigeons, for instance, can drink by using the beak as a straw, but most other birds must tilt the head up after taking water into the beak to let the liquid flow down the throat.

Children often asked if I would keep him as a pet, and I always responded that no matter how tame and even friendly Biblio seemed then, by nature he was a wild bird and therefore would never be happy living in a cage as a adult. We would release him as soon as he was able to take care of himself. As he grew, however, I found my resolution weakening. When he outgrew the encrusted-food stage, he began to have the sleek lines and gentle appearance of his species. Mourning doves are beautiful birds, and if you have read about Margelot, the mourning dove in E. B. White's *Stuart Little*, you may understand my affinity for Biblio.

When I worked in my office at home I often would let him loose in the room with me. He would walk about the floor, sit on the bookcase, or often on the back of the typewriter. He could easily fly from place to place in the small room and sometimes landed on the top of my head. He made a distinctive "whirrr" when he flew, typical of his species. He also had an ability to helicopter, which I learned is also typical. It seemed to me that he liked to helicopter over my desk more than in any other place. Papers beneath him would scatter in all directions, onto the floor, the radiator, or elsewhere on the desk, upside down or right side up, but always out of order. As I discovered later, Barbary doves can hover in the same way, and also with the same chaotic results over a paper-laden desk. His droppings were small and I never found them troublesome, though perhaps I have more tolerance, or less concern, than many people. I imagine that if I were to look behind the books at the top of the bookcase right now, I might find a small spot somewhere there that would remind me of the many hours Biblio and I shared the room together.

We often allowed him to roam about the house. He spent much time on the floor, for doves are ground feeders, like the pigeons that walk about city parks, looking for natural food as well as handouts. If a person came by, Biblio would generally move aside, in a calm manner because he was extremely tame. But one time he did not move fast enough. Jinny was going through the kitchen door carrying a large tray, and suddenly she exclaimed, "Oh, Biblio, I'm sorry. I didn't mean to hit you." I was chopping vegetables in the kitchen and vividly recall Jinny's coming back through the door, without the tray, and calling out, "Oh no!" The distress in her voice brought me over—there on the floor just inside the dining room was Biblio's tail. The whole tail. Simply lying there. We were horrified and looked for Biblio to see if he was all right, and soon we found our tailless dove quietly picking up a few crumbs under the far side of the dining room table. He appeared unphased and unhurt, but he was an odd sight without his handsome tail.

We figured that when Jinny hit Biblio she must have stepped on his tail. And, we concluded, the tail came off so easily because that was an adaptation against predators. Had Jinny's foot been a hungry fox it would have ended up with a bite of tail feathers rather than a meal of dove. Other animals have this adaptation; some lizards can lose a tail to a predator and later regrow it. Next we wondered when Biblio would again have a handsome tail, fearing that we might have to wait for molting time. The trail grew rapidly, though, and within three weeks you would never have known it had been missing.

By this time we had let our emotions rule over reason and had kept Biblio beyond the age when he could learn to care for himself in the wild. Oh yes, we had some excuses. Cold weather had set in, and wouldn't it be better to release him when food was more plentiful in the spring? I think each of us enjoyed his beauty; we had an unspoken conspiracy to postpone his release. Years earlier the girls and I

Contented Biblio sits on the dish drainer. **(Photo courtesy Kathy Feehery)**

had seen a stuffed passenger pigeon in a museum in Cleveland, Ohio. Once passenger pigeons were extremely common, but unregulated commercial hunting caused their extinction. Mourning doves resemble passenger pigeons in many ways, and maybe it was remembering the stuffed, extinct bird in Cleveland that caused us to want to keep Biblio longer.

But we shouldn't have done it. Mourning doves are so named because their cooing has a mournful quality and Biblio cooed, often. It wasn't the quality of the coo that was bothersome but it would wake us all too early in the morning. Thus, we moved Biblio's cage to the table on the side porch, and one night a raccoon reached in through the bars of the cage. Those agile raccoon front paws we understand well, and a dove perched anywhere near the side of the cage would have no chance. Sorrowfully, Biblio's story ends there.

 ## *Further Thoughts*

If you find a helpless baby bird out of its nest, try to return it to the nest. If the nest cannot be found or reached, improvise a nest from a small container and leave it with the bird inside as near to the original nest as you can. Do not worry that the human smell will cause the parents to abandon the baby. Birds have little sense of smell, and will continue to care for a baby that you have handled and returned. If you find a bird's egg on the ground, follow the same procedure. An adolescent bird, which is out of the nest, still needs parental care. It should be left alone, but, if there is a danger to it from dogs or cats, keep those pets inside or drive them away, and, if the bird is on the ground, put it on a branch for greater safety.

Should you find a truly orphaned baby bird, many of the problems are the same as with orphaned mammals. Is the baby bird injured, diseased, genetically defective, or parasitized? If so, it may be kinder to the baby not to prolong its life, and sometimes the bird may transmit disease or parasites to people. I do not know if our care gave Turvy a chance to recover from exposure to an insecticide, or whether we merely made his difficulties last longer. How can one best care for a young bird? Whatever the age of the bird, care is always difficult. Newly hatched altricial birds such as Folly are extremely difficult to rear because of their helplessness, but the older the bird, the better are its chances with foster care. Don't forget, however, that such birds should be fed frequently, even every fifteen minutes, from dawn to dusk, and that is a sizable responsibility. Precocial babies, such as quail or pheasants, will feed themselves, but both kinds usually need extra warmth. How well will the bird adapt to living in the wild when released? The first pheasant that we released did not adapt (or was the victim of an accident), for it was found dead the following day. I hope that our other orphans fared better, but it is impossible to tell. Also, some species of birds brought up by people will have difficulty adapting because they have not learned from their parents things such as song patterns that they will need in adult life. A last but most important consideration is that in almost all cases a state permit, and usually also a federal permit, is required for possessing or rearing wild birds.

The difficulties in raising an orphaned bird are great, but not necessarily insurmountable. Wildlife rehabilitation centers often accept such orphans, but their care costs, and so people bringing in orphans should be willing to make a donation to the center. If you have the proper permits, the center may be able to help with advice about care and suggest books on wild bird rehabilitation.

The robin and mourning dove are native North American species, but the other birds mentioned in chapter 5 are nonnatives, and their stories illustrate why the potential influence of a foreign species demands study before introducing individuals. Pigeons, relatives of the dove that returned to the ark with the olive twig in its bill, were brought to America by the early settlers for food. English sparrows were brought about two hundred years later. This species has accompanied people over many centuries, feeding upon undigested grain in horse, cow, camel, and even elephant dung, raiding grain in farmers' fields, and also consuming some insects. In the United States, growing cities destroyed habitats of many native insect-eating birds, forcing them to live elsewhere, and leaving few birds to eat the caterpillars and oth-

insects in city trees. *People recalled a European city bird that they believed fed its young such insects, and during the 1850s many of these birds were imported and released to control city insects. This bird came to be known as the English sparrow, though it is really a weaver finch that originated in Africa. The resourceful English sparrows consumed disappointingly few city insects but found instead a bountiful food supply in seeds supplied by horse manure on city streets, and sometimes grain in farmers' wagons. Conditions here suited these birds well, and few natural enemies were around to control their population; they took over habitats and nesting places from many native birds. By the 1880s some people began to believe that importing the English sparrow had been a mistake, but it was too late. The hardy, pugnacious birds had firmly established themselves in North American ecosystems. And their ability to adapt still helps them. Sometimes in summer they frequent gas stations to consume the insects that fall off radiators of the cars that stop to fill up.*

The starling success story in North America begins with a line spoken by Hotspur in Shakespeare's King Henry IV: *"I'll have a starling taught to speak. . . ." In the 1880s, Eugene Schieffelin, a Shakespeare admirer in New York City, who was interested in birds, hoped to naturalize in the United States all the birds that Shakespeare mentioned in his plays. Schieffelin's attempts with skylarks, song thrushes, and nightingales failed, but, undaunted, he imported 80 starlings in 1880 and 40 more in 1881. He released these 120 birds in Central Park, where they thrived and multiplied greatly. They spread to other regions, where they multiplied greatly again, and Hotspur's statement has borne indirect fruit—the millions of starlings that live in North America today. I've heard that in 1928 a United States Department of Agriculture bulletin recommended starling pie, but it would take a tremendous quantity of pies to make a noticeable dent in the starling population. No attempt at starling control has been significantly successful. One city tried an innovative approach to repel its huge roosting flocks of starlings, putting aluminum owls on the tops of buildings, only to have the starlings roost on the owls.*

The one consolation in starling overabundance is that the young ᵒᵃᵃin in the nest for three weeks, during which time the parents feed them a diet exclusively of insects: cutworms, Japanese beetles, and any other insect they can snag. Care to guess how many insects a nest of six babies requires? It's about 15,000—and that's not counting any that the parents eat. For farmers and gardeners this is an encouraging figure.

Their excessive numbers do not diminish the wonders of these common creatures. Much can be learned by observing parent starlings bringing food to their nest, English sparrows squabbling, or pigeons courting in the park. Noticing the simplest happenings nearby sometimes leads to the greatest lessons.

Chapter Six

Flying Free

The blue jay appeared as if from nowhere, directly in front of my car. With no chance to stop, I held my breath, watching the rear-view mirror, hoping not to see the tragic sight I then did see, a flopping body—I had hit the jay. On that back road with no other cars, it was easy to stop and walk back to the bird. At least it wasn't dead, but it lay there flapping helplessly. I picked it up carefully and at once saw that its right leg was broken in the middle, the end dangling.

I felt awful and put the bird in a dark corner on the car floor.

When we arrived home the blue jay was no worse and so I could hope that the only injury was its leg. I didn't think it would be hard to set, but toothpick splints and sticky adhesive tape were difficult to affix on such a small leg. My best was a mediocre job, so that two days later it was evident that the leg—toothpicks, adhesive tape, and all—was bending. Removing the adhesive tape was even more difficult than it had been to put on because of that fragile leg inside. When the leg was freed, I was surprised to find that despite the bending the bones had begun to knit. I felt a professional opinion was needed and phoned an acquaintance who knew about caring for injured animals. His advice was remarkably simple: All I needed was a big goose feather. Though Butter had not yet entered our family, I easily found a feather at a nearby pond frequented by geese. Cutting a piece off the quill end just a little shorter than the blue jay's leg, I slit the piece lengthwise. The next step was the only difficult one—I needed more hands: one to hold the blue jay, another to hold its leg out, and another one or two to open the quill along the slit and slip it onto the leg. Once that was accomplished, the bird had a splint that not only would hold its leg in position until the bones mended but also would naturally disintegrate in time. In this state the blue jay could better care for itself than I could, and so I drove it to a local bird sanctuary, where it flew from my hands, bothered not at all by the goose-quill splint. I hoped he lived a long and happy blue-jay life, never repeating that magic trick of appearing in front of a vehicle.

I was less confident about successful rehabilitation with our most memorable injured bird, Jonathan. Edie, who was twelve at the time, described his stay with us. In the story that follows, the indented portions are hers.

Jonathan came to us on a stormy night late in November. We were all at dinner when the telephone rang. Answering, I heard a greatly agitated woman saying, "There's an enormous white bird on my front doorstep! It has a long yellow beak! What is it?" From her nearly hysterical description the thought of an ostrich did cross my mind, but I realistically suggested that it might be a sea gull. "A sea gull!" she exclaimed, "How could a sea gull get here? Wouldn't something like this just happen to me!" I refrained from saying, "And what about the poor gull, lady?" but said instead that I would come over and pick it up as soon as we finished supper. That slight delay may have seemed heartless, but I felt the timing might be politic, for I had heard Tom, who had caught the gist of the conversation, mutter something like, "What, you're not going out after any bird in this weather and in the middle of supper, are you?" Soon five suppered Sissons drove off across town through the pouring storm and, after losing our way once, found Old Oak Road and Mrs. Agitated's house. She came right out, "He's right here, but, oh, I think he's dead. It has been so foggy and raining so much—maybe he flew into the house. I gave him some bird seed. . . ." And I saw the bird, lying there with bird seed scattered beside its beak. Edie describes him.

When we first saw Jonathan, he was huddled on the lady's doorstep. He looked like he had been there just soaking up the rain and sleet. His feathers were drooping, making him look dead. He had gray wings, a dirty white tail and underparts, and a brown and gray streaked head. He looked like a young herring gull, but the tips of his wings were black with white spots. Although we knew he was some kind of sea gull, we weren't sure of the species.

When we picked him up, he didn't show any resistance and hardly even moved. His neck was twisted to the right, looking as if it was broken. We put him in a box and took him home to our house and put him in a quiet corner of our kitchen. After that we looked in a bird identification book and found him to be a young herring gull.

The next morning I was delighted to find him alive. He was standing and had his eyes open. His eyes were yellow with black pupils, giving him a stern look. I touched him for the first time. It was exciting because I had never touched such a large bird; I was afraid he would peck me but he didn't. I think he was too dazed, and it looked like he had a brain problem (from the crooked way he stood); too confused to know enough to react to my touching him. He was very soft and smooth; his feathers seemed attached together like a sheet. I thought he was beautiful.

And yet his neck still twisted around as it had the night before, looking disjointed and, peculiarly, as if it were set too far back on his body. He stood up in the box several times during the day, and in the afternoon we transferred him to our big cage and put blankets over it to give him quiet and darkness.

The next morning he seemed a little better, but his head kept moving involuntarily in a twitching, twisting motion, and at times his left eye remained closed.

Sea gulls are scavengers, which means that they will eat about anything. I put some bread soaked in milk in the cage with him, but he didn't touch it. Next we tried raw fish scraps, and when he didn't touch those either it became apparent that we would, at first, anyway, have to force-feed him. Force-feeding is unnatural; to do it well requires sensitivity and practice, and this was my first experience with a gull. Edie held him while I pried open the big beak and with tweezers placed the pieces as far down his gullet as possible. He was unresisting and swallowed the pieces, but even so we ended up smelling of fish. Next day, the feeding went even better. We used bigger pieces, which he swallowed when I put them by hand inside his beak.

But that evening our troubles began. Jonathan swallowed two pieces of fish, but he was straining to escape Edie's hold, and, as I tried to put in a third piece, he suddenly opened his beak, and without so much as a cough or a burp, the first two pieces we had put in came back up and slipped out the side of his beak onto my lap. What

was up? Well, literally the fish pieces, but even though we were puzzled and annoyed we had no choice but to start the meal over again.
Jonathan was agitated. Edie had difficulty holding him still, and I had
trouble opening a beak at the end of an unsteady head. Twice I
slipped down two pieces of fish, only to have them returned. We all
three began to smell fishy, but finally five pieces went down and
stayed down, and that, we decided, was enough for his dinner.

Why was Jonathan throwing up? Suddenly I remembered reading
that gulls regurgitate partially digested food to feed their young, and it
became apparent that Jonathan's easy regurgitation was part of his
nature that we would have to accept, no matter how fishy it made us
smell. Jonathan had only to open his long beak and, with no visible
effort, pieces of fish would materialize. One time we got back one
more piece than we had put down, evidently it was one that had
gone down the meal before, and although that didn't seem fair, we
could do nothing about it except try to improve our force-feeding
technique. By chance, one day when we couldn't get fish scraps, we
tried small smelts and discovered that they were shaped better for
sliding down his throat, which helped. We found too that the less he
struggled against being held the less he regurgitated. When he
became able to flap his huge wings, it was easiest to control him on
the floor. Add a fishy floor to the fishy hands. Unfortunately, Jonathan
never ate voluntarily in all the three weeks we had him.

By day four he had begun to put his head under his wing and
hold his head still so that he could sleep normally. Also, he began to
exercise his wings, a delightful scene to watch, and his wingspread
was impressive. The white polka dots on the black wingtips had been
a surprise at first, which is why we had to check his identification. But
if you have not seen a herring gull up close, you probably have never
seen the dots. From a distance the dots don't show in the black wing
edging, and when the wings are folded they look like part of the tail.

The special opportunity we had to observe a gull closely revealed
the exquisite whiteness of his feathers, and the gray of his back had a
softness that reminded me of powder snow, just fallen. Because he
was immature, his head still showed brown-gray speckles. His
webbed feet seemed daintily small, for I was accustomed to the relative whoppers on ducks and geese. His yellow beak, with which we
were intimately acquainted, was beginning to show a red spot toward
the end of the bottom part, or lower mandible. On the bill of a parent

gull this red spot, ethologist Niko Tinbergen observed, triggers a pecking reaction in hatchlings that is vital in establishing feeding. We were surprised to find that if we looked at his nostril at the middle of the top of the beak (the upper mandible) we could see right through it. He was beautiful, but let Edie continue:

One day we suspected he couldn't see. Although he would react to new or loud noises, he gave no evidence of seeing. We had left fish in his cage, and he just stepped on it. When we put a bright light near his eyes, his pupils gave no reaction. We hoped greatly that if he couldn't see he would regain his sight, because it was not fair or right to let him live if he was not able to fly, see, or hardly even walk. If he kept on being blind I knew we could not free him and let him live a happy, normal life as we wanted him to, and we didn't want him to suffer. For his sake it would be kinder to kill him if he didn't recover his sight. Even if he wasn't blind I knew we couldn't free him because he was not acting normally. All in all, we didn't know what to do.

We did not want to make the decision for Jonathan, because his present state was bad, but he had been improving. When we first met him, he was hardly able to hold his head up. After a while he was standing, but his head was twisting involuntarily to the right and he seemed not to be able to hold it straight. Then he walked, in small, slow clockwise circles, but it was walking. Later he was slightly upset at noises and flapped when being held. And a week and a half later he was running in crazy, fast clockwise circles.

We had been discussing giving him a bath, and so one day, when he smelled especially bad of fish, we put him in a bathtub of warm water. He enjoyed being in water again. When swimming we found he had a list to the right and so he swam in clockwise circles. Also, because of his blindness he would crash into the walls of the bathtub. This made us feel terrible; although it was delightful to see him act normal as he bathed, his list and blindness were heartbreaking. To bathe he would spread his wings sightly and work the water through his feathers with a great deal of splashing.

In the tub his beautiful feet became more noticeable and the color stood out more. They were a soft pastel shade of pink

*and gray. It always amazed me the way they looked, because
although I knew seagulls have webbed feet, I had never seen
them close up. They had blood vessels and were not cold, as
they looked, but warm, not much colder than his body.
Although he was bigger than a duck, his feet were smaller than
a duck's, because sea gulls are almost equally adapted for sea
and land to get food from, while ducks depend on the water,
only occasionally eating on banks.*

When we removed Jonathan from the bathtub, he would stand on
the bath mat and preen. Preening enables birds to keep their feathers
in good condition, which is essential for flight. Preening is also done
for cleaning, which is instinctive for most animals, from houseflies to
cats. When Jonathan preened he used his beak to smooth his feathers, repair any breaks, and spread oil on them from the oil gland at
the base of his tail. The first time he preened, I was astounded,
because it was the first time I had seen him open his beak on his
own and use it for a specific purpose. This act showed that he could
eat on his own if only we could find a stimulus. According to Tinbergen, gulls have good eyesight and hearing, fairly good taste, but weak
smell. A blind gull couldn't smell or see food, nor would any noise
come from a dead fish. If Jonathan was blind, how could he know
the food was there and open his beak to eat it? How I wished we
could solve that dilemma.

When he began to walk, we moved him from the cage to an old
playpen. Soon he was running in clockwise circles, and when I said
his behavior was looney, Kathy quipped, "Mum, you should say gully,
not looney." Even though at times he could hold his head high in a
new pose that suggested alertness, his circles became faster and
faster. Edie commented that we should just feed him some grown-up
potion, change his feet, and we'd have a racehorse.

Despite his problems he continued to improve, and we moved
him from the playpen outside to the aviary, where he ran in fast, wide
circles, always clockwise, but often tripped over rocks or collided
with the chicken wire, supporting our blindness theory. He had, however, become extremely sensitive to noises and always resisted being
held, both of which were natural for a wild gull, and gave us a mod-
icum of optimism to cling to. Yet the decision about his future hung
heavily over all of us, for we all agreed that a blind or severely

demented gull could not survive on its own, and so should not be released. Nor should it be confined indefinitely. Gulls, as we had come to appreciate, are animals of wide spaces. Should we end his life? Our quandary was compounded because we were going away during Christmas vacation. Although I have taken many creatures to many places, we could not take the gull, who needed at least the space in the aviary. Our decision had to be made soon.

We needed a miracle, and we got one. At the beginning of vacation our friends, the Sterns, were visiting with their three children. Ruth and I were having coffee in the living room when Edie burst in, holding Jonathan, and exclaiming, "He flew, Mummy, he flew!" When she caught her breath, she explained that Jonathan had looked as if he was trying to fly in the aviary, and that she took him out and he flew in a small, clockwise circle around her. Ruth and I put down our coffee cups, and by that time the news had traveled so that all the other children came out with us to see what Jonathan might do next.

While all nine of us watched expectantly, Jonathan stood on a snowbank and gave himself a thorough preening. But then, without warning, he suddenly flapped his wings and flew—neither high nor far. When he landed he slipped and fell on his side. But he righted himself and, as we watched, transfixed, Jonathan flew again, and this time gained altitude to reach the top window of our loft, some twenty-five feet high. He flew several circles—clockwise, of course—and attempted to land on an arborvitae hedge but fell through to the ground.

Just as Edie had sensed that Jonathan was ready to fly in the aviary, she now sensed something greater and took him out to the field behind our house. There she put him down, and for the first time in his stay with us he walked in a straight line. As if to top it off, he went counterclockwise in a half circle. Then he took off. At first he circled clockwise around us all, then he flew in a higher, wider circle. My heart leapt. "Jonathan," I called, "Jonathan!" Higher he flew. We all called, "Jonathan!" He went in a wider circle, growing smaller and smaller as his circles became higher and wider. Finally the small speck over the distant trees at the end of the field disappeared. Seemingly a miracle had occurred, awesome and wonderful. Had beams of light opened up through the clouds and shone around him it could not have been more astounding.

Did he ever come down, and did he do it in clockwise circles or straight, and could he feed, or did he simply keep on flying higher and higher? Here are Edie's feelings.

> *At first I thought he was just flying in large circles around the field, but when he got higher and higher and farther and farther away I knew he was leaving.*
>
> *It left me with a bad feeling as he flew out of sight. Half my heart was with him, half was on the ground calling and begging him to come back. I am sad because I miss him, but I am glad he left of his own will. I would have hated to leave him somewhere or, even worse, kill him. I will always miss him. He gave us a share of all sea gulls. We never communicated to each other in any way, but still, having him with me made me love him. Even today I wonder if he will come back. I hate to think this, but I don't think he realized we were helping him, and I won't see him again.*
>
> *Today I saw two sea gulls flying over. I like to think that perhaps one of them was Jonathan and he was coming back to see me.*

The next morning we ate some of Jonathan's remaining smelts for Sunday breakfast. And Charlie Black greatly enjoyed the rest. Who was Charlie? Our household was full that winter. Not only did we have the usual four children, three ponies, assorted chickens, quail, guinea pig, gerbil, and goldfish five inches long, but we also had Jonathan, an opossum in the chicken house, and Charlie Black, a crow.

In mid-fall we were raking leaves in the side yard when a crow landed on a branch of the cottonwood tree, far above the one where Edie three years earlier had enticed Bonnie the raccoon to climb for her first time. The crow cawed in a manner that resonated within me and I looked up at the crow and said, "Hello, Charlie, come on down." The crow hesitated, cocked his head, and then flew to the ground. The children were awed but I wasn't and asked Kathy to bring bread and a bowl of water from the kitchen. Shortly Charlie went over to Kathy's bread and water and helped himself. I'm not a Dr. Dolittle, although as a child I greatly envied his ability to converse with creatures in the Dr. Dolittle books, but maybe something about the tenor of the crow's caw had reminded me of a tame crow I had known years earlier. That crow could clearly mimic a human "hello," and made many people turn around to see who was addressing them. Perhaps Charlie had been brought up by people and had learned to caw mimicking "hello" and maybe that is what I heard when he landed on the cottonwood branch. And perhaps that explains why he came down at my bidding, but I cannot say for sure.

I do know that Charlie stayed the winter with us, delighted us, and taught us much about himself, his kind, and the convenience of flight compared with our surface-bound existence. He adopted us, although he also visited other houses in the neighborhood, and every morning he flew by for breakfast. If breakfast was not served on time, he perched in the cottonwood tree, cawing loudly and letting everyone know of his impatience. He served well as an alarm clock, but smart as he was he never learned the difference between weekdays and weekends. Furthermore, if cawing in the cottonwood did not do the trick, he would appear at our bedroom window, where his loud "Caw, caw, caw" was impossible to ignore on a Sunday morning, no matter how late we had gone to bed Saturday night. How did he know which were our bedroom windows? I have no answer. He could, however, locate me when I arose early and worked in the den with a light on, but in dawn's semidarkness undoubtedly the light was the giveaway to my presence.

Once he discovered me in the attic early one afternoon. He had been served his usual breakfast but it seemed that all's fair in the mind of a crow. His "Caw, caw, caw" interrupted me as I was putting away Christmas decorations, and I turned to see Charlie looking at me through the attic window. All right, I thought, I'll go down and get something for you. You're spoiled, that's for sure. I went down the two flights to the kitchen. There was Charlie, and his way of waiting said as plain as could be, "Heavens, but it took you a long time. Why, look at me. Just a flap or two of my wings and here I was." Never before had the convenience of birds' flight come across to me so clearly. In spite of my awakened sensitivity to the marvel of flight, though, I didn't forget the point of the mission and gave Charlie a nice afternoon snack: a cornbread muffin.

Charlie's breakfast time on weekdays at least often coincided with ours. We generally fed him either beside or on the side porch, but then one day we opened the kitchen door and put his food and water on the threshold. For about two minutes Charlie stood on the porch sizing up the situation. He took a step forward, cocked his head, stepped forward again, eyed his breakfast, and then, as if he had made a decision, came forward and ate his meal as usual.

The next day we moved the food just inside the kitchen. Charlie was cautious but came hesitantly inside to enjoy his breakfast. Soon it became a regular routine to have Charlie join us in the kitchen at breakfast time. It was chilly with the door open and wasteful of heat, but both were prices we were willing to pay to have the sleek black bird in the kitchen with us. Crows are both wary and canny, and our family understood that our relationship with him stood on a fragile trust. At our breakfasts together we never approached him in any way, nor did we even contemplate the unthinkable, which would have been to close the kitchen door behind him. Had we done such a thing, he would undoubtedly have forsaken us, at once.

Outside the kitchen window is our bird feeder, and Charlie could always find little seed snacks on the ground underneath. When there was no snow, the bantams also frequented the area under the feeder, finding the spilled bird food a welcome change from the daily menu of chicken food in the chicken house. Charlie, however, eyed the chickens with misgiving. A hen came by one morning while Polly was outside giving pieces of bread to Charlie, and she tossed one small piece to the hen. This gesture maddened Charlie and he went after and attacked—not the hen, but Polly. It was *his* bread she had given away, an unpardonable blunder. Polly didn't hold the few pecks against him but felt it was an understandable action. We were learning to look at things from a crow's point of view.

A problem arose in February, in the form of a letter from an elderly neighbor.

Dear Mr. and Mrs. Sisson,

I have heard the loud sounds of a crow coming from your direction and have been told that you are feeding it. I do hope you won't encourage the crow to stay in this area when spring comes. I'm sure you enjoy Robins and other singing birds as much as we do, but if you tame the crow, it will eat their young in their nests.

One of the reasons I was glad to leave where we lived before was because of the crows. They would come into our garden and eat the young featherless birds in their nests, and we could not drive them off. I know other birds do it too, but they are not as large and voracious as crows, and other birds are afraid of them.

We both look forward to our gardens and birds in the spring, and I hope we can enjoy a peaceful time.

Sincerely yours,
Denise Knight

This letter bothered us. Ideally in a neighborhood no one will cause harm or worry about harm, to any others. Tom and I are especially sensitive about neighbors' feelings because of our numerous and varied creatures. We hold all the proper permits and comply with zoning regulations but also we want our animals to be welcomed members of the community. Our beliefs have only been strengthened by the numerous times we've been victimized by dogs owned by irresponsible persons, and so we know how unwelcome neighbors' animals can be. On the other hand we felt the letter was unwarranted.

What would be your response to such a letter? Here is mine, and I put much thought into writing it.

Dear Mrs. Knight,

We received your letter last weekend, and it is good that neighbors can communicate.

The curious crow in question seems to have adopted several families in this neighborhood, as well as frequenting other neighborhoods. It would appear that humans had already played a role in his life prior to his arrival here as he seems somewhat tame. Ultimately, this may prove to be his undoing, so probably none of us need to be concerned for too long; tamed "wild" animals are often easily victimized by predators.

Certainly the intricacies of the web of life are difficult to comprehend. We might even make a defense of the silent earthworm who so earnestly helps to till the gardens we all enjoy; his cause, however, would not be glorious since he neither looks so pretty, nor utters a single note of song, as do so many of his predators.

I am glad to know of your concerns about gardens and

*birds and the environment. These days, the environment
needs all the care we can give it!*

> *Sincerely,*
> *Edith Sisson*

Recently I checked into the question of what wild crows normally eat, especially how many "young featherless birds in their nests." In his *American Wildlife and Plants: A Guide to Wildlife Food Habits,* Alexander C. Martin reports that analysis of 1,340 crow stomachs showed that grasshoppers, beetles, caterpillars, crustaceans, amphibians, and reptiles were the predominant animal food items, although other insects, spiders, and chicken eggs were also found; the main plant foods were grains, fruits, and other seeds; no mention of young birds. But crows do have a reputation for robbing nests, and one book that I looked into supports this belief. Remember, however, that hawks, owls, raccoons, and other predators rob nests, and it's all part of nature's checks and balances.

My letter to Mrs. Knight, for whatever reason, ended our dialogue. Charlie got into deeper trouble as spring came on. Once or twice in winter we had noticed him make a low swoop over a visitor's head. The maneuver became more frequent and aggressive during March, and early in April a neighbor from across the street complained that Charlie had attacked her daughter on her way to the school bus stop. I wasn't surprised by the neighbor's report because I had seen Charlie swoop and extend his claws several times over the heads of kids in our side yard. For his own reasons he showed an affinity for girls with long blond hair. Soon we heard rumors of further attacks in a neighborhood behind us, and we don't know what happened but Charlie disappeared. Maybe he should have been called Charlotte all along and left us, as well as the trouble she was causing, to build a nest and raise a family. Though she or he never returned, being able to sleep late Sunday mornings didn't make up for our loss. I have spoken to many crows in trees since knowing Charlie, even though I know they will not come down to me, yet I keep hoping that good fortune may happen again.

By no means do all the birds that come our way survive. We often receive little boxes with birds that the cat brought home, or that flew into a picture window, or that a child found on the sidewalk on the way back from school. We do what we can, but some injuries and infections are fatal, and we are not vets. Anyway, acts that people sometimes anthropomorphize as nature's cruelty are really an integral part of healthy ecosystems. Dynamic natural balances depend on numerous and intricate relationships between the sun, climate, geographic features, plants, and animals. Here is a highly simplified example. If robins overproduce, the earthworm population may decrease. Without the earthworms' tunnels, the soil may become hard packed, eliminating some species of plants and encouraging others, and leaving an altered habitat. Meanwhile many of the robins may have died, because overpopulation sometimes opens the way for disease to spread.

We highly technological human beings with our life-sustaining techniques that now extend from before birth to after brain death are not following a natural course. We can also manipulate our environment in ways that no other animal can; thus our influence is essentially unnatural, in the sense that we can alter natural ecosystems. And if you suggest I too interfere with nature when I rehabilitate an animal, I admit the truth, but many creatures with which I have contact have been orphaned or injured directly or indirectly by human causes. But perhaps I should admit to my own selfishness: I probably receive far more from each creature that comes my way than I give, even if I succeed in giving back a life with freedom. The animals give me nourishment for mind and soul, which I try to share with others.

A few years ago while leading an adult field trip in a salt marsh, I spotted a juvenile herring gull. It was sitting beside a small pool in the marsh and, as we approached, did not take flight. When it remained there as we drew near, I knew something was wrong with the bird. Walking over, I looked at it closely; the stern yellow eyes reminded me of Jonathan's, but it did not move at all and I surmised that it must be dying. I felt the gull would best be left to die peacefully in its own environment and led my group away. We had walked on for a few minutes, my thoughts about teaching my group mixed with questions about the gull. What if a predator came? Severe weather? What harm would come from giving it a chance? The last question nagged until my mind changed. I returned to the gull, picked it up, and finished leading the field trip with the gull tucked under my arm. At the back of my car was an empty carton. I put the gull inside and closed the top.

After the hour's drive home, I was saddened but not surprised to find when I opened the box that the gull had died. I had done what I could, and then, remembering that Bruce, a friend of Jinny's who enjoyed taxidermy, had wanted a large bird to stuff, I put the gull in our freezer. I often freeze parts of creatures and sometimes the whole thing, and lately have labeled such bags "unmentionables" to avoid culinary confusion. (Mammal skulls, for instance, are useful teaching tools, especially because the teeth tell much about the animal.) About six months later we unfroze the gull and Bruce stuffed it with wings outspread. It looks as if it is just about to take off, and I enjoy the notion that in death, anyway, we have been able to give it the life that I was unable to do in reality. It is on the table in our front living room and brings back memories of Jonathan.

Two years ago we had temporary custody of another bird with wingspread as large as a gull's, one of our unusual visitors. But the story starts with my friend Binda and a fox. Binda, while watching our chickens happily scratching about in their yard, kept asking why foxes didn't eat our chickens. They would, she said, if she kept chickens where she lives in England. My response that I'd never even seen

The living-room gull still brings memories of Jonathan.

a fox about didn't mollify her. About a week after Binda's visit, a cackling and a racket came from the chickens. Generally their excitement denotes dog, and when that happens we hurry out to protect our birds. I thrust open the porch door and stopped, unbelieving. To my right on the porch was a fox. "Binda, what foxy hex have you brought about?" Before the thought had made its way through my head the fox took off, displaying a nearly hairless tail; we could recognize him again. And we did. First I did, then Tom.

In the middle of the fox episode, I was reading the mail on the sofa after a long day when a loud cackling intruded. I recalled Binda's fox, threw down the mail, and in moments was in the big chickens' house, looking through to the bantie house. No fox was there, but instead on the floor was a bird that distinctly was not a chicken. It was large and it was eating something. It looked up at me as if to say "Who are you to disturb me in the middle of my meal?" I looked, aghast, as I recognized the meal:. It was "Tack" (a little black hen whose name related to the Mrs. Nails of years back), and she was beyond rescue. I looked again at the bird, still enjoying morsels of Tack despite my presence. Yes it was big, with hooked beak and talons—a hawk? A hawk inside the henhouse? Hawks are high-flying birds and creatures that need plenty of space. How did it get in here?

And how was I to get it out? I obtained a cage, but then how was I to put the hawk inside? I've respected talons ever since an injured barred owl grabbed my wrist with his talons. The grip was unrelenting, to say nothing of strong, and fleetingly my mind had understood the efficiency of those weapons for catching mice. One talon was caught around a tendon, and I had some time in which to wonder how to unlock such a grip, but the owl finally relented and relaxed its hold. With that background I wasn't going to take any chances with the hawk. Sturdy gloves and a strong grain bag to wrap him in were the weapons I chose, and I was able to put him in the cage more easily than I had anticipated. Putting the cage with the hawk and the remains of Tack safely away down cellar, I then discovered that Little Nails, an old and favorite hen, looked mortally wounded. I gave her rest and quiet in a dark carton, but next morning she was dead.

We still had a problem on our hands—the hawk, which we had identified as a goshawk, in our cellar. Such birds of prey are federally protected, but even if they weren't we would have treated it with care and released it as soon as possible in an appropriate habitat. We needed to know how big a home range a goshawk needs—more specifically, how far we would have to move it so that it wouldn't fly over the Sissons' irresistible fast-food chicken joint again. It finished Tack in no time, and with a twinge of reluctance I gave it the remains of Little Nails. Despite being caged in the cellar, it devoured her, too.

In consulting hawk experts to learn the limits of its range, I found a possible reason for the hawk's entering the henhouse. Compared to a hawk's wide sky habitat, the henhouse is dark and confining and the two entrances are small—just chicken-sized. But goshawks, I learned, have a reputation for stubbornness, and once they choose a prey they will follow it even through bushes and underbrush, and even through a little chicken-house door.

Three days later, following our experts' advice, we released the goshawk about a hundred miles away in a relatively uninhabited area. Immediately it flew to a nearby oak and perched on a low branch, permitting us to admire it in a natural setting. And admire we did, for it was a handsome bird. After a few minutes it spread its wings, flew off, and disappeared behind trees. Good-bye, goshawk. Recently I saw a hawk flying up a hillside in the same area. It looked familiar, though I realized it wasn't likely to be our goshawk, but my heart gladdened anyway.

Further Thoughts

People can see birds flying free in almost any area, urban or wilderness, tropical or arctic, and mountainous—even sometimes in midocean. Next to insects, birds are the commonest wild animal that people encounter. No wonder, then, that bird-feeding and bird-watching are popular hobbies and that some people attract birds to their yards by growing plants that offer birds cover or food. For bird identification there are many excellent field guides available.

Herring gulls are easily recognizable and, despite their proclivity for neighborhood dumps, still are considered a symbol of the sea.

Ethologist Niko Tinbergen researched herring-gull social behavior on beaches in Holland, later receiving a Nobel prize. His books are interesting, even for lay people.

What might you do if you come upon an ailing herring gull in a salt marsh? In earlier chapters I mentioned some of the difficulties in caring for wildlife: what needs will the animal have, and can a person (with a permit), or even a veterinarian, give the proper care? Can the animal recover sufficiently to be released and survive in its environment? Is it genetically defective? Could it transmit disease or parasites to a human care-giver? What are the legal requirements for licenses or permits? For example, federal laws protect both migratory birds, such as robins, and birds of prey, such as goshawks.

Injured birds are, in some ways, easier to handle than mammals. At least birds cannot bite with sharp teeth, but they can inflict wounds with beak or feet, and they can hit with wings. Once I've acquired an ailing bird, my first step usually is to give it peace and quiet in a dark place, and also warmth, if it is cold. If a bird has a broken bone, it is often easy to spot, and the bone should be immobilized. A broken leg can be held securely by a drinking straw, if one does not have access to goose quills, as I did with the blue jay. Wildlife rehabilitation centers often take animals (many ask for a donation) or give advice. An acquaintance tells me that a wildlife center advised him to put an injured starling, which had struck his picture window, into a carton overnight, and then to put the bird in the carton outdoors next day. He followed this advice and several hours later, when he went to check the carton, the starling was gone, presumably on its own. This is good advice to remember—time for resting is often the best cure for an injured animal.

The goshawk, after its binge in our chicken house, spent three days confined in a cage in our cellar but was neither diseased nor injured. Still, it had needs for which we were responsible, such as food and water. We were pleased that it seemed in excellent health when we released it.

Hawks are birds of prey, or raptors, and are easily identified by hooked beaks, talons, and eyes at the sides of the head. Owls too are raptors, but they have eyes at the front. Some raptor species are hard to identify. Goshawks belong to the group of hawks known as accipiters, which have long tails and short, rounded wings. A particularly notice-able field mark of the goshawk is the white stripe over its eye.

Charlie Black was a common, or American, crow, an easily recog-nizable species. Although ravens and fish crows look like common crows, ravens are larger and fish crows smaller. Crows have been famous for their intelligence and canniness for centuries. Aesop's fable "The Crow and the Pitcher" *tells of a crow half-dead of thirst that found a pitcher with a little water at the bottom, well beyond reach of the crow's beak. The crow dropped a pebble into the pitcher, then another, and another, until finally the water rose so that the crow could quench his thirst, saving his life. The moral is "Little by little does the trick," but the tale attests to the crow's reputation for being clever. I can remember as a child reading in a book by Ernest Thompson Seton about the language of crows—how the tone and number of caws have different meanings. Charlie taught us that his early morning "caw caw" meant, "breakfast, please, and you'd better hurry up about it." Someday I hope to have the chance again to know one of these clever birds, and perhaps to learn more of its language than the breakfast call.*

Chapter Seven

Jingle Bells

The little black pony's name was Frisky. She walked eagerly as we
led her down the path in the field behind our house back to the nearby riding stable, but we did not feel eager, for Frisky's stay with us
was over. She looked almost fat and sassy, a vast improvement she'd
achieved in the two months that she had been with us. Only the ring
marks on her hooves were a clue to her previous health. Like tree-
stump rings that tell the good growing years from the bad, the telltale
rings on Frisky's hooves bespoke the neglect and malnutrition of her
past winter.

Nick Rodday, manager of the stable and a knowledgeable horse-
man, had seen the pony in the spring and, recognizing that she needed care, offered to take her. Her owner assented, and Frisky went to
the stable, where her health began to improve. Spotting the new
pony in its stall, I had asked Nick about it. My curiosity had an unex-
pected reward, for, after Nick explained why Frisky was there, he
asked if we would like to take over caring for her. Would I? Would
the kids? I didn't hesitate a moment—"Yes!" Little did I know that this
was the start of fourteen years of equines at our house.

Frisky stayed for the summer in our barnhole, a huge foundation
of massive stones where once a large barn had stood. It made a fine
area in which to keep a pony, and when she needed hay the kids
went down to the stable, brought some back, and dropped it into the
barnhole. Jinny and Kathy, then six years old, learned to ride on
Frisky, and in turn helped train her to become a good children's
pony. I especially remember how we taught Frisky to drive. Under
Nick's tutelage we trained her to go with long reins. Bridle the pony,
attach the long lines, and manipulate yourself into position behind the

pony without tangling the lines. If the pony moves that is easier said than done—and then, tell the pony to walk forward and you walk behind, steering the pony as you go. If the pony startles and shies at something you may be in for more entanglement, but the point of the exercise is to train the pony to being directed by reins held from behind, rather than by a rider on top. "Let the leather rein rub on her haunch when you turn," Nick said, "which will accustom her to the breaching of the harness later on."

A borrowed harness and pony cart from Nick, with assistance from him the first few times we harnessed Frisky to the cart, and we were on our own. The cart was an elegant old-timer that we nick-named the Golden Coach. Frisky took to pulling it with amazing ease and the snappy cart accorded her a stylish air. My main memory of the summer is the Golden Coach filled with children behind the little black pony.

Having Frisky that summer satisfied something within me because of a clear memory of myself, very young, sitting on my father's lap. I asked him why I couldn't have a pony or a horse. My father explained that where we lived we had no place to keep one, and perhaps I remember because he seemed to genuinely regret it. I didn't know then, of course, that my request was a common child-hood wish. I do not believe he mentioned the expense, which would have been another factor.

Finally, in that long-ago summer, Frisky satisfied my own child-hood yearning. At summer's end, however, we learned that her owner wanted her back. Probably we had avoided thinking about such a possibility; even though we knew our feelings were unreason-able we felt it was unfair after we had put so much effort into training her to be a good children's pony both for riding and driving. Thus, sadness was with us on that day when we led Frisky back down to the stable and said goodby.

But good fortune dispelled our despondency when Nick asked if we would like to keep his Sally-pony, a gray Shetland, a mite smaller than Frisky. Actually, Nick had offered us Sally before, and we had led her from the stable into the barnhole. But Sally appeared to take a dim view of being separated from her companions (horses are herd animals—they like to stay together). Furthermore, her disposition had a distinct verve that Nick colorfully described with a four-letter word. Before we realized what was happening, Sally pranced around the barnhole, found the one place where the foundation stones were lowest, gave a short gallop, a hop, and a scramble, and ran free back home.

Frisky never discovered this exit, but before Sally-pony came the second time I put in two metal fenceposts with a bar between them at the low point, and this jerry-built blockage worked. On Sally's second visit she did not escape from the barnhole, remaining with us for many years until every child in the family had outgrown her.

To think back on Sally-pony is to evoke memories that epitomize almost all that could be wished for in having a pony and children together. Sally was loved, hugged, and patted. She was fed and watered, assiduously. She was groomed almost daily—brushed, curried, and combed, sometimes by four kids at once. She was ridden bareback with only halter and lead line, or she was tacked up and ridden with saddle and bridle, which later were saddle-soaped and oiled. She was led out to graze and occasionally even led into the kitchen at breakfast time to enjoy a bale of shredded wheat with the family. She gave pony rides at birthday parties, and, if it was raining, we'd go around the dining-room table; afterward she would enjoy Hawaiian punch and birthday cake. She took part in the children's play for hours, becoming an Indian pony, a medieval charger, a fleet-footed Arabian steed, and for all I know, a winged Pegasus.

Shortly after it was apparent that Sally-pony had joined the family to stay, another Sally, the mother of a nursery-school friend of Edie's, gave me advice for which I've always been grateful. The essence of what she said (and she had kept ponies and horses for years) is that children's heads are down at the level where they are vulnerable to kicks. A kick that may break an adult's arm can cause far greater injury to a child. She suggested many techniques for enforcing pony safety, from close supervision to ways of feeding and watering that can be done without having to go into the enclosure with the pony. She also stressed wearing a hard hat when riding to protect the head if a rider has a fall or other accident. Her advice was invaluable. Neither our own children, nor their playmates, nor the countless kids who had pony rides at our birthday parties, nor the hearing-impaired children who sometimes came from their school to visit with the pony, groom her, and have rides, ever had an accident. The only mishap was the time that Kathy fell off Sally and broke her arm, but I don't count that as a pony safety hazard, because kids break arms

Sally gives rides in the kitchen.

falling off bicycles, tumbling out of trees, bowling over on the soccer field, or you name it.

It wasn't long before we began to teach Sally to drive, and this time around it was easier because we had experience with Frisky. I think though that even Nick was slightly apprehensive the first time we hitched Sally to a cart, for the high-spirited side of Sally's disposition—inherited, Nick said, directly from her mother—could have caused trouble. But Sally did not become alarmed and soon accepted driving as a normal activity. We borrowed a jogging cart from Nick, but after a while invested in one of our own. Mum contributed the largest share of cash, Jinny and Kathy the next largest, Edie next, and little Polly added in all of thirty cents. No matter how disproportionate the shares, it was truly a jointly owned vehicle.

We had fun with that cart. When the children came home from school in the afternoon it took only the flimsiest excuse (someone might need a pad of paper) and we would hitch up Sally and drive downtown to the five and ten, me sitting on the seat in the middle with a child on either side. Or we'd take someone to a kid's house to play. Or we'd go over to visit Aunt Doffie. Or we'd take friends of the children for rides. We didn't abandon the family car, because our alternative transportation required time, both to hitch up the pony and to get to the destination; it also limited us to three passengers and to fairly short trips, and in pouring rain the shelter of the car's roof was a distinct advantage.

As you might guess, people's reaction to the pony cart and its passengers was generally positive; we'd spot smiles and exchange waves. When we started driving on roads, Nick instructed me not to stay far over on the right-hand side, but to claim a position at the middle of the right-hand lane. "By doing that," he said, "if the pony acts up when a car passes you will have plenty of room to maneuver in." Most drivers were considerate. They would slow down and pass us warily. Some were even too considerate; perhaps they didn't dare to pass, and we'd find ourselves holding a long line of cars down to a Shetland pony's slow trotting speed. Then there was the other kind of driver who would swoosh by at full speed, sometimes with a loud honk just to make things worse. Perhaps these drivers were late for an appointment, or enjoyed taking risks, or maybe they disliked little gray ponies, but those were the times when I was glad that I had that room to the right of the cart to move into should we need it. It's possible, of course, that these drivers didn't know that a pony could be less reliable about staying on course than an automobile. (Some states have laws that give horses the right of way on public roads.)

Many people don't know that horses, measured against our standards of intelligence, rank far lower than their noble appearance indicates. They frighten easily and will "spook" or "shy," sometimes understandably, but often unpredictably. You are driving Sally in the jogging cart when suddenly she gives a snort and a jump to the side. As you try to maintain control you wonder what caused her fright. No bicycle had suddenly passed by on the sidewalk and no piece of white paper had been blowing in front of her by the wind, and so you look back and spot a possible culprit—a little puddle. What's frightening about an innocent puddle? Well, if you were a horse you might startle at glistening reflections suddenly appearing on your route, and your instinct would warn you not to go near. From the horse's point of view, shying away from potentially dangerous objects is a protective adaptation, however unintelligent it may seem to us.

Bridles for driving horses almost always have "blinders" on them; put your hands against your face at the outer sides of your eyes with palms facing each other and you will have an idea of what they do. Blinders prevent the horse from seeing anything behind or at the side that might be frightening and cause it to bolt. Horses are grazing animals and have eyes that are high and at the sides of the head—a protective specialization that enables them to watch for predators while they are eating. When working with a horse, as with any other animal, the human being needs to understand how the animal perceives things and then act in accordance with this understanding. When driving Sally it soon became second nature to watch out for flapping papers or innocuous-looking puddles.

This adaptation may sound simple, but it can be exasperating. One day in the country I'd been off on an all-day ride with Edie and Polly (we had another pony and a small horse at that time). We were all tired and we were almost home. In fact we were just down the hill from the cabin on the old woods road where once a bridge had crossed a small stream connecting swampy areas on either side. The bridge had long since deteriorated, leaving a ditch that in August had but a trickle running through the bottom. The other pony and the horse warily clambered down the first side and up the other, but Sally-pony took one look at the menacing ditch, snorted, and refused to put so much as one hoof over the edge. Polly kicked, Polly clucked (that tongue to roof of mouth noise that one makes to horses), Polly used a small switch from a nearby alder, Polly urged, Polly cajoled. No, Sally would not go. Polly dismounted and tried leading Sally over the ditch. She still would not go. I tried leading Sally, and Edie joined in, hitting Sally on the haunch with the switch. One front hoof, then the other gingerly placed themselves just over the edge of the ditch, causing pebbles to spill to the bottom, which was no more than two feet deep. Sally's ears were pricked forward, her nostrils slightly flared, and she tentatively tried one more step down. The hoof slipped, and with a loud snort Sally retreated in that scrambly style that I have only seen horses do, finding safety again on the hard ground of the old road. After a half an hour of coaxing, pushing, pulling, heaving, hitting, we made no further progress. We could not bypass the ditch because of the swamps on both sides of the road, and the only other way home was to go back down the road to Route 5, then up to town, around by the lake, and up our hill by the road on the other side. I don't remember how long it took the weary six of us to travel the five miles around, but finally we reached home and pasture and dinner. Looking back on this episode I wonder why we didn't try an obvious solution, which would have been to take the other pony and the horse on ahead up the hill, leaving Sally, whose herd instinct might have overcome her fear of the ditch.

A year or so after teaching Sally how to drive, our continued fortune with ponies reaped another dividend. Nick offered to let us use his boyhood sleigh. It was a picture-book sleigh, bright red and complete with sleigh bells. As soon as the first snow left enough on the ground for the runners, we led Sally to the stable and hitched her up. Although 99 percent of the time Sally was docile, especially with children around—Polly probably could have ridden her tricycle under Sally and she would have stood still—the remaining 1 percent, the other side of Sally's disposition was there too, and we knew better than to take chances. We had to quell our desire to climb aboard immediately and instead led Sally cautiously around the barnyard several times to allow her to become accustomed to the new, strange object behind her, which would feel and sound, with the bells, different from her familiar jogging cart. Sally remained calm. Then I climbed to the seat and started to drive. Between the shafts of the sleigh, Sally was farther forward from the driver than she was with her cart; she seemed strangely distant, and I realized that I was the one, not Sally, who would have to adjust to the sleigh. When Sally still remained calm, the kids came aboard. Two could sit on either side of me on the seat, and two could ride on the runners behind. We trotted off into the field, and I felt we had entered the song:

> *Jingle bells, jingle bells*
> *Jingle all the way.*
> *Oh what fun it is to ride*
> *In a one-horse open sleigh. . . .*

Yes, it was fun, and the hot chocolate in the kitchen afterward tasted especially good.

From then on whenever we had enough snow we would go out in the sleigh. We didn't even need excuses, although one time in the middle of a blizzard I decided that I just had to go downtown to cash a check. I couldn't resist the allure of taking the sleigh to the drive-up bank teller. The teller was surprised and someone from a nearby store snapped a picture, and so in the next edition of our local paper there was Sally-pony and the sleigh, loaded with the children and me, while that check, which I admit could have been kept until after the blizzard, was being cashed.

The old sleigh proves useful for modern banking. (**Photo courtesy of the *Concord Journal***)

At least once a year we would drive in the sleigh to school. It may sound axiomatic, but to use a sleigh you need snow, and even if there is plenty of snow in your yard, that doesn't mean you'll find enough on the roads. The best conditions for the trip to school came generally after a night's snowstorm when the roads had been plowed but still had a cover of snow. We would hitch up Sally and drive the mile or so to school. Sometimes upon arrival we'd give rides to playmates and other students, and once we took the principal out and around his school's playing field. After the principal got out, Polly (who was not yet in school) and I were left in the sleigh, and I decided it would be fun to go downtown. I thought of an errand we could do at the five and ten, and so we drove to the store and hitched Sally to a parking meter outside. Our errand did not take long, but long enough so that when we came out and found Sally patiently waiting by her meter, the road was nearly bare. While we were in the store the salt on the road along with warmth from the sun had melted the snow cover that we had come in on. Retribution, I thought, for my boldness in taking the sleigh downtown. It is almost impossible to move a sleigh on bare pavement, and we had difficulty getting out of the center of town, where the most salt had been applied. Then Polly, Sally, and I made it home with no trouble. In a pinch we could always go on the sidewalks, which were just wide enough for the sleigh.

One year at town meeting an article came up to discontinue using salt on the roads. Tom and I voted in favor of the article for environmental reasons, but also we thought that as a bonus we would be able to use the sleigh on the roads more frequently. Unfortunately, it didn't work out that way. The cars on the roads compacted the snow left behind by the plows into ice, and though drivers learned both caution and courtesy in handling these conditions, the pony had trouble. Sally, like many other ponies, was never shod, and so her hooves slipped easily on the ice. (Although ponies generally do not need shoes to protect their hooves, we could have had her shod, but it seemed costly to do so just for icy conditions.) I did not realize how dangerous this combination was until we were coming down our street one afternoon. Just opposite our local supermarket, Sally not only slipped but fell down, and we had a tangle of harness and pony with the sleigh shafts on the road. The mess would be cause for panic for almost any horse, let along one with Sally's disposition. I vividly remember the awful sight of that pony down on the road and how frightened I was that she'd hurt herself in her struggle to get back to her feet. Fortunately I had no passenger on the sleigh, for Sally might have turned it over. Fortunately also, traffic stopped; as I mentioned, drivers were more cautious that winter. But most fortunately of all, somehow that panicked pony managed to extricate herself with no harm to herself or the sleigh. I think we were lucky. Incidentally, at the next town meeting the no-salt decision was repealed, for reasons that boil down to our society's trying to dominate the environment. That may be my bias, but the reason for repeal was not that the no-salt practice was dangerous for ponies.

You do not need a sleigh to have fun with a pony in snow. If you can lay your hands on that part of the harness known as the breast band (the piece that does the actual pulling) or if you can fashion something like it, and if you have a toboggan, sleds, or skis and some kids, you are in for good times. Put the breast band on the pony, lengthen the traces with pieces of rope, and attach them to the toboggan or sled. Pile on the kids, lead the pony away, and look back now and then to enjoy the happy faces. Sometimes we used to make a train of sleds, attaching four or five together, with Polly's baby sled at the end. That was a procession everyone enjoyed, even the jerks of starting and the bumping together of the sleds when we stopped. Sally also pulled many children (and me) on skis. This is the old-fashioned sport known as skijoring, which I used to do when I was young, except it was behind a car.

Sally also helped us with snow plowing. At that time in our town the sidewalks were always plowed with horse-drawn plows. Sometimes these plows were kept at Nick's stable, and one day in passing them an idea came to me—I'd make a pony plow. My carpentry skill was slightly improved from my early attempts at making roosts and nesting boxes for the chickens, and so I gathered wood, saw, hammer, and nails, and started. My ideas were only in my head. The design of the plow grew as I went along. After creating the initial V shape I saw where supporting struts would be needed and how to attach a handle. When finished, it had a sturdy look, and I painted it yellow to match the town plows that were pulled by work horses.

Did the plow work? Yes, mostly. It served best for making paths. Sally and I would plow a path out to the barnhole, or to the front door (though it was seldom used), and sometimes even down to the stable for the hay-carrying route. We could help with plowing our long driveway, but the design of my plow was such that once we had made an initial pathway down the driveway, it was difficult to plow back the windrows on either side. And the plow worked best after small snowstorms, or ones that left very light snow. Sally was intolerant of trying to pull something that momentarily wouldn't budge, and that would happen in heavy or deep snow. Her reaction was to rear up, which was not a bit helpful because she'd tangle herself in the traces and display the wilder side of her temperament. Much to my surprise the plow itself endured through all the years we used it, until one spring day in backing the car out of the garage the car door somehow met the plow with a force that broke what years of stress in the snow had never done. By that time a snow blower had taken over many of the plow's duties anyway, and so I wistfully took my broken pony plow to the dump.

Earlier I alluded to another pony and a horse in the family. The horse did not come until later, but the second pony came relatively soon after Sally joined us. Zachary's arrival is a story unto itself.

It started one warm spring day when I was taking advantage of Polly's nap time to sit quietly in the sun and read the paper. A man walked down the driveway and over to me on the porch. He introduced himself as Mr. Kelley and explained that he had been to the stable to find out who that lady was who drove a pony sulky about Concord, and Phil, who worked at the stable, had directed him to our house. Mr. Kelley said he had a nine-month-old Shetland pony, but he didn't know one thing about horses himself and his children really were not interested; would I want the pony? Mr. Kelley obviously was eager to find a new home for his pony, and quickly we came to a tentative and seemingly lopsided deal in my favor: one Shetland pony for a few bantams and rabbits. That evening when I mentioned to Tom the possibility of a second pony, he was sanguine about it. And the next day I spoke with Phil, who assured me the young pony could go out and stay with Sally in the barnhole. "Go see if he has a friendly look in his eye," Phil advised, "but if he looks wild, don't take him." I went to look at him and was immediately captivated by the shaggy little buckskin whose name was Zachary. Thus the decision was made, but later I realized that perhaps I should have gone against the old adage that says don't look a gift horse in the mouth. For reasons that I did not then know, Mr. Kelley was eager to get rid of Zachary.

I inveigled Phil into taking the twelve-horse van over to pick up

Zachary. The small pony looked still smaller in the vast van, but when Phil said he thought Zachary was "kind of cute," I felt I'd made a wise decision. Ha! The problems began as soon as we got back to the stable. I had already noticed that Zachary's shaggy coat appeared patchy in places, and when I took him into the room at the stable for all present, including the vet, to admire, I received the bad news—lice. "The only cure will be to clip him," Nick said, "and he'll need a blanket and a sheltered place to stay." "Gulp," I responded to myself, "I can't keep him in the barnhole. Then where? The shed?" Phil suggested the cellar, and for some wild hours I even considered that too.

And those *were* wild hours. Nick loaned me a pair of electric clippers, and back home in our garage I tied my louse-infested pony and began to remove his shaggy yellow coat. It wasn't easy. Just try using clippers for the first time on a bucking, rearing creature and you'll understand. The only thing that was worse was using the scissors to complete the job, as I'd been advised by the mentors at the stable. I finished with only a small bite from the pony on my left ear and felt lucky to have escaped further harm. The fur under the buckskin had turned out to be gray and I wondered what color this pony was going to be. And at the end I backed off to survey my job. There stood bedraggled Zachary, his beautiful buckskin fur scattered liberally about him on the garage floor. He reminded me of a badly shorn sheep, for his gray underfur showed ridges and hollows caused by a beginner's uneven use of clippers.

What next? Keep the pony in the cellar? The shed? Make a blanket? How many hours left in the afternoon? And, thinking of the cellar, how is mother hen doing down there? Maybe you recall my telling about the bantam hen, Snowflake, who murdered several of her chicks. The day before, I'd been coping with her inability to adjust to motherhood, clutching newly hatched, injured chicks and pecked-at eggs, and throwing blankets over the cage to darken it and make the hen feel more secure. This day I had put her in the dark and quiet of the cellar with one chick under her. I planned to add the others gradually, but in the meantime I was keeping them under Tom's desk lamp in a box in the kitchen. Also, it was the end of the maple-syrup season and I had still sap to boil down. We had enough going on in the house without Zachary's distressing condition.

This was the state of affairs when Jinny, Kathy, and their friend Lesley arrived from school. They were delightfully surprised to find the new pony, they weren't bothered by his scruffy appearance, and, best of all, they were eager to help, which was exactly what I needed. By this time I'd realized that the cellar was fine for Snowflake, but we could never get the pony down the steep bulkhead stairs, and so he would have to stay in the shed. The girls pitched right in. They moved the flower pots, rakes, shovels, bags of fertilizer, and all the clutter that accumulates at the dark end of a shed. When they moved the bikes, trikes, and other wheeled vehicles back they had cleared a place big enough for a pony. And when I returned the clippers to the stable, Phil had found a blanket that we could use. Never mind that it looked large enough for a small horse—we wrapped it around bedraggled little Zachary, and although it hung way down, like a grownup's overcoat on a child, it would keep the pony warm, and what more could we wish?

We led our shorn but blanketed little pony into the cleared space at the back of the shed where we tied him, and, whew, finally everything was under control. How much control, however, depends on your perspective. Tom arrived home to find Zachary bucking and rearing in his new quarters behind all the hastily moved flower pots, rakes, shovels, fertilizers, trikes, and bikes, and he was not too happy about our newest family member.

And Zachary wasn't about to behave like a nice family member, either. The next morning before school, Jinny took Zachary out for a little walk, but shortly Kathy came in to report that Jinny was having troubles. "Why?" I wondered, as I went out to help. "Here, I'll do it," I said, but when Zach started to buck and rear, I decided that it was time to return him to the shed. I didn't think much about the problem, but I did realize that I'd have to construct a stall for him as soon as possible. He reared and pawed the floor when he was tied in the shed, and I was afraid he would break loose, wondering where he would go if he did.

Before stall construction, however, a walk to the stable seemed inviting. You see, I still hadn't fully taken in the nature of our new family member, but when that walk ended, I had. After some bucking and rearing we got as far as the field, where Zach tried to gallop in circles around me. I felt as if I was desperately holding the lead line of an out-of-control work horse, rather than a little Shetland pony that wasn't even a year old. Despite Zach's deceptively small size, the odds were stacked against me, for he was far stronger than I, and so I headed for home immediately, where further trouble awaited. Zachary would not enter the shed. I would lead, but he had only to brace his four hooves on the ground and lean back, and tugging budged him not an inch. He reared, I pulled. He pranced, I pulled harder. He bucked, I despaired. Edie and Polly, both watching from the kitchen door, offered encouraging comments: "Don't worry, Mummy, you'll be able to train him." And finally Edie quietly suggested, "Mummy, why don't you back him in?" I was ready to try anything, and so I turned Zachary around and, ready for a backing battle, was astounded when that stubborn beast backed into the shed as if he did it every day. That was one problem solved, thanks to a five-year-old's insight.

A conversation with Nick down at the stable later on did nothing to raise my spirits. It had never occurred to me that we could have any special trouble in raising a pony colt (male), but Nick graphically explained: "He may try and mount you, you know, like a dog. He will strike out with his front feet. Bite, too—you know, you've seen the rooster with the hens." And this pony was to be the children's pet? No wonder Mr. Kelley had been glad to find another home for Zachary.

Somehow I made the stall. It was not one of my best carpentry efforts, but it held our wild pony colt. By evening, however, I was ready to admit defeat, or at least the possibility thereof.

But soon Snowflake began to take to her chicks, and we were even able to bring her up from the cellar and into the kitchen. And I began to cope with the training of Zach. A lead shank with a chain to go over his nose, a strong and firm hand, and a no-nonsense attitude helped. As Nick explained, "efficient, yet nonabusive handling," and, when I started to carry the driving whip, my confidence improved greatly. Soon Snowflake and her chicks visited Edie's and Jinny's classrooms, the maple syrup was bottled and put away, and Zach began to lead so calmly that I let the kids take over.

When Zach became manageable I decided to try to take him to my parents' house, a half hour's drive away, so that they could see the new pony. Our old station wagon had a removable seat behind the front one. If I took the seat out, could I put Zach in? I tried it, and was surprised that it was about as easily done as said. I closed the door on Zach's lead line to ensure that he was firmly tied and then started the car with my unusual passenger behind me. Other than

Zachary's whinnying at a policeman at a congested traffic corner, the trip was uneventful, and when we arrived outside my parents' house I led Zach out the car door he was facing, up the walk, and in through the front door of the house. My mother greeted him with admiration despite his shorn appearance, but my father, who was not well, was upstairs. "Let's take Zach up," I said, and my mother, who enjoyed animals and had an adventurous spirit, agreed. We easily led Zach up the wide staircase and down the hall to greet my father, who said he liked the look in the little pony's eyes. We had a midmorning cup of coffee together in the upstairs sitting room, my old bedroom, while Zach waited patiently, standing beside my father's chair with a calm that belied his earlier characteristic behavior.

But what goes up does not necessarily come down, at least easily, and when we went back down the hall from the sitting room to the stairs I felt a premonition as the lead line tightened. Oh no, were we going to replay the shed episode? I glanced back and saw Zach's feet planted firmly and that he was beginning to lean back in the I-refuse-to-move position. I have learned since that horses can more easily go up something difficult than down, but Zach gave me my first lesson. How would we get him down those stairs? Even though my parents had enjoyed young Zach's visit, I suspected they didn't want a perma-nent pony resident on their second floor, and Edie's backing sugges-tion wouldn't work for stairs. Ultimately, however, the time spent in training Zach paid off. He came down those stairs. Slowly, but he did come down.

I continued training Zach, especially accustoming him to obey voice commands: walk, trot, canter, and whoa. I remember enjoying this part, but I didn't recall how much until I recently came across a paragraph in comments I'd written on our tenth wedding anniversary. "And I find now that it is the simplest things that bring me closest to realization and happiness. Back to nature, in fact. There is some-thing—perhaps only symbolic—in just going from the dishes in the kitchen to the henhouse to pause in that world for a moment while gathering eggs. Gardening, of course, brings the same—weeded the side bed just this morning—but with the animals it comes even stronger. I have loved the ponies. . . . Now, with Zachary, the time with him is an excuse to put the mind on different matters, get out of doors and away from that kitchen—I cannot even talk to the children when I am training him, so great is my concentration. These moments

Young Zach comes out of the car.

away make the trivia of life more bearable; in fact, put them in perspective.

"My baby, although Polly at three is scarcely a baby any more, is asleep on the living-room floor with her toy horsie beside her. In a while Edie will come home from school, then Jinny and Kathy. Before they come I should change the position of the lawn sprinkler—trivia—and then spend a few minutes with my other baby, Zach, for a training session—back to nature." I felt I had made the discovery that nature nurtures the soul. I didn't know then the well-known Aldo Leopold quotation, "It is by common consent a good thing to get back to nature."

When Zachary was old enough we had him gelded because geldings are more tractable than stallions (ungelded males), and later we taught him to be ridden. Despite having accustomed him to the saddle, the first riders, Jinny and Kathy (I was too heavy) had several bucking-bronco experiences, but Zach settled down soon and then Nick's advice, to consider the reins as a chute and that you push your mount through the chute with your legs, became helpful. We also taught Zachary to drive, which was easy the third time around. And now we had two fine children's ponies, and Zach, who had turned out to be buckskin with a brown stripe down his back and a black mane and tail, contrasted nicely with Sally, who was dark gray with a light mane and tail.

Soon Jinny and Kathy began to outgrow the Shetlands, although for short periods a Shetland can carry a small adult, as I learned when I had an injured foot and found riding Sally far handier than using crutches for outside work. Winter was coming on when a plot began to hatch in my mind—how about a small horse as a Christmas present for the kids? Tom agreed, I turned to Nick for assistance, and shortly I had signed an agreement to buy Lynfield's Johnnie Jump-up, a white Connemara gelding, five years old and fourteen hands, three inches tall. (A hand is four inches, an old unit of measurement like the foot. Technically, a pony measures fourteen two or less, and a horse measures anything more than that.) I wondered how to transport Johnnie from Nick's new stable across town to our neighborhood and decided the simplest way would be for me to ride him over on Christmas Eve. Oh, did I have much to learn about horses!

I was anticipating how surprised the kids would be on Christmas morning to find a new horse in the barnhole with the ponies. Phil agreed to keep Johnnie overnight at the stable near us, and on Christmas morning I planned to sneak down and lead him to our barnhole. Although the late afternoon on December 24 was bitter cold and already dark, I started my ride on Johnnie from Nick's barn with a joyful feeling befitting the season. Johnnie's first hesitation didn't bother me, nor did the second or third, but when he refused to go forward and tried to turn back to his stable, I realized what was happening. Like any normal horse, he wanted to go home, and I had underestimated his herd instinct. Perhaps my joy dissipated a little, but it continued on a steady downgrade as Johnnie stopped at more frequent intervals. I remember somewhere in the darkness reaching for a tree branch to take a small piece for a switch, and using that switch helped our progress. But by that time I was coming into a more populated area, which included Christmas lights. People may find them festive; Johnnie did not. He found them downright frightening, which inspired snorting, shying, backing, and circling into the middle of streets to stay as far as possible from the dangerous-looking, brightly colored objects. Any joy that was left in me was overcome by determination, and furthermore within the riding boots my feet were feeling colder and colder. I don't know how long that ride took, but I felt that my feet were frozen and that I was on my last emotional legs when Johnnie and I reached Phil's stable.

When I returned home to the last-minute Christmas preparations and present wrapping, I feared, like a guilty person, that something about me, maybe the unusual long, warming bath might give away the secret at the stable. But the children suspected nothing.

On Christmas morning I was able to disappear unnoticed and lead Johnnie to his new home in the barnhole. Otherwise, we followed our family traditions until after breakfast when it was pony-feeding time. The excited parents went out with the children, who discovered a beautiful white horse in the barnhole with their two ponies. He sparkled in the morning sun and had a Christmas red ribbon in his mane. Four ecstatic children patted him, led him, admired him, and rode him bareback around the barnhole. All the presents under the tree had to wait. That part of Christmas morning belonged to Lynfield's Johnnie Jump-up, and a happy time it was for us all.

That winter and spring I found our Christmas surprise had a bonus for me, for now I too could ride. Sometimes I rode the distance to Nick's new stable for a riding lesson in the morning, and brought the children down for lessons after school. Then Kathy or Jinny would ride Johnnie home. Soon, as might be expected, the kids became more serious about riding, especially Kathy, who joined Pony Club, learned much about horse care, and began to enter Johnnie in shows. Through Kathy and Pony Club we all gained in our understanding of horses and horsemanship. For instance, one way to make a horse go through a place that it doesn't want is to put a rope around his haunches and, while you lead, others put pressure on the rope. We did this trick many times in loading Johnnie into a horse van to go to a show. The technique might have worked in getting Sally-pony to cross that ditch.

Our hay costs were still minimal, but now we had large grain bills and visits from the blacksmith and the vet as well as proper attire for shows, but this phase of the horses in our family belonged far more to the children than to me. Six years after Johnnie's arrival, he developed bone spavin, which meant he should not jump. Jinny and Kathy were at college, but Edie, who was a member of the 4H horse club, and I searched for a horse that we could afford and she could train. We finally chose a black and handsome horse named Sinjon, and with sadness sold our much-loved Johnnie Jump-up. Quickly we discovered how much easier it was to groom dark Sinjon for a show than Johnnie, whose white coat easily showed dirt. Edie worked hard training Sinjon, and still feels today that he could have jumped almost anything—we never found how high he could go.

In the meantime, when Polly at last outgrew Sally and Zachary, they went to Nick's stable and Nick loaned us his large pony, named Copper after her color. Copper had one vice—she did not like to be caught. Go into the pasture, hide the lead shank behind you, shake an enticing bucket of grain, and position a few helpers where they will discourage Copper from going in any but your direction. Then meet with frustration when Copper approaches, closer and closer, but at the last moment eludes you. She did this one time when I'd been left in the country to wait for the horse van, driven by Nick's son, to come for Sinjon and Copper. Copper exasperated us with her evasions, but at least she is not still in that pasture today.

Two summers earlier a grim drama had taken place in that pasture. Johnnie, then still with us, developed colic—a dreaded sickness that occurs when a horse has eaten either too much grain or something toxic. Because horses do not vomit they cannot rid themselves of the food causing the trouble. Later we realized that Johnnie had probably consumed too much milkweed, because most of the pasture's grass by that late time in the summer had been eaten down. During our frantic trips to town to use the public telephone to find a vet, we did not know what was poisoning him. Public telephones are a boon, especially if you live without a phone, but they can twist a simple task into a farce. "Dr. so and so is not on duty this weekend, but Dr. such and such is." Then you find that the latter lives over the border in the neighboring state, but even so you call, and either the line will be busy, or it won't answer. If the latter, do you drive back up the hill to home, and come back—when? Or if the line is merely busy, how many times do you redial, how often, and what do you do when you do get through to learn that the doctor is out but "just give me your number and I'll have him call you as soon as he returns. He'll be back in about an hour, or two, at the most"? At 10:00 p.m., finally, I spoke with a vet, who agreed to come over next day. "In the meantime," he said, "you should not let the horse lie down because he may writhe and kick and knot his intestines, which could kill him. Keep him up and walking about." That doesn't sound too difficult, does it? The older children were away and so I decided to be the responsible person through the night. I arranged makeshift sleeping quarters on the porch, where I could watch the pasture, and, seeing a white horse standing in the moonlight, I lay down. But not for long. I was worried and raised myself to look over the porch railing to see a large white form prostrate on the ground. Oh no, was I too late? Grabbing the lead shank, I ran to Johnnie, who raised his head slightly, and the hammerings in my heart began to subside. Getting him up on his feet was no easy matter, but finally he arose, and, while I led, he plodded reluctantly after me. Finally, I decided I could leave him and returned to the porch to lie down. But, like a cracked record, the scene repeated itself, again, and again, and again. And if I tried to sleep, my mind kept showing me a picture of that white body flat on the ground, highlighted by the moon and, looking, frankly, dead.

By 2:30 A.M., however, the scenes were repeating less often, and I peered over the railing and saw Johnnie standing, but also I saw two illuminated eyes coming directly through the pasture toward me. They came nearer and nearer, and suddenly disappeared beneath me, where a woodchuck dwelled in our woodpile under the porch. Next I was surrounded by growls, squeals, and harsher growls, over and over. This was too much. Like a frightened child I went into the cabin, awoke Tom, and told him about the awful "growly thing" under the porch. Out on the porch together, we heard not a sound, but at least we could see Johnnie standing and swishing his tail in the moonlight. Slowly, though, I was vindicated. Almost purrlike at first, the growls started again, too close for comfort through the porch floor. I gave up and slept the rest of the night inside, and, fortunately, Johnnie's colic was far less severe in the morning.

Who was the growl maker? In the calm light of day we decided it was a fisher, a large and vicious member of the weasel family. Even so, it would have been more frightened of me than I should have allowed myself to be of it, except at three o'clock in the morning I had little inclination to stick my bare feet out on the porch steps to prove the point.

Our horses and ponies have been gone a long time now. Even Tom, however, not a rider, will sometimes point out a white horse like Johnnie, or a black like Sinjon, as we drive by. And as for me, if I spot a little Shetland, "A pony," I'll cry out, "there's a *pony* over there!"

Further Thoughts

Sally-pony and this year's winner of the Kentucky Derby have a common ancestor, and for many years scientists regarded eohippus, or dawn horse, as this ancestor. Recently, however, controversy has arisen about the evolution of equus. Some believe horses evolved from hyracotherium (formerly known as eohippus), which lived about 55 million years ago, but others take horses back only 15 million years to neohipparions, or to merychippus. However scientists resolve these theories, it seems safe to say that the common ancestor probably was small and had several toes on each foot. It may have fed on bushes and may have been adapted for moving on soft ground through underbrush. As these animals began to feed more on hard, open grassy plains they developed longer necks and heads for grazing and long, strong legs for fast running, as protection against predators. To gain speed on the hard ground, they evolved one strong toe covered with an overgrown toe-

nail—the hoof. Fast running also caused them to evolve a deep, large chest to supply more oxygen. As further protection against predators on the open plains, these animals developed funnel-shaped ears that swivel for acute hearing, as well as large nostrils for keen smell. And somewhere during the years of evolution they developed long tails as flyswatters.

Human beings found a strong ally in the horse as a beast of burden and a transporter of people. Many of the great early civilizations were horse users. John Trotwood Moore writes, "Wherever man has left his footprint in the long ascent from barbarism to civilization, we will find the hoofprint of the horse beside it." The image of the horse appeared on early coinage and on temples, and at times the horse was worshiped as divine. Until the machine age the horse was vital in many societies. Perhaps its worth is best expressed in Shakespeare's King Richard III, *when the king utters the famous words, "A horse! A horse! my kingdom for a horse!"*

Although other animals, such as oxen and donkeys, have also long been used by people for transportation, the horse was so prevalent that from it we got our measure for the strength of our machines—horsepower. I doubt that a sports car would sell well with an engine measured in ox or donkey power.

When I was very small the milkman delivered to our house in a horse-drawn wagon, but today unless you live on a ranch or have horses for pleasure riding or are among the few who still employ horses as draft animals, you probably have little contact with them. Attend a horse show or go to a country fair where draft horses engage in pulling contests and other events. In urban areas you may see police horses because they have proved effective in crowd control.

Donkeys, which were domesticated from the wild ass, are so closely related to horses that the two species can interbreed. Crossing a donkey stallion with a mare (female horse) results in a mule, which inherits useful traits from both parents. Mules can be male or female, but both sexes are infertile. Perhaps Zachary's dark stripe down the back gives a clue to the close horse-donkey relationship, for burros have similar dark stripes. Other relatives of the horse visible in a zoo are the zebras and the more distant cousins of horses, tapirs and rhinoceroses.

Do not take on ownership of a horse unless you know what you are getting into. In this chapter I remind you about some of the pitfalls, and also about some of the joys.

Chapter Eight

Squirrel in the Tree

At the other end of the telephone line was someone from the town's department of public works. "Our men were over in the cemetery cutting down trees damaged by the storm and they found a squirrel nest in one. The mother was killed in the fall, but they brought the nest with three babies here to the office, and I was wondering if. . . ." Without pause I interrupted, "I'll be right down." Never mind that it had been a long day at work, nor that we were readying the house for a visit by our friends, the Sterns. I left for the DPW building and there picked up a carton with a messy nest of dried grasses, leaves, and heaven knows what else, with three pink infant squirrels nestled together in the middle.

Once home, closer inspection revealed a host of other occupants, all tiny, all jumping or crawling about. Fleas? Mites? Lice? We didn't care which, but immediately extracted the larger occupants and threw the infested nest onto the compost pile. The baby squirrels, however, were also infested. The Sterns, who were coming, could tolerate almost anything peculiar about the Sissons, except that little squirrels with parasites hopping all over them seemed to be asking too much. Besides, the babies would be more comfortable and healthier without their guests. Polly put a white towel down in a white bathtub and set a baby at the center of the towel. We could easily see the dark parasites against the white of the towel and tub, as well as against the pink but slightly furred skin of the squirrel, and, one by one, we removed the parasites. This technique is tedious but it worked, and an hour later we had three parasite-free babies, ready to greet our house guests.

By the time the Sterns arrived Polly and I had devised a nest from a box with soft rags and had given the first of countless feedings. We had created a formula that would best approximate squirrel milk by mixing skim milk with an egg yolk and added vitamins, administering the formula with medicine droppers. Perhaps the beds weren't made, but Ruth, Frank, Naomi, and Charlotte arrived to meet clean and fed baby squirrels in a clean nest. And Frank immediately solved a problem. Polly had already called the one female Jessica, and I had named one of the two males Henry David (after Thoreau). "Call the other squirrel Elijah," said Frank, "after the prophet Elijah, for whom a glass of wine is set aside at the Passover seder. See, the baby has a reddish nose."

Care of three infant squirrels takes time, but the time shortage was solved in an unfortunate manner. The infants did not thrive; first Henry David died, followed soon after by Elijah with his reddish nose. For a while Jessica held her own, gained weight, and began to grow fur. But she developed diarrhea and became very weak. My own motherhood instinct suggested frequent minuscule feedings, primarily of water with a touch of formula. I had work to do at the typewriter, and so I kept Jessica beside me and fed her a tiny amount about every fifteen minutes. By the end of two hours she was no worse, and, by the end of the third, she was stronger. Gradually I increased the amount of formula in the feedings and after a while gave larger amounts less frequently. Next day Jessica was a healthy baby and continued in good health for the entire time that she was with us.

I've read that only about 25 percent of squirrels born live for a year. That's easy to believe considering the parasites, the unknown cause of death of Henry David and Elijah, and Jessica's illness. Squirrels are also subject to internal parasites, fungus infections, mange, and numerous other diseases. Then too, many predators enjoy squirrel meat: hawks, owls, some snakes, foxes, coyotes, bobcats, and other carnivores, including the relatives of Bonnie, Gay, Blithe, and Jesse, our raccoons. I hadn't hesitated when I decided to take on the baby squirrels; we found them cute, even at the beginning when their eyes and ears were closed and they had almost no fur. And, as Jessica grew, she was an appealing little creature. But I knew all along that squirrels could never rival raccoons in my heart. Soon I discovered how wrong I was.

Jessica had always been able to cling upside down to a hand. Adult squirrels have claws that serve as superb tree hooks, handier than crampons on a steep slope, and the babies are born with these hooks well developed—they can cling before they can see, hear, or walk.

Because Jessica's claws were always ready for use, I could walk about the house with a baby squirrel hanging on. Later she began to climb on me (the first hint of the Squirrel in the Tree game), or on anything she could reach that was climbable. She began to run rather than walk over surfaces, and soon she added short jumps to her routine. She had extraordinary balance and agility, and her supple body was perfectly adapted for her gymnastic talent. Gradually we became captivated by her graceful acrobatics and her seeming joy in performing them. At breakfast she would hop across the table, jump to the basket of apples on the counter, next an upward leap and spin that can only be described as a jump for joy, then a scurry through the open dishwasher, and finally a leap and a cling onto a house plant, which toppled to the floor, but never mind, we would be laughing too much by this time to care. Yes, she was making inroads into our hearts.

The Squirrel in the Tree game, invented by Jessica, was a special delight. One of us played the part of the tree, and Jessica, the squirrel. She streaked up and down and around with a swiftness that was unbelievable; she sidled from front to back, paused abruptly, totally motionless on a shoulder, then bolted down the back and the game began anew. All the tree had to do was to stand and enjoy the game. Trousers for the tree were a necessity, Kathy pointed out, to protect against scratches from Jessica's tree hooks. Ours was the simplest part, but by this time we had come to realize that the common squirrel had vitality and talents that we had never perceived, and then Jessica began to challenge our prejudice for raccoons. You may wonder and shake your head if you have never seen anything exceptional about squirrels in the park, in the woods, or on your bird feeder. I can only respond that I was surprised by the wonders of squirrelness, but my descriptions give only a pale image of the real thing. I wish you could have come into my kitchen to see for yourself.

She did not always stay in the kitchen, for she loved to roam about the house. She would hop under the dining-room table into the living room, where she enjoyed climbing up the curtains and leaping across to the top of the bookcase, invariably knocking off a small metal vase, and she often sprinted up the stairs to see if Polly was in her room. If you went to look for her you might look under the sofa where you'd just heard her, only to find her gazing silently down at you from the back of a chair across the room.

Often I tried to have her in the den with me when I worked at

Jessica's tree hooks work well. (**Photo courtesy Polly Fleckenstein**)

the desk. She would leap onto the desk as if to check what I was doing, scattering orderly piles of papers as well as disorderly ones. Then a hop over the telephone and across the radiator top to the bookcase and the file cabinet, and on to other areas. Small clunking noises indicated that she had knocked something over or to the floor. The larger noises generally got my attention—what's been broken? Ultimately she would come back over the floor, hop onto the chair and me, and then back to the desk. She often nibbled at the top end of a pen, which sometimes resulted in squirrely designs on my paper. Once she actually added some squiggles to a page of manuscript. When I sent the manuscript in, I pointed out the special addition on page 1 of chapter 3 and suggested to the publisher that perhaps this was the first contribution they had received from a squirrel.

Of course she had long since outgrown her formula and formula mixed with baby cereal and had been eating all kinds of solid food. Peanuts, sunflower seeds, apples, peaches, pears, strawberries, bread, crackers, potato chips, corn chips, cookies, chocolate—yes, Jessica ate junk food, if given the chance. Wild squirrels eat widely varied fare: acorns, of course, other nuts, fruits, berries, bird seed and other seeds, tree sap and buds, mushrooms (including some poisonous to us),

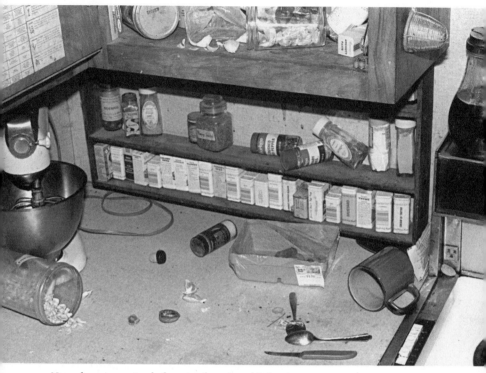

Never leave a squirrel alone too long in a kitchen!

insects, birds' eggs, and even hatchlings. Sometimes we would see Jessica sitting by our kitchen sink gnawing vainly on our metal tea egg. We make tea with the tea egg every morning and then leave it in the sink, which is where she used to find it. Perhaps she thought it was a walnut because it has about the same shape, but I doubt that with her keen sense of smell she was fooled. Maybe she found the smell of wet tea leaves enticing.

The tea egg was comical. The time she ate the seed corn was not. Tom had been soaking red-dyed corn prior to planting, and I came into the kitchen to discover that Jessica had found the bowl of corn, and it seemed that she had eaten some. "Tom," I called, "Jessica has eaten some of your corn. What's on it? Anything poisonous?" Soon we were perusing the back of the seed packet together and found that some long-named chemical had been added as a fungicide. Fear and panic gripped me though Jessica was saucily sitting on top of her cage flicking her tail. I called the poison clinic and even though my question about the long-named chemical and corn and a squirrel might have seemed implausible, especially at such an early hour, after only one repetition of the problem, the answerer set to work, looked up the chemical, and told me that, as I feared, it was toxic in some amounts. But what quantity would poison a squirrel? "Lady, perhaps you should call a vet. Squirrels aren't exactly in our line."

I called a veterinarian. "How much corn did your squirrel eat?" she asked. I had to admit that I didn't know. I was reminded of the time when one of our kids had gotten into some strong medicine, and how the doctor had advised ipecac, even though we didn't know if she'd actually eaten any of the pills. My thinking was on the right track, for the next thing the vet and I were discussing was how to make a squirrel throw up. We could not figure out a way, and the only alternative was to give Jessica extra water to dilute any poison and hope for the best.

After the telephone conversation Jessica was sitting on the kitchen counter grooming herself. She used her forepaws to clean her head, much as a cat does, and then she set to the task of keeping her fluffy tail in order. Grooming is a normal and vital activity for squirrels. Certainly Jessica was behaving normally, and when she continued to do so for the rest of the day I finally stopped worrying about the corn.

A day later Jessica had gone on one of her house explorations—I had unwittingly left the kitchen door ajar. I searched everywhere and, frustrated, began to look in Polly's room. Suddenly I spotted her. She was sitting atop Polly's bedpost, calmly regarding me. At the same time I felt something crunch under the rug beneath my foot. How did something crunchy get under the rug? I turned up an edge and found a broken peanut in the shell on the floor. I looked up and the culprit was still gazing at me from her bedpost perch.

After this we'd often find a walnut tucked under the sofa pillows, pistachios under the living-room rug, or an acorn under a seat cushion. Jessica was following her instinct, no matter how humorous it was for us to watch her take a peanut in her mouth, jump to a window sill, look around, then scratch with her forepaws at the corner of the sill and solemnly place the peanut there. We couldn't explain to her, "Look, dummy, that peanut's still in plain sight, and the ones you put under the rug have been smashed." Her instinct bore fruit, in a manner of speaking, the spring after she had left us. Watering a houseplant, I discovered a little oak tree growing in the pot.

One day when Jessica was still with us, I was just about to lead an adult class on an hour's field trip when someone came in with an orphaned infant squirrel. It was cold, but there was no time for any usual action, and so I simply tucked it under my shirt and sweater next to my stomach. And, with my jacket on, no one was the wiser. I knew this would be fine for the squirrel, but I had overlooked something—me. About half an hour into the class I began to feel a few itches around my middle. Then I felt a lot. Good grief, how could I have forgotten those parasites after our experience with Henry David, Elijah, and Jessica? But also I was surprised, for many parasites are host specific—they dwell only on selected species. Whatever it was that was enjoying the baby squirrel found me just as tasty. At least the squirrel was warm when, as soon as the class ended, I removed him and his little buddies. But at what expense? I awoke the next morning to find myself covered with welts around my midriff and some as far away as my shoulders. Itchy, too.

We cared for the new little squirrel, but somehow he never entered our hearts as Jessica had. He scarcely had a name, although in a pinch we used Squeezix. Perhaps I had a premonition about his future personality, which showed up surprisingly early. We were vacationing in a house so large that it had an entire room we could use for the squirrels. We put their cage on a big table, with the cage door open so that they could sleep in their familiar quarters, yet also have the freedom of the room. One day I noticed that when I did anything to the cage Squeezix made noises that undeniably told me he objected. A few days later he did the same, and also threatened me, when I refilled the water dish on the table. Then I began to understand: the cage, and now the table, were Squeezix's territory, and I was an intruder. The day before we were due to go home I entered the room, barefoot as usual, and without hesitation Squeezix hopped across the room to me. I scarcely had time to finish thinking what a friendly action that was, when he bit, hard, on the top of my foot. He had taken over the whole room.

We took the two squirrels with us in their cage next day, and shortly after our arrival home I took Squeezix to a wooded and uninhabited area, where I let him go. As he scurried up an oak and I turned to leave I had not the slightest doubt that with his disposi-

Baby Squeezix traveled in a cooler turned into a "warmer."

Squeezix drinks his formula from a medicine dropper. (**Photo courtesy of Polly Fleckenstein**)

tion he would make out just fine out there in the real squirrel world.

When I came back home I gave Jessica a walnut as a special treat. She took it with her front paws, which had four toes with the toenail tree hooks and a curious little stump, known as a tubercle, where a thumb would be on our hand. The toes and tubercles effectively held and rotated the nut while she gnawed through its shell with her two lower front teeth (incisors), at the same time using the two top incisors for support. When she had made a hole in the nut large enough for the bottom incisors to fit inside, they broke open the shell and Jessica busily ate the contents. Her handy can-opener incisors grew constantly. She had to keep filing them down by gnawing on hard objects.

These incisors are the trademark of the rodent family. Off and on during the years we've had other rodents in our household, including Squeakie the guinea pig with a special bantam friend. None of these animals ever fascinated us as did the squirrels, but I'll digress to tell about some of them.

Woodchucks or groundhogs, which are marmot relatives, are rodents that we now know too well. They have a penchant for our vegetable garden and find the Sissons' young bean plants, broccoli, cauliflower, and any number of other vegetables irresistible. Tom had used a number of techniques to discourage them, but sometimes they even have the audacity to tunnel under the fence right into the garden. My foot slipped into one such hole, otherwise hidden by raspberry plants, while I was enjoying a lunchtime treat of fresh raspberries last summer.

My first close encounter with a woodchuck was years ago. His name was Rug and, for reasons I've forgotten, he could not be released into the wild. He was kept at the nature sanctuary where I was teaching, and I had used him with a class about hibernation late in the afternoon. When I returned to the building where Rug was kept, it was locked and I found myself with a guest for the night. The children were pleased, and George, a friend who stopped by, enjoyed Rug as we sat in the kitchen, I with Rug on my lap. He was a lapful, for like a wild woodchuck that gains almost a third in body weight anticipating hibernation, Rug was fat indeed. "You can hardly tell which end is which," said George, "Don't you thing he looks like a hot-water bottle?" Our hot-water bottle, however, had strong claws and easily escaped from the large wooden crate that I had thought would make a fine bedroom for our guest. Poor fellow, he had to spend the night in the sanctuary's little traveling case, which, though cramped, was escape-proof.

Next morning I was awakened by Jinny carefully putting a fat woodchuck on my bed. Rug was a friendly fellow, and this was a pleasant surprise. But woodchucks have an unerring instinct to dig tunnels, and within moments Rug had tunneled under the bedclothes, ending up next to my feet. I can report that a woodchuck in bed is tickly on the toes.

Years later the tunnel instinct brought us the only baby woodchuck we ever had. Edie was riding Sinjon the horse in the field behind our house when she spotted a little woodchuck on the ground ahead. She stopped and the woodchuck attacked Sinjon's right front hoof. Not that Edie was worried about the hoof—a feisty young woodchuck couldn't so much as scratch it—but, thinking about such a youngster being out of its tunnel home and away from its mother's care, she dismounted, took off a riding boot, and lay it on the ground beside the baby. What did the little woodchuck do? Just as Edie thought he would, he perceived the boot as a long dark tunnel and immediately went inside. When I came home, Edie told me that she had a surprise for me in the kitchen.

At first he was easy to care for. He drank a milk formula easily and thrived. I used him at times with my teaching, but the last time I did that was a day when he'd been enjoyed and patted by three-year-olds in the morning and by a group of elderly people in the afternoon. Somehow during the ride home he got out of his cage, and when I picked him up to put him back in, he snarled and tried to bite. Was this the same creature that the kids and older people had met during the day? I always tell my classes that wild animals do not make good pets, but this one was proving my point at an early age. After that I had to wear thick gloves every time I fed him, and there was something ironic about feeding a little one that in turn was trying to bite. Another irony was that inside the kitchen I was rearing a young woodchuck, while outside my husband was trying, as always, to get rid of woodchucks. You may have noticed that I have not called this woodchuck by a name; we must have given him one, but I've forgotten it, perhaps for psychological reasons. The moment that unlovable youngster reached the age at which he could fend for himself, I abandoned him, and in an area that was far from gardens.

We've also had various semidomesticated rodents. Aside from the guinea pigs, for many years we had their relatives, another South American animal, the Octodon degu. Degus look like overgrown hamsters, with rich brown coats and a tuft at the end of a long tail. These were scurrying creatures, always on the move it seemed. Thus the first two, which my friend Biz gave to Edie, were aptly named To and Fro. In generations that followed we had such personalities as Hither and Yon or Here and There. Also we had one Mrs. Bitey, her self-explanatory name a reminder that many small rodents bite, and the wounds from those sharp incisors can be painful. I speak from experience.

Once Hither got loose in the house, and because ours is an old house with many nooks, crannies, and small holes, we felt the chances of recovering him before he starved were slim. We searched all over, aided by a neighborhood couple who had stopped in just after we discovered the loss. No luck. Two days later a scuttling sound under the dining-room radiator revealed the escapee, we were able to catch him, and Hither rejoined his family.

With so many animals in residence, whenever we go away we need an animal sitter. Elizabeth, our current sitter, has been doing the job for several years and has become like a nanny to our creatures; Butter the goose is particularly partial to her. When we had the degus we had several sitters, and I'll never forget the sight that greeted us after a ski weekend with the family. Everything seemed fine: we were unpacking the car, I was putting things away in the kitchen, and I opened the freezer compartment at the top of the refrigerator. Smack in the center beside a carton of vanilla ice cream and looking directly out at me was Fro, one of the original degus. It took me a moment to realize that he was frozen, and the mystery was solved when our weekend sitter explained that Fro had died while we were gone, he didn't know what to do, and so put him in the freezer. It did make an unusual homecoming.

Recently we had a colony of Siberian hamsters. A friend of Jinny's was doing her doctoral dissertation on the social habits of these animals—her little darlings, she called them. And they are beguiling creatures, smaller than the common pet-store golden hamsters, colored brownish gray with white beneath, and a face with twitchy whiskers, cute looking enough to make you feel they must have emanated from illustrations in children's books. It wasn't long before I found an excuse to have some of my own "little darlings"—I would use them in teaching. And I did. They lived in a large aquarium in my classroom and spent much of the time sleeping in a heap in a coffee can because, like other hamsters, they are nocturnal. They were too small and quick for children to handle easily, but that problem was solved when I found the top of a car luggage carrier at the dump. Turned upside down, it made a fine hamstorium. Kids sat around the edge, watched, patted, did food-preference experiments, and made mazes. The little darlings were loved by all. They are short-lived creatures, however, and although we had several families, natural attrition finally claimed them all.

Kathy's Flopsy, Edie's Cottontail, and Jinny's Peter were our first rabbits, long ago, before Polly's time. Rabbits belong to the order of animals known as lagomorphs. They are not rodents, although you might think they are, because if you look at their teeth from the outside you see the two pairs of incisors that are typical of rodents. But if you look inside—not easily done with Flopsy, Cottontail, Peter, or any other living rabbit—you will see two little teeth behind the upper incisors.

These were Dutch dwarf rabbits, small enough for two-year-old Edie to hold easily. Flopsy and Cottontail were gray and white, and Peter was black and white. Flopsy was especially loved—Kathy carried her often around the house, in the car, into stores. Flopsy became tamer than the others, but even so, if she escaped outside the rabbit hunt was as difficult as for the others. "Kathy, look, she's right under the car. You and Jinny go to the other side, and perhaps. . . ." Flopsy, frightened by her view of feet that she may perceive as predators, scoots out from under the car, naturally at a spot where no one is around to catch her, and runs under the lilacs. We approach the lilacs, and she's off to the thicket between us and the neighbors. Then it's on into the neighbor's back yard, where finally we corner her between the house and the three of us, and as she attempts an escape, Kathy intercepts her, picks her up, and carries her back home.

Baby rabbits we had in abundance, usually around Eastertime and by "planned parenthood." How do you limit reproduction with such fecund creatures as rabbits? Easy. Peter lived in a separate cage from the two females. Then how can you plan for Easter bunnies? Easy again. Put Peter in with a female about thirty days before Easter. Female rabbits can almost always conceive immediately. Your chances are good that, after putting the male with the female, the latter will kindle (give birth) in about a month. The mother pulls fur from her breast to make a nest, and the babies are always covered with this wonderful fluffy blanket. If you have worn an angora sweater, you can appreciate the warmth of rabbit fur. When we had our first litter we were worried because Cottontail did not appear to be nursing her babies. We interfered, and several times daily brought Cottontail to the nest so that the babies could drink her milk. Only later did I find that wild rabbits nurse their babies at dawn and at dusk. Otherwise they stay away from the nest, so that they will not reveal its position to predators. Because domestic rabbits also nurse twice daily, our interference was unnecessary, possibly even harmful, because we were causing the mother to act in an unnatural way.

Three or four times over the years we have taken over for a wild mother cottontail rabbit. Substituting for a mother raccoon or squirrel is easy by comparison, for of all the cottontail bunnies that have come to our kitchen, only one survived to adulthood. He was a healthy rabbit and reminded me (as most cottontails do) of the young hare painted in watercolors by Albrecht Durer. I was happy when I let him go in a nearby forest. Of course the survival rate of cottontails in the wild, baby or otherwise, is low. Rabbits rank high in the diet of many predators, from owls to foxes: a staple, so to speak. And yet if they did not we'd probably be knee deep in rabbits. Fortunately most ecosystems have a similar dynamic, natural balance between rabbits and their eaters.

Infant cottontails must be kept warm and fed a suitable formula. We generally fed ours more than the twice a day they would be fed in the wild, assuming that smaller, more frequent feedings would be beneficial. In the wild the mother rabbit stimulates elimination by licking the anal and genital regions; we used a piece of paper towel wet with warm water as a substitute. We sadly found that, if fed too rapidly, a little rabbit may get the milk into its breathing system and drown. And we found out how subject these infants are to pneumonia. I have a vivid memory of putting one severely ill baby into our incubator with the hope that the body-temperature warmth would help pull it through. It didn't.

Our first lot of cottontails came from a nest that Kathy and Jinny's friend, Ellen, discovered on top of the manure pile, perhaps a wise place because it was a cold spring and decaying manure generates heat. Although they had none of their mother's fur around them we waited several days, hoping the mother would take over. After three died, however, we took them in. Our last orphaned litter came from a nest that Tom, who had no inkling that a nest was there, rototilled in his garden, and coincidentally the mother was found dead outside the garden. I came home to a surprise box of baby bunnies in the kitchen. As I pulled them out to feed them, I named them Flopsy, Mopsy, Cottontail, and Peter and saw that some showed severe injuries from the accident with the Rototiller. At the next feeding I pulled out Flopsy, Mopsy, Cottontail, and Peter, and then I found one more! Peter lived longest, but he too succumbed, whether to injuries or unnatural mothering, I don't know.

A happier rabbit memory is of Polly's Willie, who was medium-sized and black and white. Polly often put one of the old raccoon harnesses on Willie and took him out with a leash. When he had been with us less than a month and produced a litter of babies, though, we learned her sex. For year's we've had a Volkswagen Rabbit, known as Willie in honor of our last domestic rabbit.

But let's get back to squirrels. At about five in the afternoon on a day early in September, Jon telephoned. He had been one of Polly's teachers, and had just found an infant squirrel in his yard. Although we still had Jessica I couldn't resist and went to pick up the infant, which was cold to the touch and curled up in a hibernating position—he was near death. Back home I hastily pulled out my yogurt maker, plugged it in, threw in some crumpled paper towels, and on top gently placed the baby, which I had decided to call Littlejohn if he survived, and then I closed the cover. Several hours later he was alive and had become warm. I fed him a small amount of water with a touch of honey and a pinch of powdered skim milk, and then continued these feedings about every twenty minutes, increasing the proportion of milk and amount of feeding as we went along. By bedtime he had improved from the brink of death to a creature that crawled and could hang on to my hand upside down. Littlejohn and his tree hooks were in good order, and I awoke in the morning to a lustily hungry baby squirrel.

He had probably come from a second litter. I hadn't known that sometimes a mother squirrel will produce two litters in a year, but his late-in-the-season arrival caused an interesting problem. I was just starting a new teaching job and didn't have a squirrel sitter. Thus, Littlejohn came with me and, because he was so young, it was easy to stress with the students that he needed calm and quiet. The children enjoyed watching him nurse from the medicine dropper, and first grader Chris wrote afterward: "Edie Sisson brought in her Squirrel; his name was Littlejohn. He drinks warm milk but Squirrel milk is better for him, because it has more nutrients. Like when You are a baby you get nutrients from Your mother's milk." The punctuation, capitalization, and correct spelling are all as they appear on the double-lined sheet of paper, but I especially like how Chris explained an important idea.

By this time we had released Jessica, and Littlejohn came to be my teaching assistant throughout the school year. The children continued to respect his need for calm and quiet, because squirrels by nature are hyperactive, at least by our standards. Together the students and I observed, enjoyed, experimented, and learned much about squirrels.

We noticed, for instance, that his nostrils were relatively large. I had read accounts of how squirrels locate buried acorns under several inches of soil and snow by smell and how they can even detect if the acorn is whole, empty, or worm-infested. The third and fourth graders were eager to experiment, and so they hid cookies in the room. I think I was as surprised as the kids when Littlejohn unerringly found each hidden treat.

We saw how his ears could swivel and cup to face downward or forward, and how he could lay them flat. We had no need to devise hearing experiments. A dropped book, a sneeze, an opening door—almost any different noise caused him to startle and watch, motionless and on guard.

His eyes at the sides of his head gave him a wide field of vision, like those of many animals constantly subject to predation. Even the kindergartners could understand, if I held Littlejohn so that they could look at him from above and see his eyes, that, in turn, Littlejohn could see them. I've heard that squirrels' eyes protrude under stress, which sounds like a good protective adaptation. But we never noticed it happening, although I can't say that Littlejohn was never under any stress at the school. Imagine the commotion in the hall at 8:25 in the morning: children walking with their books, talking with friends, hanging up jackets, taking off snow boots, dropping lunch boxes. Then imagine me with Littlejohn riding on my shoulder walking to my room. But, without warning, Littlejohn hops off and lands in the melee. Do his eyes bulge? Who can see? But, well-versed in squirrel-

Littlejohn seems contented. **(Photo courtesy Polly Fleckenstein)**

ness, a child or two would say calmly but loud enough to be heard, "Oh, Edie, Littlejohn is over here." And I would easily retrieve him.

Once I was unprepared for a kindergarten class but suddenly thought—whiskers. I drew a quick picture of a squirrel without its whiskers, made a copy for each student, and then we looked at Littlejohn's whiskers and added them to the pictures. We started out with the most obvious, the whiskers on his muzzle, which are the most numerous as well as the longest. Then we spotted whiskers under his lower jaw. The kids were using their pencils and making whisker lines on their squirrel drawings. Next, Caleb pointed out, "His eyes—there are whiskers both up on the tops and down on the bottoms." The eye whiskers were added to the drawings, and I thought the pictures were then complete. But Sarah, whose quietness sometimes obscured her ability, softly said, "Look, look there on Littlejohn's front legs, there's a whisker on each one." We all looked and right at the back of each "elbow," a whisker protruded. The children added the elbow whiskers to their drawings while I talked about how squirrels could use all these whiskers in a dark hollow tree to find their way about. The pupils understood, and when they are older and

Littlejohn's tree hooks stick easily on a sweater. **(Photo courtesy Polly Fleckenstein)**

My typewriter fascinates Littlejohn. **(Photo courtesy Polly Fleckenstein)**

learn about mammalian tactile hairs, perhaps they will remember Littlejohn and his whiskers.

In a class with second graders we found acorns outside and fed some to Littlejohn. He ate a few using his chisellike incisors but then "buried" one under a paper towel. This act gave the children an idea. They wanted to copy Littlejohn, and so we found flower pots, dug up earth to fill them, put several acorns in each pot, and were rewarded by little oaks sprouting. We kept the pots inside until spring, when we planted our little trees outside near the playing field. If even one has survived, it is a tribute to a squirrel.

During the winter when Littlejohn came to school, I took many classes out to look for squirrel tracks in the snow. We found plenty between trees at the edge of the playground and also on the playing field; the school's urban location did not limit its potential for squirrel tracks. It took the children a while to figure out which way a squirrel was going, for squirrels hop, setting their hind feet down in front of their front paws. The longer prints are in front of the small prints, indicating the direction of the squirrel's travel.

Rabbit tracks form a similar pattern, and once at home I had set a large piece of paper down in the kitchen, dipped one of our rabbits' feet into food coloring mixed with water, and then let the rabbit go on the paper. Except for a little scattered food coloring, the rabbit tracks showed up well. I thought it would be fun, and educational, to do the same with my class of fifth and sixth graders. We pushed several tables together, brought a long piece of white paper down from a roll in the art room as well as green poster paint, and put the paper down over the tables. But how could we best get the paint on Littlejohn's feet? We found a small tray, laid a few paper towels down in it, poured in green paint, and there we had the perfect stamp pad for squirrel feet. At least, so we thought. Even as I picked him up I could almost feel that Littlejohn took a dim view of the proceedings, and it wasn't easy to get him to put his feet on the green stamp pad. By the time I was sure all his feet had paint on them he was objecting. He scrambled out of my hands, leapt down our carefully laid paper, scattering globs of green on the nearby walls, the floor, the tables, and yes, some on the paper but not in any form that resembled squirrel tracks. It was a total and chaotic failure, and at that moment Paul, the building custodian, walked through the classroom. I can see him still, surveying the ubiquitous green paint and shaking his head. "Oh, don't worry," I plunged in, "we'll pick it all up." Which the kids did, but I had a worse problem to face: a frightened gray squirrel that had turned mostly green. Littlejohn did not like it when I tried to wipe the paint off with paper towels; he liked it less when I used wet paper towels, and, because he still was green, especially on the white of his stomach, I tried to give him a bath, which he took as the ultimate insult. I'm probably lucky he didn't bite, but I did learn that squirrels do not like baths. Any leftover green Littlejohn could clean off himself.

Littlejohn had a beautiful tail, from which we learned a lot about squirrel specialization. The tail is primarily a balancer, especially useful to a tree dweller. It works as a balancing pole does for an aerialist. If he was caught off balance we easily noticed how Littlejohn swung his tail until he felt secure. He also used his tail as a signaler—rapid flicks, we learned, indicated annoyance or anger—but many of his other signals we couldn't decipher. The students could see how Littlejohn used his tail as a blanket, as an umbrella, and even as a parachute. And I'm told that when a squirrel swims it uses its tail as a rudder. What a marvelous implement is a squirrel's tail.

From the very first day when Littlejohn came to school I made it clear to the students that he would stay with me only until he was old enough to be able to take care of himself. As a wild animal he would not enjoy staying in the cage in my kitchen and he might bite if he felt threatened. I explained too that, although I was doing my best as his foster mother, some customs and mores of squirrel society I could not teach him, which might cause him difficulty in relating to his own species in the wild.

After school was over I knew it was time to let Littlejohn go back to the woods. He had been as enjoyable at home as ever Jessica had been. He ran and frolicked seemingly for the sheer joy of it, exploring the house and getting into mischief, and we played Squirrel in the Tree countless times, but he was ready to take care of himself.

The day before I planned to let him go, Tom had helped me take some pictures that showed the bottoms of Littlejohn's feet. But the next day I decided I would try a few more, and thought I wouldn't bother Tom this time. Picture me, holding Littlejohn with one hand, trying to keep his foot in a photogenic pose, holding the camera in the other, and then trying to hold Littlejohn far enough away from the camera that his foot would be in focus. Over and over we tried, but each time Littlejohn squirmed, sometimes immediately, but sometimes just as I was

"May I have a sip of your tea?"

ready to take the picture, and I had to reposition him and try again. On about the twentieth try, Littlejohn bit—hard, with a crunch as his rodent incisors hit the knuckle bone of my right forefinger. "Ouch," I cried. From inside the house, Tom called, "Are you all right?" "No," I said, as I entered the house to douse the bitten knuckle with running water. Actually I was all right, but it hurt, and furthermore I knew what a mistake I had made. I had pushed Littlejohn far beyond the limits of even the tamest squirrel—the bite was completely my fault. And the next fall

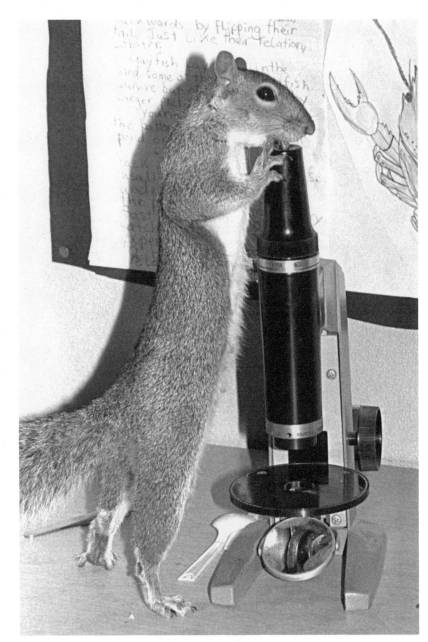

Littlejohn shows scientific curiosity.

Tom holds an infant red squirrel.

back at school I told my students about how Littlejohn had bitten me at
the end, and I believe a point was made.

A postscript here is about two orphaned red squirrels that I raised
a few years later. Ever since my brother and I, as children, vainly tried
to trap red squirrels in a wooden orange crate baited with peanut butter, I have admired these saucy creatures, so I looked forward to having them in the family. They proved disappointing. As they grew their
rapidity seemed to increase exponentially. To say that they were
speedy is an understatement, and the game of Squirrel in the Tree
became a farce. As a tree, I felt I had a pair of whirling dervishes
twirling in a blur around me. I wasn't sorry the day I discovered that
somehow they had managed to escape from the outdoor cage they
were occupying, and I have a feeling that with their dispositions they
had no trouble adjusting to life in the wild.

I have greater pleasure in remembering our beautiful gray squirrels. I think of Jessica and Littlejohn with the same nostalgia that I
have for Bonnie, Gay, Jesse, and Blithe, the raccoons.

Further Thoughts

"Squirrel" comes from the word the ancient Greeks used, skiouros, *formed from the roots,* skia, *shade, and* oura, *tail, meaning shade tail, and squirrels do sit in the shade of their tail. The Ojibwa Indians called the red squirrel* ahjiduhmo, *which means "tail in the air," and presently in many parts of North America the squirrel's multiservice tail features in local names: silver tail, shade tail, banner tail, or bushy tail. Of the eighteen or so inches in a gray squirrel's body length, about eight inches are made up of that wonderful balancer, parachute, blanket, umbrella, parasol, and rudder. Beatrix Potter, in her* Tale of Squirrel Nutkin, *describes squirrels floating on pieces of wood while using their tails as sails. A bit of fantasy, but another conceivable use.*

Squirrels are found on all continents except Australia. In North America, Indians hunted and trapped squirrels for their meat and fur, and, when the colonists came, squirrels were so numerous that bounties were placed on their heads—in 1749 Pennsylvania offered three pence for each squirrel scalp. The dish known as Brunswick stew was originally made with squirrel meat, although chicken has now replaced the squirrel. And yet human settlement destroyed so much of the squirrel's habitat that in the early 1900s conservationists worried about gray squirrels' becoming extinct.

Extinct? Impossible, it seems, for today gray squirrels abound in their range. They are easy to find, and watching them can be a simple and rewarding way to observe wildlife. Make behavior studies of squirrels in a park, in a wooded area, or at your bird feeder, learning how to tell the different ones apart by their appearance and actions. Try to determine which ones dominate the others. How do they communicate? Can you determine signals or expressions from their tails, ears, faces, and sounds that they make? At what time of day are the squirrels most active, and how does this time correlate with weather and seasons?

You may find rewards in recording your squirrel observations in a journal, and perhaps extending the journal to other animals. Less is known about the natural world than most of us realize, and information gathered by lay people often adds to our knowledge. Have you noticed the number of unanswered questions in this book? Perhaps I could find answers to some by consulting the proper person or source, but I will never answer them all, and furthermore new questions keep arising.

If you wish to make a squirrel feeder, almost any bird feeder will do, if located where squirrels can reach it (and often, as people who feed birds know, even if placed where you think squirrels can't reach it). A flat platform with a slightly raised edge serves well, because the squirrels can sit on the platform and eat while you watch. If you wish to make a nesting box for squirrels, it should be about two feet high and twelve inches square. Make a three-inch hole near the top of the front and attach the box to a tree, just over a limb for easiest squirrel access, about twenty-five feet above the ground.

Sometimes peoples' emotions run high about squirrels, and in fact they can be a menace. They can gnaw through television antenna wires, electrical power lines, and telephone lines. If they gain access to your house they can create havoc, as well as the potential for fire should they gnaw through the electrical wiring. Furthermore, many people prefer to feed birds rather than squirrels, and it is not easy to get rid of squirrel freeloaders.

Have you ever seen a black, or even a white, squirrel? I've seen black, or melanistic, squirrels in Toronto, Ontario, and in Princeton, New Jersey. Although their black coats give them a sleek, handsome appearance, they lack the subtle shadings of the grays. In Olney, Illinois, white squirrels live protected by regulations; they have become the city's trademark. The squirrels have the right of way on the streets, every policeman and fireman wears an outline of a white squirrel as a shoulder patch, police and public-works vehicles display the white squirrel emblem, and money is even allotted in the city budget for feeding the squirrels.

Undoubtedly you have encountered some of the close relatives of the gray squirrel: the red squirrel, the chickaree, the tassel-eared squirrel, the fox squirrel, and the flying squirrel. The latter, the only noctur-

nal species, has a membrane that connects front to rear legs. With the membrane spread out it can glide some distance between branches. More distant relatives are the members of the rodent order of animals, such as beavers, porcupines, prairie dogs, muskrats, gophers, rats, mice, lemmings, and voles, as well as the woodchucks.

Often we fail to find beauty in the commonplace. As I admitted, I didn't expect Jessica to captivate us. But she did, as did Littlejohn—their grace and agility, their seeming joy at being alive, these are deep, rich memories. Furthermore, when I see a squirrel scuttle to the side of a tree as I walk by, I am rewarded with an appreciation that is a legacy from Jessica and Littlejohn.

Chapter Nine

The Little Ones

She was called simply "the frog" for about a year and a half. The mundane name, however, belied her amazing adaptations. These we had learned right from the start.

The start was a rainy mid-September evening. We were driving on a back road when suddenly the headlights highlighted small hopping creatures in front of the car. The hoppers became more numerous and we might have felt we were driving through a migration of fleas, except that these animals were a little larger than Ping-Pong balls and their hops averaged a foot and a half into the air. By this time we realized that our tires must be crushing dozens, although we had slowed way down and ultimately stopped out of curiosity. In the glare of the headlights it was easy to grab one of the hoppers. It was a frog that looked slightly like a toad but without lumpy warts. What kind of frog? Our car had killed so many, we reasoned that one fewer in the herd would make no difference, so we brought the frog along to identify it. Little did we know that we had just picked up a four-year guest.

Back at our cabin with kerosene lanterns we examined the frog. It was a little more than an inch and a half long with slightly bumpy, mottled gray skin and a darker crosslike marking on its back. We looked at its feet and discovered discs at the end of each toe, and when it hopped to the side of its pail container and stuck there, we realized that the discs served as suction cups. This clue told us it was a tree frog, but of which species? Finding it in our guide book was easy: our frog was the common tree frog, a member of the hylidae family, known as *Hyla versicolor*. The *versicolor* part of its scientific name became clear the next day; we discovered that the frog could slowly change color from a darker gray on a dark background to a lighter shade on a light background: an amazing creature with its suction cups and color changes.

Amphibians become disoriented if removed from their own area, and in the darkness the night before we had not noticed where we were on the road. That may be partially an excuse, but we took the frog back to our suburban home. I found a leaky old aquarium that we couldn't use for fish, but it was just right for our frog, which didn't need water for swimming. Although tree frogs have slightly webbed hind feet, they spend most of their life on land, in trees, and return to water only to mate in the spring. I put sandy earth at the bottom of the aquarium, a small container of water for drinking, a thick piece of bark going from the bottom at one end and resting halfway up the glass at the other, and a screen over the top. When we put the frog into its new home it treated us to a show of its suction-cup acrobatics on the glass walls. The frog had a spritely air about it. It enchanted us, and from being mere admirers, we became attached to this small being whose talents held us in awe. Finally it settled down on the bark, about two-thirds of the way up, and its effective camouflage explained why common tree frogs are not commonly seen.

As we knew well, frogs eat live insects. Where would you go first if you were responsible for live-insect meals? I thought of my kitchen, where every fall some houseflies buzz around. Yes, some were there, but catching one alive was another matter. Finally I got one by using the old trick of putting a glass over the fly, then slipping a piece of paper between the top of the glass and the countertop. I brought my captive to the aquarium, carefully lifted the screen top, but the fly was quicker than I and flew off. My second try was more successful. I closed the top hastily, and there inside the aquarium was a fly, walking upside down across the top, and a frog that did not appear either to see or care about an upside-down meal. I watched. The fly went into a corner and cleaned its antennae with its front legs. I watched. The fly walked down a side wall. Another suction-cup creature, I thought, when suddenly the fly flew toward the piece of bark, only to be abruptly intercepted by a jumping frog, which landed on a glass wall and, with a blink of its bright eyes, swallowed its first meal with us.

It was a novel experience to be responsible for providing live insect meals, along with meals for a human family of six. But I had helpers, and all the kids enjoyed feeding the frog. It thrived. And I began to see insects in a different way—as food. I had read and taught for years about insects as a vital link in food chains, but now I had become part of such a food chain, though only an intermediary. A fly settled on my arm in a restaurant: a meal for Felicity, I thought, carefully capturing the fly and popping it into a little plastic box with magnifier lens in its top, which I carry with me for teaching, but which I found was useful for frog feeding as well. I hoped no one had noticed, for my new role in a food chain might have been difficult to explain.

Insects were becoming scarcer as the weather became colder. Soon the frog's food supply would run out, and what were we to do then? I consulted my herpetologist friend Dan, and he told me that, in the wild, common tree frogs hibernate, generally in the duff on the forest floor. (Dan also mentioned that tree frogs often move together in vast numbers in the fall, which was the phenomenon we had witnessed when we originally found our frog.) It was not difficult to re-create a forest-floor habitat with leaves, duff, and earth in a small cage, and so when the October cold set in I put the frog into its forest-floor cage and put the cage down in our root-cellar room, where we keep apples, cabbages, beets, carrots, potatoes, and (that winter and three more), a tree frog. Several days later I went down to look at the frog—it had disappeared. Some cautious poking through the leaves and earth, however, revealed a quiescent frog, which I hastily reburied. After that my responsibilities were minimal. The frog in hibernation would neither eat nor drink and its metabolism would slow down to conserve energy until spring. But it did require moisture, and its simulated forest floor in our root cellar could dry out. I needed to sprinkle water into the frog's small cage periodically, but somehow that was a task unrelated to my normal housework, and I might go to fetch a cabbage only to realize three weeks had passed since I had last watered the frog. In guilty haste I would fetch a glass of water and sprinkle some into the cage. In all the four years the frog was with us, remembering to water it in the winter was a task that never became routine.

Next spring when catchable insects appeared, I brought the frog out of hibernation in the root cellar and returned it to its aquarium home. Immediately it resumed its old position two-thirds of the way up on the bark. We found ourselves in the live insect-catching business again, although at first the frog was lethargic and did not jump with alacrity at the exoskeletoned morsels that we provided. Soon, however, it was back to its spritely self.

The easiest frog-feeding times came when we were in the country. For reasons I do not know, our outhouse in early summer always had an ample supply of crane flies, which resemble grossly overgrown mosquitos but do not bite. The frog was well fed, perhaps risking obesity if that is possible for a frog, because every family member was glad to bring back an outhouse crane fly for the frog after every visit. The frog would leap to catch them, then sit blinking as she swallowed, looking as if she relished the crane flies, including their long crunchy legs, which often stuck out of her mouth until the final swallow.

Yes, we had decided the frog was a she. Tree-frog mating season had come and gone, but our frog had not given the trills with which male tree frogs entice females, and so we figured ours was a female. Also, she gained a name, as a result of this next story.

How well I remember Edie running up the stairs, crying out, "Mummy, Mummy, I'm sorry, but I've killed your frog. I gave her a honey bee to see what she would do, and I thought she would know if she shouldn't eat it, and she did try to eat it, and she spat it out because I think it stung her, and I think it killed her, and. . . ." We ran down the stairs together and found the frog on the floor of the aquarium, now a pale putty color. I picked her up, carefully. No, she was not dead, but for three days she remained that color, and for three days she stayed down on the sandy earth instead of sitting in her usual position, two-thirds of the way up on that piece of bark. She was a sick frog, but we knew of nothing we could do to help her; we could only worry. Gradually, however, her color improved and occasionally she resumed her usual spot on the bark. We enticed her to eat by holding an insect in front of her wide mouth and wiggling the insect a little. It worked: she ate. She also learned to eat food that we held in front of her. This maneuver eased the feeding chore because a dead insect is easier to handle than a live one, and if the supply is abundant, you can freeze the surplus, and you have frog-style TV dinners on hand.

The frog soon was back to her normal self—except that something was different about her left eye. The change was subtle: was the eye becoming covered by a membrane? Had the bee sting injured it? Was that eye going blind? What had happened? Delving into books helped us come up with a plausible explanation. When a frog eats it blinks its eyes, which lowers them in their sockets into the mouth cavity, where they help push the food down the frog's throat. We guessed that when our frog tried to eat the honey bee, the bee stung the inner portion of her left eye, which had lowered to give the normal assistance to the frog's swallowing. Our hypothesis was probably correct. After a year that left eye had become opaque. It was blind and the frog could catch live prey only with difficulty because the one blind eye had diminished her ability to judge distances. We generally fed her by hand—easier for her and easier for us.

None of us could help but admire our spunky little frog's recovery from the trauma of the bee sting. She deserved an appropriate name—Felicity—and the name suited her well from then on. We did wonder why she had chosen to eat the bee. Would she have done so in the wild? Our guess was probably not, but that within her aquarium she had become accustomed to leaping after anything that moved.

Felicity, like so many of our creatures, came with me for teaching. That she was an accomplished acrobat, I've already explained, but she could perform engaging tricks on a pencil, astonishing onlookers. Take Felicity out of her carrying jar, put her on a pencil, then turn the pencil and she hangs on with agility, demonstrating the wonders of her suction-cup feet. This was years ago, but still today people from an adult class that Felicity entertained ask about her. That little tree frog made a reputation for herself.

In the summer after Felicity's fourth hibernation with us she began to react more slowly to tempting insect morsels. The change was almost imperceptible, but she seemed less spritely. I wasn't worried, however, and when cold weather came put her in her forest-floor cage in the root-cellar room as usual. In mid-November I remembered to sprinkle water on her, but perhaps a premonition made me open here cage to see how she was doing. Scarcely under the leaves I found her, a lifeless little frog—she had not even started hibernation. We had lost a special, elfish creature, but I like to think that she is still with us, which I mean in a literal sense. I buried her at the base of a small oak we had recently planted in the side yard to replace the old cottonwood that had died. The oak has grown well and I know that Felicity is a part of the tall tree.

Near the oak is the small fish pool, where Butter the goose likes to swim. It's only a few feet deep, and the children used to play in it long before Butter's days. After the kids outgrew it, the neighborhood mosquitos found it a breeding haven. Fish, we thought, would eat the mosquito larvae, and Edie undertook the project and purchased three of the lowest-priced goldfish at the five and ten. She released them into the little pond but within a week when we looked for them we couldn't see them anywhere. That's the way things go, we thought; too bad they didn't survive.

That fall we were in for surprises, and big ones at that. We looked into the pond and saw a flash of golden orange. Then appeared a fish, but not the little one Edie had put in last spring. This fellow was big, at least by comparison—almost three inches long. And shortly we spotted the two others, which were equally large—mosquito larvae certainly had proved a healthy, growth-promoting diet. Given ample room, goldfish can become large, and also they can stay out in winter under the ice of a pond. Our little fish pond, however, was so shallow that it froze solid, and so we brought Edie's three fish inside for the winter, and they graced our kitchen with their golden hues.

Next spring we put them back in the outside pond, and in fall, when we brought them inside for the winter, the fish had another surprise for us. We found not only three huge goldfish—four or five inches long—but a whole lot of little fish. Some of the little ones were black, some were golden-orange, and some were mixed. Our kitchen aquarium reminded me of a slow-moving kaleidoscope that winter. People find beauty and variety in tropical fish, and for several years Polly had a fine aquarium of them in her room, but I found I could be transfixed by watching gossamer golden tails gently swerving, as by watching flickering flames in our Franklin stove. Edie's original three giants were eventually replaced by others of equal size and beauty. Generations came and went, and winter after winter we had our delightful aquarium display.

Currently, however, we are reduced to one large fish, dwelling in Kathy and Rick's living room. They have purchased a small friend for it, and who knows, maybe we'll start all over again.

In the meantime, I used the aquarium one winter to accommodate a snapping turtle. We spotted the snapper plumb in the middle of a cloverleaf ramp, an approach to a superhighway. To drive by was to leave it to be killed, and so Tom stopped the car and, being wiser in the ways of trucks and cars than the turtle, I was able to pick it up unharmed. It was not a large snapper, as snappers go. It was about nine inches long and had the slightly peaked back and spiked tail that I feel give snapping turtles a dinosaurian look. Its upper shell or carapace, and especially the lower one, were relatively small for its body size, because snappers cannot retract as far into their shells as can most other turtles. I suspect their aggressiveness has limited the need for more protective covering. Snappers can and do bite, hence their name, and I realize that they are not on many people's list of good guys. Their reputation is bad: They dine on cute baby waterfowl, which they obtain by the stealthy means of grabbing a small webbed foot from below; they bite swimmers; and an anti–snapping-turtle person could give you a longer list. I've been led to believe, however, that, like other creatures, snappers have their role in an ecosystem. They are a part of the cleanup crew, garbage collectors, so to speak. As scavengers they eat the remains of organisms, a vital though not revered, task, in return for which I can't begrudge them a few young waterfowl.

And as for the swimmers, a snapper is far more afraid of any human being in water than the person may be of it. I once spent several hours mucking about in a small offshoot of a beaver pond, and when I probed the dip net under a rocky shelf, I found the net became unusually heavy. With effort I hoisted to the surface something large. Large indeed: before I had time to grab its tail, a snapper more than a foot long slithered off through the murky water toward the little pond's outlet. Despite my respect for snappers, I was unnerved to think it and I had been so close for so long, and I would have preferred to make sure of its exit by taking it downstream myself, holding it by the tail, which is a safe way to handle a snapper. Do not misunderstand me, a threatened snapping turtle can and will inflict damage in its own defense.

Over the winter I kept the turtle from the highway in the aquarium because, like amphibians, reptiles such as turtles are reputed to become disoriented if placed in a new area. We could not have left the turtle on the highway, which was a part of its habitat, and, because winter was near, we felt it wouldn't have a chance to adjust to a new area before hibernation time.

The quiet, obscure guest spent most of the winter under a corner of a rock in the aquarium; I seldom saw it even though the aquarium was on a shelf beside my desk. Midway through the winter I discovered that my address book was missing. I searched, and searched again, in all possible places, but to no avail. I never thought to look in the aquarium, which doesn't seem much of an oversight. In spring when it was time to release the snapper, I emptied the aquarium and—surprise—there was the address book, soaked. Somehow it must have fallen in. My Aunt Eleanor had given it to me when I was a college junior, and so it had sentimental as well as practical value. I opened its looseleaf binder and carefully took the pages apart to dry them. Today my address book is in its accustomed place in my desk drawer; some of the addresses are blurred but legible, and, if I stop to think about it, they have an interesting memory for me to recall.

What happened to the turtle? Before releasing it I took it to school for the students to see. I put it in a clear plastic container that gave the children good views of the turtle from the top, sides, and underneath, but prevented them from touching it. I'm generally a "hands-on" teacher—why not let the kids touch the turtle? Turtles (though rarely) can carry a salmonella bacterium that, though not fatal to people, can cause illness requiring hospitalization. If you do handle a turtle, wash your hands afterward, as a precaution. Many classes enjoyed the snapper and learned a lot about its specializations, and I was relieved not to worry about adequate handwashing and salmonellosis. That afternoon I let the winter companion of my address book swim away in a small local pond, where I hope it found its niche and did its work as part of the cleanup crew.

Another encounter with snapping turtles started with the eggs. A nonlover of snapping turtles dug them out of a nest on her property and gave them to me. Might as well give them a try, I thought, and buried them in sandy soil beside our garage. At first I thought about them every now and then, but when time for hatching passed, I forgot them. But I came to surprised remembrance when I found a tiny snapper walking on the grass in our back yard that September. And a day later I discovered one more. They were cute little creatures, miniatures of the large adults, only a little more than an inch long. After consulting with Dan, the herpetologist, I decided to put them down in the root cellar for hibernation. Dan told me that they would have enough energy left from the yolk-sac food to sustain them through a winter's hibernation. I looked forward to enjoying more of the little turtles in the spring, but something went wrong and both little snappers died within a few weeks.

Felicity the frog's aquarium held two land snails for many years, and, like the snapper, the aquarium was on the shelf beside my desk. I hadn't realized that even snails could be captivating, but I became fond of these two, even though I couldn't tell one from the other. They would move about in the aquarium, slowly, of course, using their antennae to sense where they were and where to find the piece of lettuce that I had put in for them. Their needs were so slight that I confess to occasionally forgetting their care. When memory caught up, inevitably I would look into the aquarium to see two dead-appearing snails. Pick one up and its horny "door," or operculum, would be well closed and back nearly a quarter of an inch into its shell. After this happened a few times, I concluded this was the snail's protective mechanism for conserving moisture as well as energy.

Sprinkle in moisture and add a few succulent snail victuals, and slowly, extremely slowly, the snails would come out as if I'd never forgotten about them. Just as I was beginning to wonder how close to immortal snails could be (they had been beside my desk for some years), one died, and the other died in the following year. Probably, as snails go, they had both lived to ripe old ages.

We've had many small animals in aquariums and similar containers over the years: crickets, crayfish, and creatures of the pond, as well as mealworms, sow bugs, and also bats and snakes. The snakes were small ones—green snakes and garter snakes—and generally we released them after a time, the green snakes especially, because they are hard to keep in captivity. Snakes are creatures of wonder, if you think about how all their insides fit into such a long, thin shape, and how by unhinging their lower jaw and other remarkable adaptations they can swallow prey larger than their circumference. If you have grown up with a dislike for snakes my few words of praise may cause you to shiver—such primal prejudices are difficult to dispel. I should know: it took me a while to feel comfortable with spiders, and even now I find them a bit leggy. Our baby garter snake, Slip, however, could appease snake prejudices like no other snake I've known—it was hard for any one to truly dislike his eight-inch-long little self. Whereas zoologists give reptiles credit for having "invented" the hard eggshell, garter snakes and a few others bear their young alive, and we must have found Slip soon after his birth. He enchanted many students before his release.

Another animal that gets about as bad a press as the snake is the bat. Students found the two bats, which we have had, hanging low on the school wall within easy reach of kindergartners, one in early spring one year, and the other in the following year. Because bats can bite, my response to the excited bat finders each time was to go out with them and put the bat in a container before small exploratory fingers could be harmed. We brought the bats inside, and I don't know if the children or I got more out of watching these special creatures close up; they are, after all, the only mammals that can truly fly. We saw how their leathery wings spanned the space between their fingers and ankles, and even stretched to the tail, and how they hung upside down by their thumbs, but also used a number of other small hookers, which probably helped them cling to cave ceilings or attic beams. Their eyes were small but their ears large—useful for the bat's remarkable specialization, its system of echolocation, or, as the students called it, sonar, which enables bats to catch flying insects in the dark. Both of our bats had probably come out of hibernation too early, and although I received ample instructions on bat care and feeding from my friend Chuck, who also shared with me his enthusiasm for these unique animals, neither bat survived—I suspect their metabolism hadn't properly readjusted after hibernation. They would never have flown into your hair, nor have bitten you (unless threatened), nor have performed any of the other sinister deeds that folklore attaches to bats. I've heard that they spend more time cleaning themselves than we do, and carry fewer parasites than do dogs or cats. In China, bats are considered a symbol of happiness. I admire them.

My students have always enjoyed tadpoles, which gives me an excuse to bring some to school in spring, for I like them too. But I've found it hard to raise them through to the adult stage, even though I'm careful to take only a few frog eggs to ensure that they all receive enough oxygen, and to limit the number of tadpoles for the same reason. The safest procedure I've found is to replace them in the pond they came from after they have grown a leg or two. When my own children were young we once kept a bullfrog tadpole, which takes two years to mature, in the refrigerator over the winter, to simulate its natural winter conditions. We would sometimes forget to warn a visitor who went for something in the fridge about what was inside, and that person inevitably was taken aback to find a tadpole contentedly sitting in a container of water amid the cranberry sauce and mayonnaise.

In summers by the ocean we often had bowls on the kitchen table as temporary aquariums for salt-water creatures, but their visits were brief because we couldn't provide the oxygenated cold water these creatures needed. We watched sea anemones send out their tentacles like blooming flowers, brittle stars moving with their five rickety long legs, and barnacles swooshing planktonic food in with their feathery-looking feet. But the most notorious personality, anyone in my family would tell you, was Miss Squish, our first sea cucumber.

She bore a repulsiveness that defies description. Her color was a dirty off-pink tan. Her shape? She didn't have any—she could appear nearly as round as a ball or she could lengthen out, and worse still, she could grotesquely undulate almost any portion of her body. She also had a tiny ringlet of tentacles at one end, which presumably was the front. All that we found unattractive, however, you might not, although it is hard to imagine Miss Squish winning anyone's beauty contest. In fairness I admit that Miss Squish belongs to a group of animals I've always admired, the spiny-skinned animals, or echinoderms. In this group are starfish, brittle stars, sea urchins, sand dollars, and sea cucumbers. Also, these creatures are our closest relatives among the invertebrates. Since Miss Squish we've had other sea cucumbers of different species, far more solid appearing, in fact looking greatly like the vegetable for which they are named. And to give final credit to Miss Squish I recognize that sea cucumbers are relished as delicacies in France and Japan. That taste stretches my imagination, but perhaps *bêche de mer* is made from a different species than our infamous Miss Squish.

Honey bees are another kind of small animal that we have—Tom has been a beekeeper since 1936. We eat honey, cook with honey, and sell honey and honey products. As an onlooker I've learned a lot about bees—their social life is extraordinary—and I find that many people are curious about them. Mention honey bees in a group of neighbors, in a class, or at a dinner party, and a string of questions will pour forth.

At times, generally when Tom wasn't home, I've had direct experiences with the bees. I've caught swarms, which is fun to do, and generally the bees are so preoccupied with swarming that they seldom sting. You can even pick them up by handfuls, as I did once when they had gathered on a bush that was nearly on the ground. Once Tom had ordered a package of bees through the mail, and I took the telephone call from our post office, which went something like this: "We have a package for you—it's bees." Followed by, "Perhaps you might like to come down and pick them up—soon." Next, "Or, maybe if it's convenient, right away." I pictured people in the post office worrying about what would happen if the contents of the box escaped, and obligingly said "fine," even though it wasn't. Then came the last comment on the phone, "And don't bother to come through the front door. You can just drive up to the back and pick up your package there." I've never been admitted to the hallowed back of a post office before or since, but that day they wanted those bees out of there—quickly.

Tom now does all his own extracting of honey, but years ago he used to take the honey, in its wax combs in the frames that beekeepers use, across town to another beekeeper, who extracted the honey for him. One September day he had many frames of honey in the back of the car, ready for extracting, and, as he left for work in the morning, he warned me, several times over, to leave the windows of the car tightly shut when it was at the house, because in the fall bees are desperate to get every last bit of honey that they can for their winter food supply. "Leave a window open, even a crack," he cautioned, "and you'll have the bees coming in after the honey."

This caution I understood because I knew how a bee could communicate the exact location of a new food source to other worker bees in her hive. She transmits this message by a dance, as Karl von Frisch discovered (he won a Nobel prize for his work). Von Frisch found that a worker bee that has found a new source of nectar, upon her return to the hive, dances—her pattern of movement, body position, abdomen waggles, and the speed of the dance are all signals, and the workers near the dancer can fly directly to the new source of nectar. "Of course I'll remember about the car windows," I reassured Tom as he left.

Polly, then four, and I went to the supermarket later that morning. It was hot, especially in the car, and so in the supermarket parking lot I opened all the car windows. Errands completed, we returned home to find that a friend had just arrived. Together we went inside for a visit, during which I started an old hen cooking in the pressure cooker, but after a short time (no more than twenty minutes) when my friend had to leave, I went out with her to say goodby, and to my awful astonishment found the driveway amass with a cloud of flying bees. The car windows! I had forgotten to close them, and bees were everywhere. I looked in the car and the bees were thicker there than in the driveway. Something had to be done and right away. I went upstairs, put on a pair of trousers, not taking time to remove my skirt. Put on a long sleeved shirt, but it seemed loose at the cuffs, and so I put on another over it. Put on socks and pulled them up over the bottoms of the trouser legs. Then shoes. What else? A bee veil—where had Tom put it? In the garage? I found it hanging off the end of a ladder, put on the old felt hat with the veil around it, and tied the bottom of the veil down around my chest so that it would protect my face from bee stings. Polly? I had no bee veil for her, and so I could only say, "Stay in the kitchen, and don't come outside." But the end of the statement was unnecessary, because so many bees were outside it was not at all enticing.

Wearing all my layers of protective clothing I opened the car door and carefully sat on the seat, hoping not to sit on any bees. There were bees on the steering wheel, but I held the wheel where the bees were not, started the car, moved down the driveway and out onto our road, spewing bees out the windows right and left as I went. I thought the local supermarket parking lot might be a good place, but upon arrival I had second thoughts. I didn't think a car exuding honey bees was a welcome addition, and I left. Where to go? I felt as if I were carrying the plague. Then I thought of the field behind our house and sought refuge there. Moving slowly, I began to take the frames of honey out of the car, one by one, carefully shaking the bees off each as I had seen Tom do many times. It worked, and I wasn't stung. When I finished the last frame, I went back to Polly. And you can believe I had every car window securely shut. Still a cloud of bees swarmed to the car the moment I entered the driveway, and I realized I shouldn't leave the car there long. Inside, Polly was fine, and the pressure cooker with the chicken hadn't boiled out of water. I looked out the window and saw a mailman I hadn't met before walking across the side lawn with a package. I went out to greet him, then suddenly remembered my appearance: old felt hat, veil over my face, two shirts, skirt with trousers underneath, socks pulled up over trouser legs—an apparition. Lamely I tried to explain—trouble with my bees. The mailman handed me the package quickly, and to my knowledge he never delivered anything to our house again.

Next I drove with Polly over to Uncle Horace and Aunt Marie's

I have seen Tom shake off the bees many times.

house, a few miles away. They were startled by my appearance, but at least they understood my explanation, and besides, by that time I could remove a few of the layers. I called Tom, confessed about the windows, and asked if my aunt and uncle's house was far enough away, or if the bees might still find the car. He assured me that the car would be fine there, and my uncle gave Polly and me a ride home. Aside from a number of bees still hovering about the driveway, it was life as usual. I do sometimes wonder what that mailman really thought.

Further Thoughts

Are all the little ones mentioned in this chapter animals? Yes. But what is an animal? Many people equate animals with mammals, and become unsure if birds are animals or if they are just birds, to say nothing of invertebrates such as honey bees, which could be insects, or animals, or both. Furthermore, zoologists' studies sometimes result in changed classifications. In the nineteenth century, sponges were classified as plants, but for a long time now we have considered them animals. When I studied biology amoebas were animals, but now they are in a different category, known as protists. Generally speaking, an animal is an organism that, unlike a plant, does not make its own food, and usually, though not always, is capable of moving, a definition that embraces all the creatures in this chapter, even though the land snails moved very slowly and Miss Squish seemed to belong to no one's classification of anything.

We share the earth with animals, and no matter how far modern industrial society strays from intimacy with other animal species, our lives are inexorably connected. Albert Schweitzer wrote in The Philosophy of Civilization *(Macmillan, 1949), "Man can no longer live for himself alone. We must realize that all life is valuable and that we are united to all life. From this knowledge comes our spiritual relationship with the universe."*

In the Stone Age, people lived closely with the animals around them, and their interest in them is shown by their paintings of animals on their cave walls. Much later, people's domestication of various species demonstrated how animals can be useful to us, while further-ing our understanding of these animals' behavior. Aristotle, in the fourth century B.C., wrote about various species and their habits, and he was the first to describe the inherited animal behavior drive that we call instinct. Consider the force of honey bee instinct on that day when I left the car windows open—one bee's instinctive dance resulted in the droves that came for the honey and the monstrous problem they caused me. Charles Darwin, in the nineteenth century, studied instinctive behavior and conducted other observations of animal species that led to his belief in survival of the fittest and his theory of evolution.

In about the same period John James Audubon was extending the study of birds with his observations and paintings, and other natural-ists were recording their observations and deductions. Among the fas-cinating literature by naturalists of the nineteenth century and the early twentieth, I recommend works by Henry David Thoreau, John Muir, John Burroughs, and Aldo Leopold. I also suggest Gilbert White, who wrote in the eighteenth century. Because everything in nature is connected, all these naturalists include information on animals and their behavior.

In the mid-1930s Konrad Lorenz and other scientists developed the study of animal behavior, known as ethology. They based their research primarily on observations of different species in the wild, and they brought new insights into the genetic codes that transmit abilities from one generation to another and discovered that a few primates learn and teach crude forms of language. Lorenz's writings on the imprinting of geese helped me to understand Butter. More recently, sociobiologists have theorized that instinct causes altruism among ani-mals in order to ensure survival for their genes. A worker honey bee, for instance, may sting you in trying to protect her hive, which con-tains her genetic material, even though the stinging pulls out part of

her innards, causing her death. Sociobiologists also suggest that geneti-
cally derived instinct governs some behavior in human societies.

Beyond instinctive behavior, animals develop learned behavior;
certainly most of our domestic animals are trainable in many ways;
and scientists now talk about the "cognitive life of animals." Think
how Felicity the tree frog learned to consume dead insects offered to
her by hand, although instinctively frogs eat only live insects (or ones
that are artificially animated, but we had never bothered to try to
make our dead offerings seem alive). Even "simple" animals show
seemingly intelligent behavior. James Gould, a Princeton University
scientist, recently discovered that when he moved a supply of sugar
water regular distances away from a beehive each day, after several
days the bees began to anticipate the move. With their elemental
brains, how did they do it? Professor Gould says he doesn't know.

My friend in the country, Josephine, has a basic description for the
cognitive life of animals: "Well, I'll tell you, working with animals, that
some has got more smarts than people does." Among the recent books
about modern theories on animals' "smarts," I recommend those by
Edward O. Wilson or Donald R. Griffin. If you are interested in learn-
ing more about the creatures mentioned in this chapter, I suggest gen-
eral field guides, books that may be available on the animals in your
area, writings on honey bees by von Frisch, and also the Stokes' Nature
Guides *(Little, Brown), which offer a unique combination of field*
guide and behavior information.

Chapter Ten

Black and White

I put down the telephone, peered around the door, and saw him still picking up glass pieces from the broken jar and the spilled rice on the floor and under the freezer: "Tom, dear, a lady on the phone wants to know if we'd like a baby skunk." Tom's response, considering the conditions, was restrained but negative. I returned to the phone and responded, "I think we can. I have just one point I need to clear up, and I'll call you in the morning."

For Tom's sake I admit that we had just taken on ten so-called mallard ducklings and their parents. My telephone, serving all normal functions, also brings news of surprises such as orphaned squirrels and injured starlings, and the ducks' arrival was another that came courtesy of the telephone company. Their owners didn't want to keep the mallards any longer, and I felt it wouldn't be difficult to finish raising them and to release them all together next fall. Over the phone I gave the owners directions to my house; they arrived shortly, deposited two large cartons, and left.

I opened a carton and was baffled. The "ducklings" appeared nearly full-grown. And, whatever they were, they were not mallards. I put all twelve into the chicken house, whereupon a broody hen took one look, and whoosh, ran to the safety of the chicken yard. Parent ducks and youngsters commenced loud, alarmed-sounding quackings, and outside hens clucked, roosters crowed, and to complete the cacophony, the guinea fowl added their loudest danger cries. When the racket subsided slightly, a guinea fowl approached the door, cocked its helmeted head, retreated at sight of the intruders, but returned, reinforced by a few roosters. I left them all to become acquainted and went to the books to see what kind of ducks had been dumped on me. My conclusion? Khaki Campbells, a domestic duck, which obviously canceled the release plan, and they are an egg-laying breed at that. More eggs of any kind we did not need, and egg layers would have little meat for eating. (It turned out I was wrong about the latter point. Though small, they were gourmet treats.) To top off the mallard mixup, my preoccupation with the ducks had caused me to forget my chicken soup on the stove. The soup burned, badly.

Burned soup, a dozen useless ducks, along with the smashed bottle of rice, were the backdrop for the skunk telephone call. By the following morning, however, the caller's inappropriate timing was forgotten and Tom assented. Tom later became one of the skunk's most ardent admirers. In fact he finally solved the name impasse. My Clover, Stripey, and, in desperation, Linnaeus (for the scientist who founded the system of scientific nomenclature) had all failed to suit, but Tom knew what he was about when he suggested Lorenzo. Skunks do have a magnificence about them, as did the Medici bearer of the name, Lorenzo the Magnificent.

When I went to pick up the black-and-white baby its benefactor, Mrs. Fitzgerald, a self-described animal lover, told me how her grandson had found the skunk by Route 126 near its run-over mother. Mrs. Fitzgerald had done well by the orphan: it was in a carton with water, cat food, and blueberries, as well as soft towels to provide a cozy denlike atmosphere. The baby appeared alert, healthy, and miniature.

Back home I put him in an enclosure with a box for a den lined with old flannel pajama bottoms, a potty (like the one used for the raccoons, an old pan with earth), and a dish with raisins and Mrs. Fitzgerald's leftover cat food. I mixed a formula of skim milk with egg yolk and served it in a doll's baby bottle. The little skunk showed no inclination to nurse, but when I put the formula into a dish he lapped it up eagerly. Then he dug around in his potty using his nose for a shovel, much as a pig does.

His nose was the color of black-raspberry ice cream, and he was constantly sniffing with it. Like all skunks' heads, his seemed small in proportion to his body. His eyes were small and his ears tiny; they scarcely showed. A thin white strip ran from his nose to his forehead, and on his back was the white V-shaped marking that distinguishes the striped skunk. He was white on the nape of his neck, though I noticed a tiny fleck of about four black hairs, and over his shoulders the white divided into two thin stripes that continued to the base of his tail. At the end of that black tail were white hairs. One night I happened to look through his tail with the light from behind. If you share my opinion that the tail of a rat or an opossum is, well, ugly—that is what I saw inside the hairs of the little skunk's tail. How superficial attractiveness is—a basic tail with a layer of hairs or fur added becomes esthetically pleasing. For such a little fellow (upon arrival he weighed only eleven ounces) he had long front claws, which I knew were for digging grubs and other ground creatures later on, but I did not then appreciate their tunneling potential. His back feet were plantigrade like those of the raccoons; sole and heel both touch the ground in walking. As a whole he was a bundle of black and white fluff, and adorable—we had already succumbed to our usual prejudiced-parent syndrome.

And yet we worried about raising a non–de-scented skunk. Tom had asked, "Why not de-scent him?" My response, "Do you want a pet skunk for thirteen years or so?" caused him to understand that de-

The bundle of black-and-white fluff sits on Tom's lap for the first time.

scenting was out of the question because we couldn't release a skunk that had lost its protection. Tom felt our raising the skunk was a culmination because his weapon was a challenge and it called forth all our knowledge and understanding of animals; furthermore, I had not been able to find in our library any helpful information about raising skunks. Tom compared our need to adjust to skunk nature to cousin Ellen's work with her sheep dogs—working with the dogs, she stresses, depends upon understanding both the instinct and nature of the dog.

Our respect for this foster child caused us to observe his behavior closely. I was amazed I could work all day at one end of a table while he stayed at the other end, sleeping, sniffing, eating. A squirrel or a raccoon would have created constant interruptions. After another day the most mischief the little skunk did was knock over a small vase of wildflowers because he was sniffing a daisy at the top. If a paper blew on the table, up went his tail—such flagging is a skunk's first warning signal. And yet he was as amiable a companion as one could wish for. Friendly, he loved a snuggle; independent, nonetheless. If he'd been a person, I'd have enjoyed knowing him—something I could never say about anyone with the frenetic disposition of a gray squirrel. And despite his small size he bore an air of magnificence, well deserving the name Lorenzo.

Except that shortly we decided he was female. What should we do about her well-suited name? Change the O to an A, we decided, and she became Lorenza.

She ate a variety of foods. Like raccoons, skunks are classified as carnivores, but they are omnivorous, and Lorenza ate dog and cat food, pieces of meat, cheese, peanuts, raisins, and green beans, to name a few. She had a passion for bananas, and we used to joke about all the banana trees she would find in the woods when we released her. Sometimes she was fickle about food. Yesterday a dog biscuit would be refused—today, devoured. She used the potty in her cage and always wiped her bottom on the sandy soil after defecating. She also groomed her fur. Skunks are clean animals.

Lorenza used her nose much as a blind person uses a cane; skunks depend greatly on their sense of smell because they are nearsighted and have generally poor vision. Sniff, sniff, sniff, you could hear if you were near, and see from the way she moved her nose. As our friend Josephine said when she met Lorenza, "She's sniffing away at sixty miles an hour." One evening I noticed that the sixty-mile-an-hour sniff located mosquitoes outside the window screen. I went out, caught a few, put them on the table, and Lorenza came sniffing over and scooped them up like a vacuum cleaner. Thus I found myself in the food-chain business again, as I had been with Felicity the tree frog. Later that evening I walked down the hill to the beaver pond and put each mosquito I swatted into a sandwich bag. It gave me a new perspective on mosquito bites, especially if I thought about my own role as nourishment if I let the mosquito bite for awhile, and I came back with a small heap of tiny delicacies for Lorenza.

Lorenza's next natural foods came from a rotting log. From the moment I put it down she began instinctively to rip it apart with her long front claws to find tasty grubs, while her nose was working overtime sniffing. How about earthworms? I wondered. They are easy to find in the compost pile. I dug a mess of them and put them in a bowl, but the sniff-sniffer ignored them. What's wrong? I mixed the poor creatures in with dog food. Lorenza ate, without enthusiasm, and, like a picky child, avoided many of the worms. I concluded that skunks don't like earthworms and haven't tried them again.

More successful was outdoor foraging. My young friend and country neighbor, Angela, was visiting, and we put one of the old raccoon harnesses on Lorenza and took her out to find her own food. With only a little help from us, she found a grasshopper. Her sniffing became monumentally loud, and then crunch, crunch, crunch—down went those crispy hind legs and thorax, succulent abdomen, and fibrous antennae. We also discovered that Lorenza ate junk food. Angela gave her one of the creme-filled cookies she had brought for a luncheon dessert, and Lorenza gobbled it with as many crunching noises as she devoted to a big grasshopper.

After Lorenza had been with us a while, I began to wonder why she didn't play as other young mammals do. I remembered how Bonnie and Gay the raccoons tumbled over each other, biting, pulling, pawing, and pouncing. Lorenza seemed downright serious, and when

I moved her into a larger carton, along with her den box, potty, food, and water, almost immediately she flagged her tail, stamped her little front feet, and had the audacity to turn her rear right around in my direction so that her body was in a U shape with her head and back end both facing me. These are the three warning signals a skunk gives before it sprays. Goodness, I felt, Lorenza's certainly become territorial about her new abode in a hurry. Relations between us for the rest of the week were strained and subdued.

Later in the living room, however, Lorenza went through the flag, stamp, and turn routine again, then again, until finally I caught on. She wanted to play, that was all, and that was what she was trying to tell me when I moved her into the large carton. After that we had grand games of mock spray. On all fours, I would stamp on the floor with my hands and turn my rear as much as possible toward her. Then she would advance and show me really how to do it—and get in the practice that she needed for her future. I felt honored to be admitted into such skunkhood play, and also I felt assured that she would be able to defend herself in the wild.

But she never sprayed once while she was with us, and we couldn't even see the two scent glands at the sides of her anus. I can tell you only what I've been told or read about skunks when they spray, which is that the scent glands protrude only when spraying and skunks are accurate with their spray, up to about fifteen feet. The victim is subjected to a nauseating smell, and, if the spray hits the eyes, it causes strong stinging and even temporary blindness. Because skunks have only enough liquid for five or six shots at one time (although afterward their body replenishes the supply), they exercise restraint in spraying. They also hold their tail up and out of the way of spray, apparently because they don't like the smell either.

Most animals learn to avoid the skunk's powerful weapon, which is advertised by the black-and-white coat, the white showing up clearly in darkness. With such a reputation, skunks don't worry much about predators, which can be a fatal mistake. When you smell skunk and then see one dead on the road, you can guess at the cause. Skunks, like Lorenza's mother, assume an automobile is going to turn and go away as do other animals, and so they are frequent highway victims. Great horned owls, however, are skunk predators. Perhaps their sense of smell is poor, as it is with most other birds. I've been told that often their nests smell awful. Also, I've read that coyotes, bobcats, foxes, and even eagles will risk the stench for a meal of skunk. Were I one of those creatures, I think I would have to be extremely hungry.

Not only did Lorenza play many mock-spray games with me, she also played as raccoons do, but in much milder form. Trundle your fingers out before her and she pounced, tussled, and bit. Sit with bare feet on the floor and along came sniffs, a cold nose, and then marauding long claws and teeth sharp as needles. I would tuck my feet up; Tom put on his shoes. Tie a crumpled piece of paper at the end of a string, dangle it in front of her, and she would chase it, just like a kitten.

But she could also bite—fiercely. Angela and I had her out for another grasshopper- and cricket-eating foray in the meadow. I heard a car door slam, which meant that Tom had arrived, and on my way to greet him I scooped Lorenza up and turned her to give tummy tickle, which she always enjoyed. But I must have been too abrupt, because without warning Lorenza bit the knuckle of my right forefinger, hard, and I thought I heard a crunch, the same as with Littlejohn's parting bite. My knuckle hurt, but it was my own fault. Many months later we were having a picture-taking session with Lorenza and Tegan, our granddaughter, and I held Lorenza against her will one time too many. She bit the end of my finger hard and painfully, and again it was my fault.

By that time my niece Dorrie, who is a veterinarian, had told me that skunks can carry rabies even though they don't show any of its symptoms. I was worried until I figured that, because I had already once been bitten by Lorenza, who had no opportunity in the meantime to come in contact with a rabid animal, I would be all right. Rabies, however, is spreading rapidly in many wild-animal populations and is becoming a severe danger, especially with skunks.

During the summer as Lorenza grew larger her small ears began to stick up and she appeared to have more white in proportion to the black. In the dark her pure white was especially noticeable. She still

I admire amiable Lorenza. **(Photo courtesy Biz Paynter)**

had the little black dot, bigger of course, amid the white over her shoulders. She gathered nesting material in her den box—rocks, newspaper—anything she could find she would drag in. If I held a chicken bone in front of her den, out she would come, sniffing with seeming indifference to the bone, but then she would gently take it in her mouth and back into the den. It was an ethereal appearance and disappearance, reminding me of a slow-motion jack-in-the-box. And the gentleness with which she took food from our hands contrasted markedly with any of the other animals we had raised. This little skunk, despite her intimidating weapon, continually surprised us with the marvels of her ways.

Toward summer's end we took her with us on a visit to Jinny's. Lorenza traveled in a small box, and so Jinny kindly let her occupy her kitchen, blockaded with packing boxes at the entrance, and proffered her walnuts, which she found delectable. Kathy, the researcher of the "little-darling" Siberian hamsters, came especially to meet Lorenza, and, considering the competition, we were pleased by how much Kathy enjoyed and admired our black-and-white darling.

When we returned home Tom suggested we let Lorenza have the freedom of our kitchen. I closed all the doors and put a sign out back, "Enter slowly or knock loudly. Skunk loose in kitchen." At first she went exploring and sniffing, especially under things like the toe spaces under bottom cabinets, and came out with distinctly dusty whiskers. I set up her den box, potty, and food and water dishes in a corner and left her. After half an hour I looked in on her; still roaming about. After two hours I checked again, and she was not there, but searching revealed her at the back of her den box, which somehow she had pushed behind the potty. I was learning that skunks are strong pushers and pullers.

Shortly Tom and I went for a visit with Aunt Marie, and came back to no skunk in the kitchen. She wasn't in her den box. I noticed that the bottom of the dishwasher was askew, but no space seemed large enough for a skunk to pass through. The bottom piece of the refrigerator, however, was off at one end and hanging at an angle. I looked under in the darkness but couldn't find her. "Lorenza, Lorenza, come," I kept repeating, while my imagination conjured up electricity or some other malevolent refrigerator mechanism killing her. Tom fetched a flashlight, gave a thorough search under the refrigerator, and declared, "She's not there." As one, we turned toward the dishwasher, looked underneath, and under pipes, a valve handle, and other plumbing and electrical parts, there was Lorenza, denned up way in the back. I lay down on the floor and in trepidation reached my hands under the dishwasher toward Lorenza, remembering how Gay had growled at me when I had removed her from a kitchen cabinet, and wondering how a skunk would react to being summarily removed for a brand-new den. Bite? Spray? I spoke reassuringly to her so that, despite her nearsightedness, she would know whose hands were approaching. Then I picked her up slowly, and, amiable animal that she was, her only reaction was to enjoy a cuddle in my lap. I took the skunk warning sign off the back door, and that was the end of Lorenza's stay in the kitchen. Several times later we had her come in for a visit but it was always cut short because, not only did she remember her dishwasher den, but also, no matter what we put in front of the dishwasher, it did not deter her from reentry.

After the kitchen failure I tried having Lorenza in my den. She didn't go under the radiator and all was well until I looked in after supper and found she had moved a third of the books from the bottom shelf of the bookcase to the floor. She looked as if she couldn't decide which one to read. Next we kept her in an old mesh playpen until she clawed too many holes in the mesh, then we reluctantly put her into our big metal cage that was smaller than the pen. Just two nights of hearing her rattle about in that cage and we decided that she had to have space—we would risk putting her in the aviary. We knew she could dig her way out under the wire, but that would have to be left up to her.

While we worried, Lorenza enjoyed the space in the aviary. She made her den in the shelter at the far end, until one day I found dug-up earth and no Lorenza. Then my foot slipped into a soft spot. I looked down, and out came an earth-covered skunk. While I breathed a sigh of relief she shook off all the dirt, looking as clean as ever and ready for a game of mock spray. How could I resist that little black-and-white creature, with tail up and little feet going stamp,

stamp? We played, but when I left, she nosed around trying to follow, and I asked myself if we were really rehabilitating her.

That night over a soybean casserole Tom and I discussed our puzzle in releasing her. We couldn't take her to the country and abandon her because she was not yet nocturnal and her hunting skills were questionable. If only we could stay with her there for a time, we could supplement her food until she learned to be on her own. That would be the best solution. How about adjusting her to life in the aviary and then releasing her from it? But neither of us could bear the thought of finding a dead skunk on the road, and Lorenza would always be recognizable because of that little black dot in the white over her shoulders. And what if she sprayed a neighbor? Our decision was to wait until she became nocturnal, which meant I had to resist temptation to visit her during the day, give her plenty of food so that she would gain some of the weight she would need to survive the winter, and then later take her to the country when we could stay for at least a few days to help her.

Lorenza foiled the plan by taking things into her own paws. I had been planning to bring her to school for a visit, but was waiting until I knew my classes well enough to be certain they would be respectful when she came. John, the head of the school, was understandably skeptical about having a non–de-scented skunk visit. Finally on the first day of fall I decided everything would be all right, put her carrying box in the car, and went to get her from the aviary. Surprise. I saw a tremendous pile of sandy earth under the shelter, a tunnel, and no skunk. I called in vain. And I had to go so as not to be late for my classes. On the drive to school I worried. Might the tunnel through our sandy soil have collapsed on Lorenza? Should I have dug down with a shovel? When I returned from school, still no sign of her. I thought I saw something white in the tunnel and wriggled down to touch it, but it was only a stone. Perhaps her tunnel had another end, and so I went outside to look around, but when I happened to glance back at the aviary, there was Lorenza, ambling nonchalantly about as if she hadn't done anything extraordinary by excavating. She was giving us a good education in the ways of skunks. We didn't know they dig a long tunnel on the first day of fall to be certain to have their winter den all ready. Tom thought her front claws looked worn down by the digging—anyway, we knew she had settled the question of where she would spend the winter. She did come to school with me a few days later. The children behaved admirably, and so too did Lorenza, which was asking a lot of an animal that on her own was beginning to make the transition from a peopled world to a tunneled and more natural skunk world.

Several nights later I heard her make a noise for the first time. I gave her some chicken bones, reached over to pat her, and thought I heard something like a hiss or a sigh with a touch of growl. Was it my imagination? I tried another pat and heard the same strange but angry sound. She didn't bite or spray, but the meaning of her hiss-growls was clear. I wondered that such a peaceable animal's first comments were so defensive.

In October I put hay near the entrance to her tunnel. The next time I went out the hay was gone, except for a few whisks at the tunnel's entrance. Because I thought she might be hungry I called to her, but heard no rustling under the hay. As I was leaving, however, she materialized as if out of nowhere—a skunkish trick. Even if she was hungry she was gladder to see me than supper, and allowed me to pick her up and to go in to visit Tom. Back outside I put her down, she sniffed at dinner, carefully chose a chicken neck, and galloped off with it toward her hole.

After early November we did not see her at all. We left food about every other night and it disappeared. It had been hard enough to remember to feed a nocturnal animal; leaving food for a tunnel was worse. I felt silly, taking Thanksgiving dinner leftovers—bits of turkey, cranberry sauce, and rice with a few walnuts and pecans as treats—out to a hole, even talking to it: "Lorenza, here's your Thanksgiving dinner. Come on out and eat it." On Christmas she had the neck of our Christmas goose. But still, it was hard to remember to feed a hole.

In mid-January I went by the aviary and saw a squirrel scamper out with one of Lorenza's peanuts. How could I be sure that it was Lorenza who was eating the food? Perhaps hungry raccoons, opossums, or squirrels were taking it. Was she all right? Our question was answered a few days later after a snowstorm. We saw beautiful skunk footprints near the entrance to her tunnel.

Without a real skunk to enjoy, we began to fantasize about her down in her cozy tunnel. We imagined that we'd given her a sofa and a little television set for Christmas and that she was curled up on the sofa watching the tube, in black and white of course. One time Tom came in from feeding her and said he found that she had tried to take her yellow bowl down into the tunnel, but it had become stuck. Would she want a knife and a fork next? John, the head of my school, often asked after her (I think she won his heart when she visited, despite his uneasiness), but he thought that what she was doing in her tunnel was catching up on reading old skunk books.

And so it went until the first of March, when I went out, saying firmly to that hole, "Hey, Lorenza, do you realize that this is March? It's time you came out!" It was raining, but as I put her dinner down, I thought I heard a thumping noise. Just the rain, I thought, but I turned the flashlight toward the hole and beheld a pinkish nose and whiskers. She wouldn't come farther, but I ran in to Tom: "Lorenza exists. She really does!" It wasn't until next day that I wondered if the thumping sounds were warnings. Had she forgotten her mom? Or would spraying mother be the perfect adolescent rebellion for a skunk?

On March 22, the second day of spring, I went out to the aviary with a bowl of sunflower seeds, peanuts, and a piece of banana. I opened the outer door, and in the darkness glimpsed something white in front of me. I held my breath and watched. Was the white moving? Yes! My heart leapt. It was Lorenza—my first real view of her since early November. She ambled toward me and in typical skunk fashion sniffed the bowl of food and went on by as if she wasn't interested. During the winter I had decided that when and if she reappeared, I would wear thick gloves if I wanted to touch her, but I threw caution to the winds and gave her a tentative pat, then another. And I couldn't resist: I boldly picked her up, and she was the same animal that I had held last November. She sniffed me, and when I excitedly brought her in to Tom, she sniffed him. I was ecstatic, but for whom, me or her, or both?

She was gorgeous; her white seemed whiter, but still there was the little black spot between her shoulder blades. And if she wasn't fat, she certainly was plump. No hard winter for her. Tom said, "So, you are unable to let her go." And again we were faced with her release.

She had her own home in her tunnel, and she knew the environs inside the aviary. Should I leave the doors open some night? Or, with her tunnel now opened right next to the fence, might she move the entrance slightly and thereby release herself? Then she could come and go, outside the aviary or inside, and we could continue feeding her in the aviary until she learned to find enough food on her own. But what about the neighbors? Might they or their dogs be sprayed by our skunk? They are good neighbors, but would we be asking too much? What about visitors to our house who might inadvertently seem threatening to a skunk on her nightly rambles? But the worst problem by far was the street. It's a busy street and near our house and the aviary, surely within Lorenza's territory. And, because she was brought up with many noises and goings-on strange and unusual for a skunk, her reflexes toward danger would probably be less appropri-

Granddaughter Tegan enjoys Lorenza at dinner. **(Photo courtesy Gretchen O'Connor)**

ate than those of a wild skunk. No, if a car came near she wouldn't have a chance.

Our alternative was to release her in the country, which would mean taking her away from home and hole. She would be in an entirely new environment, although she might remember her foraging places from the previous summer. She might go off so that we could not continue to feed her while she adjusted. On the other hand, she would have no neighbors or their dogs and no lethal road to face. That road was the deciding factor, and we agreed that natural risks would be fairest for her.

On the night of her move to the country she was excitedly ambling about in the aviary. No, she was not anticipating travel, she was eager for supper. During the previous weeks she had been skittish when I went in to feed her, as if she were dehumanizing herself on her own. To be on the safe side I wore Tom's thick work gloves. As we went out I heard Tom say to Angela, who had been staying with us for a few days, "We'd better watch out; Lorenza may spray." Yet, the moment my gloved hands reached her, I knew we had nothing to fear. I held her, Angela and Tom gave last pats, and Lorenza was sniff-sniffing. I put her into our big cage with her old den box and potty inside (fortuitously, I had never removed them), and she appeared to feel right at home. We put the cage in the car and I drove off to the country.

The next morning I moved her in her cage underneath our woodshed, which to my eyes seemed like an ideal place for a skunk to take up residence and dig a new tunnel. I left her inside the cage to accustom her to the new area, and next morning I opened her cage door. I peeked several times during the day, put some food in her cage, and thought she was sleeping in her den box. Just before going to bed I went out with a flashlight and found her den box and cage empty, but all the food was still there.

When I awoke in the morning I went out first thing to the woodshed. I wasn't hopeful, and leaned down to see her cage. She was not there, nor was the food eaten, and I understood then that she was gone, completely. She had returned to the wild in the woods.

Good luck, Lorenza, good luck—and farewell.

Further Thoughts

The striped skunk inhabits North America roughly from the southern half of Canada to a portion of northern Mexico. Its relatives, the spotted, hooded, and hognosed skunks, all have more southern ranges. All these skunks belong to the family of animals known as the mustilidae, or musk carriers. Although these animals vary in color, they all have anal scent glands, and they generally have long bodies and relatively short legs, like the weasel, marten, mink, otter, wolverine, badger, and the fisher that frightened me off the porch when Johnnie the horse had colic.

The North American skunk population increased after early settlers cleared much of the eastern forests for farms and houses and urban centers. Skunks find more insects, berries, seeds, and mice in fields, bushy areas, and borders than they do in dense woods, and their penchant for such insects as Japanese-beetle grubs makes them a boon to farmers. Ernest Thompson Seton wrote in Lives of Game Animals *(Charles T. Branford, 1953), "Every skunk is the guardian angel of a garden acre. To destroy that skunk is to devastate that acre." Even though Lorenza went to live in our woods, I did not worry about her food supply because the woods include open areas left by logging, and nearby are fields. Like raccoons, skunks coexist with people; life in the suburbs offers porches for skunks to live under, garbage for easy meals, and I have read about wild skunks and domestic cats eating peaceably together from the same dish.*

With or without a cat, if you do not live in an urban area you might like to lure one of your black-and-white neighbors. At night put out a dish with cat food or dog food, or any of the items that Lorenza enjoyed. Then, sprinkle flour in a light layer on the ground around the dish. If the food has been eaten by the next morning, look for the footprints the eater left in the flour. You may recognize the prints of the neighbor's cat or the dog from down the street, but if you see prints that look like a baby's foot, only thinner, you may be looking at the print of the plantigrade hind foot of a skunk. To be certain, consult a field guide to animal tracks.

Do you worry that by inviting a skunk to your yard you may risk being sprayed? If you meet it, speak to it in a soft voice to let it know you are there and do not make sudden motions that the nearsighted creature could misinterpret as aggressive. The skunk is accustomed to respect and sprays only as a last resort. Generally it scurries away from danger, and, if not, flags its tail and then stamps its front feet, giving ample warning.

The skunk's spray contains butymercaptan and, as you probably know, the smell is difficult to eradicate—it persists, especially in damp weather. I have no experience with the odoriferous problem, but the common remedy that I have always heard is to wash in tomato juice whatever has been subjected to the spray. Also, I have read that gasoline is effective, and even catsup. As a positive note, I've heard that skunk oil was once used as a treatment for rheumatism.

The skunk's spray is one remarkable weapon but, thinking of my animal family, I recall many weapons used, both for defense and for procuring food. First prize should go to Butter the goose's beak—biter par excellence and efficient grass clipper. Next among bites, I think of Littlejohn the squirrel's parting gesture, and how useful his chisellike teeth were for gnawing through the hardest nuts. Other rodents using their incisors as weapons against us were the territorial young squirrel, the little woodchuck caught in Edie's riding boot, the South American degus, and even the little-darling hamsters. The raccoons' teeth, arranged in the carnivores' way with large and sharp canines (look into a friendly dog's mouth and you can easily see those canine teeth) gave us enough trouble in play, worried me, and in the end enabled our last raccoon, Jesse, to bite Jinny. How useful carnivore teeth are for killing and eating meat, I know from many examples, but none so graphic as the time when little Gay the raccoon decapitated the quail. The opossum that Polly found in the henhouse would have bitten if we had done something stupid, like try to pick it up, and the snapping turtle never had a chance to demonstrate the reason for its name because I always held it by the upper shell. But Lorenza the skunk's bites were puzzlers because she had a more powerful weapon that she never used against us. My guess is that she bit me because I was holding her and she couldn't do her flag-and-stamp routine.

Chickens cannot bite but they can peck. Try to take eggs from under a chicken in a nest box and you may get pecked, though usually not hard. And yet, Snowflake pecked hard enough to break her own egg, though she was aiming at my hand. And our guinea fowl peck viciously when we handle them. Some birds use their wings defensively. Even our doves, if cornered, would try to fend me off with a wing. Although I have never seen Butter use his wings, perhaps his first-prize beak is weapon enough. I was bit once by the forward edge of an angry goose's outstretched wing, and it felt as if I had been given a hard whack on the shin with a piece of kindling wood. And some roosters use their spurs. It's okay when they use them defensively against each other, which is their main purpose, but not against us, and you may remember how quickly Henry Wallace was dispatched.

Alfred Tennyson's poem "The Eagle" starts with the line, "He clasps the crag with crooked hands," and those crooked hands, the talons of eagles, hawks, and owls, rank high on the scale of effective predaceous weapons. I remember my wrist gripped unrelentingly by the talons of an injured barred owl, and I cannot forget how the goshawk caught, killed, and consumed our little bantam, Tack.

Our honey bees are well known for their defensive stings, as are other bees, and also wasps and hornets. Their stings are poisonous enough to cause pain, and some people get allergic reactions, which can be fatal. Generally, like the skunk, these insects use their stings only as a last resort. Stand still, move slowly, and do not cause the insect to feel threatened, and you can avoid being stung. When Tom works on his beehives, he always moves slowly and carefully; when I watch, it is like seeing him in slow motion.

Another weapon that worried me as much as the raccoons' teeth were the hooves and strong legs of our ponies and horses. These animals defend themselves by kicking, and they do it effectively, although, fortunately, ours did not. Some of us were stepped on by a misplaced hoof, but that, though painful, is another matter. (Of course, head injuries can result from a fall while riding, which is why wearing a protective hard hat is important.) Rabbits also defend themselves by kicking, as we found with ours, especially right after catching one that had escaped. Their claws can inflict painful scratches during the kick. Both the rabbit's hind legs and the horse's legs and hooves are adaptations for running away, perhaps one of the commonest defense strategies among mammals. Raccoons, opossums, and skunks also run from danger, although the latter two are on the slow side. Ground birds run also, and I'd hate to add up the hours in all my years of chicken keeping that I've spent trying to catch escapees. My mind says that chickens are speeders, but I may be thinking subjectively. Of course the chickens can fly, which makes things worse. The wings of all birds can take them up and away, a fail-safe escape route from terrestrial predators.

Another common defense device is camouflage. Felicity, the tree frog, was a master of the art, but a broody brown bantam sitting on a nest among pine needles at the end of a woodpile can be invisible unless you look closely. Most rabbits use camouflage, but I recall a cottontail that hopped across our driveway as I drove in, and then hopped to the bright spring-green lawn, where it froze. Its instinct said it was camouflaged, and I giggled at the obvious brown rabbit on the green grass. Lorenza exemplified the opposite of camouflage, but her black-and-white coat served a defensive purpose, identifying her as owner of a powerful weapon.

Skunks are not popular animals in literature, though in the children's rooms of your library you may find an informative book or two. I find that many times books about animals that are written for children give me all the information I need, whereas sometimes adult books are either far too technical or hard to find. As a child I read about Jimmy Skunk, a character in stories by Thornton Burgess, and I remember Jimmy as an amiable creature. Amiable too was Lorenza, yet to call a person a dirty skunk is an insult. In the first place, skunks are clean animals. If someone likened me to a skunk, I would feel complimented.

Chapter Eleven

Butter's Family

After Butter lost his mallard babies he went about business as usual, but I felt that, given a chance, his instinct would still prompt him to be a father goose. Tom's birthday was in twelve days and in that time I found a person in our town who raised various waterfowl and who would be willing to sell me a gosling. Should I present the gosling to Tom on his birthday, or . . . and I thought of the solution. I would make him a certificate that would read on one side, "Good for the ownership of one gosling," and on the other "Good not to have the ownership of one gosling." He could have a choice in the matter. I forget entirely other presents I may have given him that day, but I remember his opening the certificate, reading it, and stating that he felt he had only one choice—the next day we went and picked up a soft brown and yellow female gosling. When we put her down beside Butter, he cocked his head to look with a blue eye at the diminutive bundle of fluff and within instants arched his neck protectively over her. She reciprocated with dulcet "queep, queeps."

To say that Butter assumed total parental responsibility for the gosling is an understatement. Seemingly proud, he strode across the lawn to the fish pool with his gosling scurrying behind, occasionally flapping her useless, tiny wings. Carefully, he swam with her; attentively, he grazed with her; and watchfully, he lay down to rest beside her, her small, dark body contrasting sharply with the bright white of the large gander. Butter hissed loudly and aggressively at anyone who came near and would have fiercely bitten anyone who did not heed his warning. As the gosling grew, Butter let us approach closer, but no matter from which direction we came, Butter always was between us and his gosling, and yet positioning himself so subtly that it seemed like chance. We were not to be allowed near that gosling and had to be satisfied with seeing her on the far side of Butter. She was so much his sidekick that it became her name—Sidekick, or Side for short.

From a distance we could see that Side grew rapidly, but, just as other people's children aren't as engrossing as one's own, her progress lacked the excitement that Butter's had for us. Assuredly, though, it was easier to leave Side in Butter's care than to be the responsible parent. Not until she was fully grown did we discover that we were deeply fond of her. Tom and I had been Christmas shopping together at the mall, and before returning home had stopped to have some croissants. I enjoyed mine but at the same time had a strange feeling that for some reason we should be on our way home. When we did return, my premonition had a basis in fact. It was time to put the geese to bed, but Side was missing. We could not find her anywhere, and, greatly worried, we put Butter into the pen alone.

In the morning we looked and longed for Side, but she did not return, and, as in the parable of the prodigal son, we realized how much we cared for her. The second day was gloomy and we gave up hope. But on the third day when I came home from work, Side was in the yard as if she had never disappeared. What had happened? Tom reported that at about ten in the morning Side had come flying high over the road from the vegetable field on the other side where a number of wild Canada geese were foraging. Side had been carousing with the flock for three days. Maybe it was an adolescent fling. She never did it again.

During the winter we gave the geese their water in a rubber pony bucket, about three feet in diameter. We would break out the ice, put in fresh water, and be rewarded by Butter and Side's enjoyment of their baths. Toward the end of February, however, we began to notice splashings beyond the usual and that both geese were in the water at the same time. Never having been offered a goose sex-education course, it took us a while to catch on to what was going on in the water. First was the courtship ritual, often initiated by Side, in which she nibbled at Butter's feathers at the base of his tail. He would reciprocate and they appeared to be chasing each other in circles. Then Butter grabbed Side firmly with his beak at the back of her head and mounted her to copulate. Afterward, he assumed a nearly upright position in the water, beat his wings, and made a cry that can only be described as ecstatic. In the house, even without being near a window, if we heard that cry we knew what had been going on.

Around the first day of spring, Side presented us with an egg
that was huge and white and beautiful. I blew out the contents and
it sits on my desk today. Then came a succession of eggs, about
every other day. One of her eggs made an omelet or scrambled eggs
for two; one, fried by itself, made a whopper that covered the plate.
We ate and gave to appreciative individuals a number of Side's wonderful eggs. Then uncertainty nagged us—how many would she lay?
Would she brood on them? When? As gosling insurance we put
three eggs into Polly's incubator. In the meantime Side laid three
more eggs. When the incubator eggs hatched four weeks later I had
difficulty restraining my gosling-motherhood inner self, but a hiking
trip in the mountains ("no goslings in a backpack," said Tom) dispatched the three babies to their true parents, who anthropomorphi-
cally speaking, were delighted. And Butter lowered his long neck
and chased away anyone who came within thirty feet of his new
family.

What to do with Side's remaining three eggs? We put them in the
incubator, and twenty-eight days later in the morning I came home
from shopping and a miracle, as it always seems to be, awaited me: a
wet, dark little gosling splayed out on the incubator's mesh floor.
Another gosling, a yellow one, hatched during the afternoon, and
from the third egg queeps could be heard.

But I faced a dilemma because I was going to leave for the country and I had two hatched goslings and one unhatched. I needed to
invent something that would contain both in the proper conditions. I
started with a thick Styrofoam cooler, a remnant from a biological
supply house that bore fluorescent labels saying, "Live Animals—
Open Immediately." I put a bottle of water into the incubator so that
it would heat to about 100 degrees, wrapped the bottle in cloth, and
put it into the "Open Immediately" container. Next I placed the
unhatched egg, which already had a crack in it, beside the bottle on a
wet paper towel, to ensure the high humidity it needed. Beside the
egg I put a soft piece of flannel as a cuddler, and on it, the two
goslings. I left the top slightly ajar for air to get in, and during the
entire trip in the car I worried. Were they too cold? Too hot? Suffocat-
ing? Should I check and thereby diminish heat and humidity? What
was going on in that box beside me?

Upon arrival I opened the box and found two and a half goslings,
and shortly the half gosling became a whole one—wet and very large

and very yellow (looking just like its Dad when he hatched). My Styrofoam gamble had worked.

When we returned home I decided to mother the dark gosling and to let the two yellow ones join their true family, but I was uncertain how the parents would react to the sudden arrival of two more offspring. I should not have worried about Butter and Side; they included the two new goslings immediately, and the newcomers had no difficulty imprinting on their goose parents. But I should have worried about the two older siblings. Were they acting hostile toward the new arrivals? I kept an eye on the family during the day, but not enough, and I was unprepared for fratricide. When I was not watching, the two older goslings murdered their small siblings. We were astounded. Why had they done it? We understand sibling rivalry in human families, but in the goose family it had run amok. I still do not know why.

Soon after the misfortune, my friend Biz took the surviving gosling and me canoeing to explore her beaver pond. As we passed a wetland shrub called leatherleaf, its scientific name floated into my mind, *Chamaedaphne calyculatta*. "Daphne," I announced to Biz and the gosling, "we'll call the gosling Daphne." From the bottom of the

A gosling takes a first view of the world.

Grass provides comfort for a gosling's rest.

canoe Daphne queeped through her beak that looked as if it were made of black plastic. Her feet matched her beak color, and her fluffy down varied from a soft yellow-olive green to brown.

Little Daphne gave us many of the same pleasures as Butter had two summers earlier, but none of the problems (no motel visits, no police-station escapades), which makes her upbringing seem bland in my memory. In the fall she served as an assistant teacher with me, and because my teaching schedule was especially busy, I am still grateful. She visited many classes and, in an after-school program known as Homesteaders, she became the homesteaders' goose. She followed the group everywhere—to the cider press, to feed the goats and sheep, to forage for materials for natural dyes—and the children enjoyed her almost as much as the activities we did. If Daphne's webbed foot could have held a candle, we felt she'd have joined right in when we were candle-dipping.

Butter swims with his family while Side keeps a lookout at pool's edge.

Daphne and I enjoy a moment of companionship. **(Photo courtesy Rich deCampo)**

Daphne followed the same route as Butter, but this time we understood the implications of her increasingly aggressive actions and quickly realized that we had another gander. We could not dispatch him to the freezer, as we had done in the fall with the other grown goslings, to whom we were not particularly attached. A year later we found another home for Daphne, on a farm; we needed to limit the number of geese that we kept permanently because we didn't have enough space. Until then Daphne took on the guardianship of our truck, and in spring he tried to kidnap one of Butter and Side's second crop of offspring. Daphne appeared with a little yellow follower, and his disposition, even more problematical than Butter's, showed marked improvement, which was a welcome surprise. The personality change lasted just a few hours, because when Butter discovered the kidnapping, he immediately retrieved his gosling. Shortly after, perhaps still upset by the kidnapping, Butter vehemently attacked Kathy's familiar Jeep entering the driveway. Fortunately, Jeeps are tougher than ganders.

In this past year Side laid her first egg on March 21, the first day of spring. After many omelets and scrambled goose eggs, we faced the usual questions. How long would she lay and when would she brood? We tried to encourage her to brood by leaving her eggs in the nest she had made in the pen, but the eggs only spoiled. On July 1, I gave up and put a number of her eggs in the incubator, and almost immediately thereafter Side began to brood on one more egg that she had laid. I have returned to her the eggs that were in the incubator, and if you go into the top of the pony shed she hisses loudly from her nest at the corner of the goose pen. Her meaning is absolutely clear.

Butter is perhaps lonely without his mate for most of the day, and when I leaned down beside him the other day to tell him that "his" book was nearly finished, I'm sorry to report that his only response was a particularly painful bite on my arm—unwarranted, I felt. But he will probably embrace fatherhood with his usual verve, for already this year he has again been trying to adopt chicks—this time fifty-four of them. The chicks had been in the kitchen until even I could no longer stand either dust or smell. Kathy kindly gave a thorough cleaning and disinfecting to the pen beside Butter and Side's, and we moved the chicks there, but perhaps we should have known better. Butter instantly appeared by their pen and would not leave, and Side, left alone outside, began to complain, "honk, honk, honk." Finally, I closed Butter out of the shed and put old sheeting around the pen so that he wouldn't be able to see the chicks. In the meantime Butter hung around outside the window of the chicks' pen as if he were trying to look in at them. Again, perhaps I should have known better because, despite the sheeting, Butter returned to stand by the chicks' pen, leaving droppings all over the floor. We didn't want him in there all day, deserting his mate and lusting after fathering the fifty-four chicks, and so we moved all the chicks out of Butter's earshot.

During this annual season of Butter's fathering compulsion we acquired an unusual orphan by the usual means, the telephone. Our beekeeper friend, Frank, said, "There's a baby screech owl under a sycamore tree right beside Monument Street. And up in the tree is a hole, probably its nest hole." When I arrived, we looked at the nest hole. The baby could not be replaced by ladder because the hole was high and fenced by telephone and electric wires. We worked out a plan that I would keep the owlet overnight, and in the morning the town's "cherry picker" would replace the owl in its nest. Frank, who is a birder, and I both knew it was essential for the owl's interests that it rejoin its family. It needed to remain imprinted on its own kind, and if it didn't have its owl parents to teach it to hunt, it would never learn how to find its own food, vital skills for a predator in the wild.

Our overnight guest was only a little more than two inches tall. It was a mottled gray, a shade that would easily camouflage against tree bark, and the down on its body was so soft that you could scarcely feel it. It could walk clumsily, but could not fly. Its tiny toes were covered with gray down, and little whiskerlike feathers stuck out on either side of its hooked beak, but its most important features were its large, bright yellow eyes with black pupils, which changed in size with the nuances of the lighting about it. The owlet was enchanting. And probably hungry, but I could not feed it then because I had to go and teach.

I took the owlet and pieces of meat off a chicken neck from the freezer with me, and because my schedule was jammed, I had no choice other than to feed the owl during a class. I knew the students well, had explained to them all about the owlet, and it was hardly necessary to tell them to be as quiet as mice, which we thought appropriate for an owl. I let the owlet sit on my hand, took a small piece of chicken with tweezers, and nudged the meat at the side of its beak (as suggested in some pages on owl care I had hastily scanned before school). The children, all on the floor in front, were even quieter than mice, and the owlet opened its beak, took the chicken, and swallowed it. We were spellbound. Next I offered a piece at the front of the hooked beak. It opened and the piece was gulped down. Incredible. Again and again, the little owl devoured the chicken pieces, as if it had been brought up eating food from tweezers held by a human being in a sunny classroom before a bunch of kids.

At 7:00 the next morning the owlet and I were at the Department of Public Works building as scheduled. Dan, the town's director of natural resources, and I led the cherry picker to the sycamore tree and I had the fun of a child watching the thing work. The operator in the basket was skilled, slipping it through the wires with inches to spare. He arrived at the hole, peered in, but gave us bad news: "This isn't even a real hole; doesn't go into the tree at all, and there's not so much as a feather here." When the operator came down, Dan asked if he would mind trying a tree down the road, where we had spotted two holes that looked active because the bark was scratched and worn around the edges. The operator checked both holes—no owls, not even starlings or squirrels; each hole was empty. Dan and I looked at each other. We could have spent the whole day fruitlessly looking into holes, but we concluded that we had done all we reasonably could to return the owl to its family.

Thus, the Sissons gained another foster baby, which I named Sage. After all, owls have a reputation for being wise. His color also resembled that of sagebrush (as I remembered it anyway) and I had to overlook Jinny's objection that the name reminded her too much of the mundane kitchen herb. Most of the time we referred to Sage as he, but sometimes as she, because we didn't know which he or she was. With owls the only sex differentiation is that the adult female is slightly larger than the male.

In the one day that we had him, Sage had become more alert, brisker in his movements, and when he wanted food he made chittering noises, which reminded me of sounds our raccoons used to make, but which also were akin to the noises nestlings make when they anticipate food. If he was upset he clacked his beak, a common sign of owl displeasure. I worried about his future, though, telling my students, "I may have some accomplishments, but I cannot fly through the woods at night and catch mice, which is how the owlet would learn hunting naturally from his own parents." Was Sage doomed to life in captivity, or could I devise ways to teach him to hunt?

At least I could feed him the type of food he would eat in the wild. When an owl eats it holds its prey in its talons, tears off pieces with its beak, and swallows it all—skin, bones, fur, feathers, innards, outards—everything. About twelve hours later the owl regurgitates the indigestible portions in the form of a pellet. Although wet at first, owl pellets do not smell and can be fascinating to take apart, for they include interesting bones and even the skulls of the animals eaten, such as mice. The chicken pieces, supplemented with canned dog food, which I had been giving Sage, didn't have the necessary roughage. From a nearby farm I obtained a number of small pullets that had been killed by a weasel. I cut the little birds into pieces to freeze, gave a piece to Sage, and, when he produced his first pellet, felt like a proud mother whose baby has uttered its first words.

Within a week he was no longer a little ball of fuzz but had grown to be more owl-shaped, and his little ear tufts had become noticeable. These tufts, incidentally, are nothing more. They help to break up the shape of a screech owl as it camouflages itself against a tree; the owl's ears are at the sides of its head, looking like the holes of chickens' ears but much larger. I read that they are canted—one is placed higher than the other—the owl therefore has binaural depth perception. Also, owls have facial discs, with feathers flattened to make a disc shape to help concentrate sounds like a dish antenna. You and I can tell the direction from which a sound comes; an owl can tell not only the direction but also exactly how far away it is.

Also, Sage began to triangulate. He moved his head back and forth sideways, bobbing it slightly while keeping his eyes fixed on an object. He could pinpoint the object's location both by sight and hearing. Jessica and Littlejohn would sometimes triangulate before making a leap to determine the exact position of their landing place. You may notice a squirrel in a tree using this technique.

One morning when Sage was sitting on the breakfast table with us, he chittered so loudly that I offered him a spoonful of granola with milk. To our astonishment he ate it, or as much of it as he could, because spoons are definitely not designed for hooked beaks. Despite the clumsy utensil, Sage enjoyed seconds and thirds of the granola. Why was our little predator eating granola? We didn't know, except that his foster mother offered it. A few days earlier he had gulped a small portion of cottage cheese from my hand, but then opened and closed his beak as if the cheese had tasted bad. When I offered him more he backed up, stood tall, and tucked his beak down into his fluff—a distinct, "No thank you," which I had met on other occasions when he had enough to eat.

Soon he began to fly. Although I could hear him when he flew, his flights were quieter than those of any bird I have ever had. Owls are known for their silent flight, which is why they have a reputation for being spooky and are associated with Halloween. Owl feathers have soft edges, and their legs and toes are covered with soft feathers, both adaptations enabling them to fly so quietly that they can hear where their prey is, but their prey cannot hear them approach.

Sage enjoyed flying freely on our large porch in the country, especially at night, but by day he would sit high up on a beam. When he peered down at me he looked appealing but enigmatic in an owlish way—his big eyes, when they focused directly on me, seemed all-seeing and all-knowing. These eyes gave him good night vision, and their forward-facing position gave him the same binocular seeing that our eyes give us. We can move our eyes in their sockets, but owls can't. If you wish to look behind you, you can turn your head to the side and then turn your eyes to see farther back. Owls, though, can turn their heads 170 degrees, and so they can look behind for possible prey. It is a myth that they can turn their heads completely around, but for extra flexibility they do have fourteen vertebrae, while we, and even giraffes, have only seven.

One hot, sultry day on the porch, I discovered Sage on the porch floor in a surprising position. His wings were stretched out with the feathers spread, so that with his outspread tail feathers he made a half circle. In the middle was Sage's body; he looked as if he were sitting down with a ball gown spread about him, except that the gown was of soft feathers, of varied shades of gray. Why? Was he trying to cool off? But he was in the sun! And yet, I saw him do this exercise several times on cold days, always in the sun. Sunbathing, perhaps?

And, as for bathing, several times I heard Sage jumping in the little water container in his cage. I thought it a silly notion but fetched a small baking pan with water and put it on the floor. Sage flew down, perched on the side, and looked about him for at least five minutes, perhaps watching for possible predators. He then splashed in the water, a poor imitation of Butter's baths, but a bath it was, and at the

Sage peers down. **(Photo courtesy Biz Paynter)**

end he shook himself, spraying drops of water in all directions. His breast feathers looked still wet, but by this time nothing could surprise me much more, for I would never have believed that an owl would take a bath had I not seen it for myself.

I had heard about training an owl to be on its own by leaving its cage outdoors with the door open, so that the bird could fly out at night and learn how to hunt, and yet could return to its cage for a human-placed meal if necessary. To prepare for this operation I hung Sage's cage from a beam on the porch, left the cage door open, and at evening put his dinner in the cage. In the mornings dinner was either finished or well hacked. I had hope for Sage as a hunter because sometimes he indulged in a kind of catch-the-mouse play. He would walk along and pounce; once on the floor he repeatedly pounced on a rug corner, as if pretending it was a mouse. Another time above me on a beam I heard him rattling and playing with something I guessed was an old chicken bone, but was surprised to see, when I climbed on the table to look, that he was playing with one of my pencils. Because I don't put pencils on beams, Sage must have flown the pencil up as a mock mouse.

To give him practice with his catch-the-mouse play, I set a small live trap baited with cheese and peanut butter. (I had already begun to adapt a predatorial outlook.) The dead baby barn swallows that had fallen from their nests this summer were no longer the small tragedies they used to be: I saw them, instead, as a good change in diet from Sage's usual chicken. My predatorial side was pleased when I found a little deer mouse inside the live trap next morning. My friend Angela visited that day. "Oh," she said when she saw the mouse, "he's so cute, how can you feed it to the owl?" I admitted to having the same problem, but after all, I had become a predator's mother, and what else could I do?

The story of that mouse ended in comedy. After dark that night I put Sage in his cage, and Tom tried to put the mouse in. The mouse had other ideas and jumped out and onto the porch floor. Then ensued a flashlight chase. "He's over here," I said to Kathy and Rick, "in the corner—oops. . . ." Then Kathy, "He's run by me," and Rick, "I think he went under the table." We were on all fours or other curious mouse-chasing postures, and someone wondered if we needed gloves in case the mouse bit. Next came scurrying mouse sounds, and the mouse hunters were after it again, except that the mouse vanished, probably through a crack somewhere. As we turned off our flashlights, I thought that Angela, anyway, might be pleased.

The second mouse story ended with success, perhaps depending upon your point of view. I put the next mouse in an old five-gallon can, the container in which years back farmers used to put milk for pickup, and then I put in Sage and covered the top with mesh. I heard Sage try to fly out a few times, but then I heard a few squeaks. In due time I took the mesh off the top, and next morning Sage was sitting contentedly on a beam, and no trace of the mouse was left in the milk can.

For a few nights the mouse hunting was unsuccessful, but when a frog hopped out from under a stone I caught it as a different treat for Sage. That evening I put the two together in a carton, originally used for shipping daffodil bulbs and with small holes around the sides, and covered the top with an old screen. In a little while I looked inside and there was Sage, but no frog. Rather a quick dispatch, I thought, and let Sage out. But next morning I was astonished to find a perky frog sitting on a chair on the porch. Sage had gone hungry while little Houdini had slipped out one of the small holes in the carton, I concluded. That evening I covered all the holes with tape, giving Sage another chance for frog legs. As if vengeful, he pounced on the frog immediately, but then let it go. What was wrong? I recalled the incident when Blithe the raccoon discovered that toads emit a foul taste, and wondered if frogs could taste bad to owls. I knew that some tree frogs protect themselves with poison, but this was not a tree frog. Had it been a tree frog, I couldn't have given it to Sage anyway. Irrational, I know, but Felicity's memories preclude my extending my predatorial outlook to tree frogs. During all these thoughts Sage tried again with the frog. Peeking in occasionally, I could see that he held the frog in his talons and that he appeared hunched over, using his beak to eat the frog. This brief story has an unfortunate ending. After about five minutes, when I looked in again, Sage was at one end of the carton and a lifeless frog was at the other. I removed the screen on top, Sage flew out, and I picked up the frog, finding no visible wound anywhere on its body. What had Sage been doing, and why had he not eaten the frog? When I told this tale to Tom, he responded, "Sage must have hugged the frog to death with his talons." I did not like the needless loss, and still I do not know why the screech owl did not eat the frog.

Because my mouse hunting was still unproductive and I figured that Sage was hungry, I bought a can of dog food as a treat and gave him a generous helping that night. But, to my surprise, it was still in his cage in the morning. At least I could imagine an explanation for this taste quirk of the young owl. I figured that, like the squishy white bread that my family calls pap, the dog food seemed like pap to Sage—no crunch bones, no fur or feathers, no other interesting pieces, just pap.

Soon we returned to our suburban home, where the freezer was still well stocked with pieces of weasel-killed pullets, and I watched as hungry Sage ate. He held the piece in his talons and used his beak as a puller and ripper, but did he close his eyes? Another surprise from our little owl? I watched closely: he narrowed his eyes to slits as he lowered his head to the food, then closed them and did not open them until he was upright again. Again, why? All I could think of was frogs, and how they blink their eyes down into their mouth cavities when they eat, like Felicity the tree frog and the bee. But it didn't seem logical that owls would work on the same principle, and several people have suggested that perhaps the owl closes its eyes to protect them against wriggling, and possibly clawing, prey.

Kathy and Rick had invited us to go on an overnight hike with them and their daughter Tegan. Pleased with the invitation, I had overlooked Sage. We needed an owl sitter—Angela, I thought—and, when I asked her, she was delighted, as were her parents, Steve and Sally. Sage's cage fit well on the winter stove in their kitchen, and Angela carefully put Sage's pullet pieces in the refrigerator. I went off hiking with my family without worries.

Upon returning home I called Sally because I couldn't pick him up for two more days. "He's doing fine," Sally told me. "He raises his ear tufts and clacks his beak at Sheba" (their dog). "And when the cat came in," Sally said, "and ate right under the edge of his cage, Sage raised his ear tufts, peered down at the cat for a few moments, and then clacked his beak and flapped around so furiously in his cage that the cat ran upstairs and hasn't dared return to the kitchen since." I asked about Sage's food: "He's eaten all the chicken," Sally said, "but we'll find something." When I went to pick him up, there he was on the stove, our wonderful little owl, and in his food bowl was something that looked suspiciously like a lamb-chop bone, and something else that looked like a half-eaten chop. Steve said, "He's the best-fed screech owl ever. We gave him one lamb chop and he liked it so much we gave him another." What a come-down weasel-killed pullets and mice would be. I asked Sally how Sage preferred his martinis. "Dry," she said, "and he prefers black caviar to red." I took my spoiled owl back to his porch, where he accepted chicken the first night and fresh mouse the next.

Although I hoped my work in preparing him for release into the wild would be successful, I also had to realize that I might not succeed. If that were to happen, the best solution would be to use him for educational purposes. To do that, he needed to be trained to sit quietly on a hand with a jess (the "leash" used by falconers that is attached to a leg of the bird) as a restraint. A jess is often made of soft leather, but I fashioned one from a piece of cotton material, and it worked well. Although at first Sage tried to remove the jess with his beak, he became accustomed to it and generally stayed quiet while it was on. My main problem was his objection to my getting the jess on or off his foot. He clacked his beak, a sure sign of anger, and even tried to bite, but his bites were not strong. Fortunately, he now accepts even my putting the jess on and removing it.

And yet, will we need this training? Must he be kept by people for the fifteen years or so that an owl can live in captivity? Or will he be able to adapt to the wild? He has had ample flying practice at night on the porch, with occasional excursions into the house, and sits quietly by day on the back of a beam, where, if it were a tree, he would be well camouflaged. Although he is friendly to human beings, he is not likely to encounter people in the woods. Nor will he see dogs or cats, but his innate response to them at Angela's house leads me to believe that he will take care of himself if he meets a fox or a raccoon, and I hope he will be watchful for hawks and the larger owls. He still plays catch-the-mouse, but better still, for several evenings in a row he has been catching live mice out of a large, open carton, as well as a few crickets and grasshoppers. I am hopeful. And I plan to hang his cage where he can return to it for food, if needed.

Yet these may be overoptimistic thoughts, because Sage is imprinted on me. This unnatural imprinting would not allow him to lead a normal owl life in the wild and may ultimately preclude his release. Many raptor rehabilitators keep out of sight, feeding their orphans using appropriate raptor puppets to prevent wrongful imprinting. For Sage's future, only time will tell.

In the meantime Side is still brooding the twelve eggs in her nest. She is guarding them zealously with hisses that are meaningful enough that I haven't dared go nearer to see what she might do. She does leave her eggs once or twice a day. We see her feeding with Butter or swimming in the pool. Once when she was out I sneaked into the shed and carried her twelve eggs carefully to the cellar, where I candled them. Small shadows showed in each one. I replaced them gently in the nest, and Side was never the wiser.

We don't count our goslings until they hatch, though. If they do

Owls are reputed to be wise. Can Sage work the computer?

hatch, will Butter charge at anyone who comes within thirty feet of his family? Will he attack an intruding car and intimidate any stranger who enters the yard? Will he and Side lead the goslings to the pool for a swim? Will he graze with them? Lie down with them? Will he care constantly for them? Will he watch over them in every way? Yes, I believe that my father goose will.

Further Thoughts

Butter and Sage have not met. They are as different as day and night, literally and figuratively: Butter is a web-footed grazer and Sage, a taloned predator. Butter is large and domestic, Sage, small and wild. Geese have a reputation for intelligence, and yet we have the well-known expression, "you silly goose." Owls have a reputation for wisdom, and the ancient Greeks associated them with Athena, daughter of Zeus and goddess of wisdom.

My care for each also differs. Butter has long been a family member, Sage is young and we do not know how long he will be with us. My appreciation for the wonders of each, my reverence for their lives—these feelings do not differ for the goose, the owl, or any of the animals in our family. Even Miss Squish deserved respect for her wondrous specializations adapted to her mode of living.

In his autobiography, The Story of My Experiments with Truth *(Beacon Press, 1957), Mahatma Gandhi explains how his faith in* ahimsa *includes the belief that people gain in compassion when they try not to harm, but to save, even the tiniest creatures. And "underlying* ahimsa," *he says, "is the unity of all life." My hope is that compassion for all living beings and the unity of all life is the message you receive from this book.*

About the Author

A childhood love of animals, coupled with her husband's beekeeping and gardening and the curiosity of her four children, rekindled Edith Sisson's interest in the natural world. With the raising of the first orphaned racoons, the family developed a true back-to-nature lifestyle.

Mrs. Sisson began her career as an educator/naturalist and science teacher when the youngest of her four children went to school. Currently, she teaches elementary science and heads the science department at Wayland Academy in Massachusetts. She frequently holds seminars and lectures for groups such as the Boy Scouts and U.S. Fisheries and Wildlife. She has also worked for the Massachusetts Audubon Society for more than twenty years.

Born in Boston, Massachusetts, and brought up nearby, Edith Sisson remains a New Englander to this day.